# ACADEMIC
# CONNECTIONS 4

# ACADEMIC
# CONNECTIONS 4

## JULIA WILLIAMS

PEARSON
Longman

**Academic Connections 4**

Pearson Education, 10 Bank Street, White Plains, NY 10606

Staff credits: The people who made up the *Academic Connections 4* team, representing editorial, production, design, and manufacturing, are Pietro Alongi, Andrew Blasky, Aerin Csigay, Christine Edmonds, Ann France, Gosia Jaros-White, Caroline Kasterine, Sherry Preiss, Karen Quinn, Robert Ruvo, Debbie Sistino, Paula Van Ells, and Marian Wassner.

ETS staff credits: The ETS people who made up the *Academic Connections* team, representing research, test design and scoring, item development, statistical analysis, and literature reviews, are Matthew Chametzky, Terry Cryan, Phil Everson, Elizabeth Jenner, Kate Kazin, Dawn Leusner, Brad Moulder, Jan Plante, Jonathon Schmidt, and Jody Stern.

Project editors: John Beaumont, Nan Clarke
Cover art: Art on File/Corbis
Text composition: Kirchoff/Wohlberg, Inc.
Text font: 10.5/12.5 Times Roman
Reviewers: See page xxiv

**Library of Congress Cataloging-in-Publication Data**

Academic connections. -- 1st ed.
    p. cm.
  ISBN 0-13-233843-2 (Level 1) -- ISBN 0-13-233844-0 (Level 2) -- ISBN 0-13-233845-9 (Level 3) -- ISBN 0-13-233841-6 (Level 4)  1.  English language--Rhetoric--Problems, exercises, etc. 2.  Report writing--Problems, exercises, etc. 3.  Listening--Problems, exercises, etc. 4.  Reading comprehension--Problems, exercises, etc. 5.  College readers.  I. Cassriel, Betsy. II. Martisen, Marit ter-Mate III. Hill, David, 1937 Oct. 15 IV. Williams, Julia
  PE1408.A223 2010
  428.0071'1--dc22

                                                          2009017781

ISBN-10: 0-13-233841-6
ISBN-13: 978-0-13-233841-7

Printed in the United States of America
1 2 3 4 5 6 7 8 9 10—CRK—14 13 12 11 10 09

# CONTENTS

# WELCOME TO **ACADEMIC CONNECTIONS**

*Academic Connections* is a four-level, integrated skills course designed for students **preparing for academic study** as well as for **standardized tests**. A systematic, building-block approach helps students develop and sharpen their language skills as well as their academic and test-taking abilities.

## The ACADEMIC CONNECTIONS Series Is

**INTEGRATED**

- *Academic Connections* **integrates** all four language skills—reading, listening, writing, and speaking.
- *Academic Connections* teaches students **how to integrate skills** and **content** in real-world academic contexts.
- **Integration of various media** empowers students and instills confidence.

**ACADEMIC**

- Academic skills and content prepare students for **success in the classroom** and on **standardized tests**.
- Explicit, **step-by-step skill development** leads to student mastery. With careful instruction and engaging practice tasks, students learn how to **organize information**, **make connections**, and **think critically**.
- Key **academic skills** are introduced, reinforced, and expanded in all four levels to facilitate acquisition.

**AUTHENTIC**

- **High-interest** and **intellectually stimulating authentic material** familiarizes students with content they will encounter in academic classes. Readings and lectures are excerpted or adapted from textbooks, academic journals, and other academic sources.
- Course content covers five **academic content areas**: Social Science, Life Science, Physical Science, Business and Marketing, and Arts and Literature.
- **Authentic tasks**, including listening to lectures, note-taking, participating in debates, preparing oral and written reports, and writing essays, prepare students for the demands of the content class.

**ASSESSMENT-BASED**

*Academic Connections* provides a **variety of assessments** that result in more effective student practice opportunities based upon individual needs:

- A *placement* test situates students in the appropriate level.
- *Pre-course* and *post-course* tests allow teachers to target instruction and measure achievement.
- *Multi-unit* tests track individual and class progress.
- *Formative assessments* monitor student skill mastery, allowing teachers to assign individualized exercises focused on the specific learning needs of the class.

**RESEARCH-BASED**

- *Academic Connections* was developed in cooperation with the **Educational Testing Service (ETS)**, creators of the TOEFL® test. The blend of curriculum and assessment is based on research that shows when English language learners are provided with authentic tasks, individualized and target practice opportunities, and timely feedback, they are better able to develop and integrate their reading, writing, speaking, and listening skills.

**PERSONALIZED**

PEARSON LONGMAN
myacademicconnectionslab

**MyAcademicConnectionsLab**, an easy-to-use **online** learning and assessment program, is an integral part of the *Academic Connections* series.

MyAcademicConnectionsLab offers:

- **Unlimited access** to reading and listening selections with online glossary support.
- **Original activities** that support the *Academic Connections* program. These include activities that build academic skills and vocabulary.
- **Focused test preparation** to help students succeed academically and on international exams. Regular **formative** and **summative assessments**, developed by ETS experts, provide evidence of student learning and progress.
- **Individualized instruction**, **instant feedback**, and **personalized study** plans help students improve results.
- **Time-saving tools** include a **flexible gradebook** and **authoring features** that give teachers **control of content** and help them **track student progress**.

# THE **ACADEMIC CONNECTIONS** UNIT

## UNIT OPENER

Each unit in the *Academic Connections* series begins with a captivating opener that outlines the unit's content, academic skills, and requirements. The outline mirrors an authentic academic syllabus and conveys the unit's academic purpose.

The content in *Academic Connections* is organized around five academic disciplines: Social Sciences, Life Sciences, Physical Sciences, Business and Marketing, and Arts and Literature.

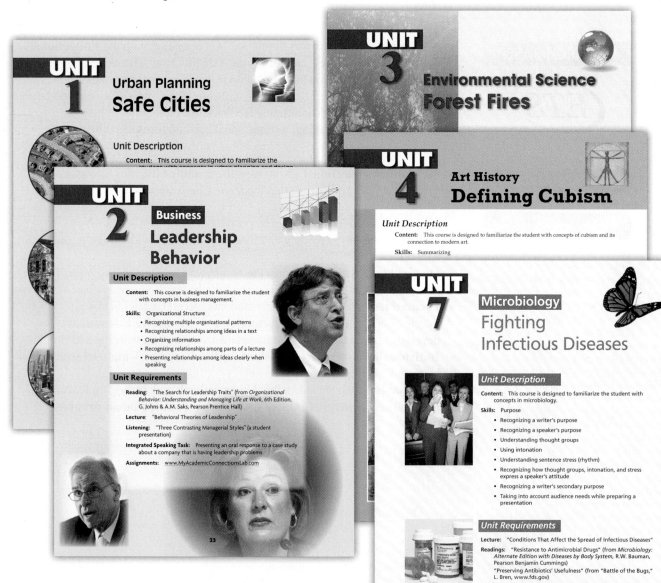

**UNIT 1**

Urban Planning
**Safe Cities**

**Unit Description**

Content: This course is designed to familiarize the student with concepts in urban planning and design.

**UNIT 2**

**Business**
**Leadership Behavior**

**Unit Description**

Content: This course is designed to familiarize the student with concepts in business management.

Skills: Organizational Structure
 • Recognizing multiple organizational patterns
 • Recognizing relationships among ideas in a text
 • Organizing information
 • Recognizing relationships among parts of a lecture
 • Presenting relationships among ideas clearly when speaking

**Unit Requirements**

Reading: "The Search for Leadership Traits" (from *Organizational Behavior: Understanding and Managing Life at Work*, 6th Edition, G. Johns & A.M. Saks, Pearson Prentice Hall)

Lecture: "Behavioral Theories of Leadership"

Listening: "Three Contrasting Managerial Styles" (a student presentation)

Integrated Speaking Task: Presenting an oral response to a case study about a company that is having leadership problems

Assignments: www.MyAcademicConnectionsLab.com

23

**UNIT 3**

Environmental Science
**Forest Fires**

**UNIT 4**

Art History
**Defining Cubism**

*Unit Description*

Content: This course is designed to familiarize the student with concepts of cubism and its connection to modern art.
Skills: Summarizing

**UNIT 7**

**Microbiology**
Fighting Infectious Diseases

*Unit Description*

Content: This course is designed to familiarize the student with concepts in microbiology.
Skills: Purpose
 • Recognizing a writer's purpose
 • Recognizing a speaker's purpose
 • Understanding thought groups
 • Using intonation
 • Understanding sentence stress (rhythm)
 • Recognizing how thought groups, intonation, and stress express a speaker's attitude
 • Recognizing a writer's secondary purpose
 • Taking into account audience needs while preparing a presentation

*Unit Requirements*

Lecture: "Conditions That Affect the Spread of Infectious Diseases"
Readings: "Resistance to Antimicrobial Drugs" (from *Microbiology: Alternate Edition with Diseases by Body System*, R.W. Bauman, Pearson Benjamin Cummings)
 "Preserving Antibiotics' Usefulness" (from "Battle of the Bugs," L. Bren, www.fds.gov)
Integrated Speaking Task: Preparing and delivering an oral presentation about combating the spread of infectious diseases and antibiotic resistance
Assignments: www.MyAcademicConnectionsLab.com

135

# 1

## Preview

This section introduces students to the theme of the unit.

**Previewing the Academic Content** gives an overview of the topic, engages students in it, and exposes them to key words they will need in order to proceed.

---

## 1

### Preview

For online assignments, go to

myacademicconnectionslab

### Previewing the Academic Content

More than half the world's people live in large cities, forming a growing urban population. Almost all future population growth is expected to occur in these urban areas. With large numbers of people living closely together, personal safety is a concern. In the cities we know best, there are places where we feel safe and places where we fear for our safety. How can urban planners—the people who design cities—reduce, modify, or eliminate unsafe areas?

**1.** Label the illustrations with the key words. Two of the adjectives apply to one of the illustrations. Compare your answers with a classmate's.

_____ area

_____ area

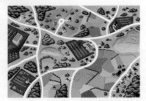

_____ area

**2.** Look at the table on the next page. It compares the rates at which victims experience property and violent crime in urban, suburban, and rural areas of the United States. This rate is called the victimization rate. What can you say about the victimization rates in urban, suburban, and rural areas?

---

This unit will help you recognize coherence and cohesion in readings and lectures. It will also show you how to create coherence and cohesion in your own writing.

### Previewing the Academic Skills Focus

In Units 1 and 2, you learned about expository essays and lectures, which provide information in an organized pattern. In this unit, you will learn about persuasive essays and lectures, which attempt to persuade the audience to agree with the author's main point.

#### Coherence and Cohesion

There is coherence in a reading or lecture when all the paragraphs of the reading or lecture are connected in a clear and reasonable way. Coherence makes a reading or lecture easy to understand as a whole

There is cohesion in a paragraph when all the sentences, clauses and parts, are connected in a clear and reasonable way. Cohesion is essential for readers and listeners to understand the text.

Coherence and cohesion are similar. However, coherence refers to how paragraphs are connected in a larger text, while cohesion refers to how sentences are connected in a paragraph or how clauses are connected within a sentence.

**1.** Read the persuasive essay about the beneficial effects of forest fires. As you read, underline the thesis statement and the concluding statement, and consider how they create coherence by connecting the paragraphs. Remember, a thesis statement states the essay topic, the author's opinion, and the author's main points, often in a single sentence. The concluding statement is a restatement (not repetition) of the thesis.

#### The Beneficial Effects of Forest Fires

1 Forest fires are undoubtedly a menace. They ruin valuable stands of trees, destroy animal habitats, kill woodland creatures, pollute the air, and endanger human life, homes, and communities. In the mid-1900s, all forest burns were considered undesirable, and firefighters responded to all of these fires whether or not they were burning close to human habitation. This approach to forest fires was both expensive and risky. However, more recently, forest managers began to see that forest fires did have benefits. Foresters saw that forest fires were beneficial for trees, soil, and animals.

2 Previously, people believed that forest fires caused irreparable damage to trees; however, now forest managers know that trees are the major beneficiaries of fires. Many naturally occurring forest fires, often caused by lightning strikes, are surface fires that burn the understory—the shrubs and herbs from the forest—without damaging the trees in the overstory. In this way, the fire eliminates competition from the smaller trees, allowing the larger trees to flourish. Once the understory has been burned away, the forest is less likely to burn from high-temperature fires—the combined crown, surface, and ground fires that can do real damage to the tall trees. Burns are also a natural form of control for tree disease and insect pests. Furthermore, the heat from a fire can

**Previewing the Academic Skills Focus** gives an overview of the academic skill for the unit. The material activates students' awareness of the skill and then prompts them to use it on a global level.

# 2 and 3
## Building Academic Reading and Listening Skills

Sections 2 and 3 focus on academic reading and listening skills. First, students read a text or listen to a lecture on a topic related to the unit's academic discipline. They acquire reading and listening skills through careful instruction and engaging practice tasks.

Every unit includes both reading and listening.

**Before You Read/Listen** introduces students to the topic of the selection with pre-reading or pre-listening activities. The activities may include discussions that activate students' prior knowledge of the topic; they may also include vocabulary or brief academic skill practice.

**MyAcademicConnectionsLab** icons remind students to complete their online assignments.

---

1. Compare your answer with another student's. Do you agree on which paraphrase is best? Why?
2. What are some of the paraphrasing techniques from the skills box on page 75 that the writer used to paraphrase?
3. What is similar about the first sentence in paraphrase 1 and 2? Why did the writer start these two paraphrases in this way?

## 2 Building Academic Reading Skills

In this section, you will learn more about paraphrasing techniques. These techniques will help you summarize information later in the unit. You will also learn how to recognize summary and concluding statements. For online assignments, go to

myacademicconnectionslab

### Before You Read

#### Using Synonyms

Synonyms are words that have the same, or similar, meanings. Using synonyms is one key technique you can use to paraphrase—express in your own words—someone else's ideas. Using synonyms can also add variety to your speaking and writing.

**1.** Write each synonym next to its definition in the chart. Pay attention to the forms of the words.

| artist | far-reaching implications | impact | painter | subject |
| artwork | figure | (the) legacy of | painting | subtle clues |
| broken down | float | lingering influence | repercussion | work of art |
| creator | fragmented | monochromatic | single color/tone | |
| dissected | hover | object | small details | |

| Definition | Synonyms |
|---|---|
| Something created by an artist | artwork (n), work of art (exp) |
| Someone who creates art | |
| Something larger that has been reduced to smaller parts | |
| Not easy to see unless you pay careful attention | |

## 3 Building Academic Listening Skills

In this section, you will practice recognizing relationships among various pieces of information from spoken sources. For online assignments, go to

myacademicconnectionslab

### Before You Listen

Over the last two decades, people have slowly become aware that pollution is damaging the global environment. Many people now believe that they need to change their behavior in order to prevent environmental damage that may endanger future generations. This approach to protecting the environment is an example of innovation on a grand scale. How did so many people become aware that the environment requires protection? What forces are encouraging people to change their behavior?

#### Key Words

**channel** *n* a system or method that is used to send or receive information

**diffusion** *n* the spread of ideas or information among a lot of people

**inundate** *v* to receive so much of something that you can not easily manage it all

**mass media** *n. pl.* all the people and organizations that provide information and news for the public, including the Internet, newspapers, magazines, radio, and television

**1.** Work in groups of three. Read the list of forces that are encouraging people to change their behavior in order to protect the environment. These forces are channels of diffusion. What other channels can you think of? Rate the channels of diffusion from most influential (1) to least influential (10).

_____ mass media (Internet, television, newspapers, magazines)

_____ education systems (elementary and secondary schools)

_____ other people's behavior—social norms

_____ advice from parents

_____ opinions of friends

_____ governmental rules/policies

_____ business policies

_____ protests

_____ intercultural contact

_____ other

**2.** Now compare your rankings with other groups'. Overall, what do you think is the most influential channel of diffusion?

**Global Reading/Listening** presents a selection that is adapted or excerpted from higher education textbooks or other academic sources. Comprehension and critical thinking activities lead students to an understanding of the selection on a global level. Students are also introduced to an academic skill that they practice by completing engaging tasks.

---

### Global Reading

#### Finding the Main Idea when Reading Quickly: Skimming

When you skim a text, you read it strategically to understand its general meaning or main idea. Here are some strategies you can use to skim a reading. Notice that some of these strategies were listed on page 4.

- Read the title, headings, and subheadings of a text.
- Read the first and last sentence of each paragraph.
- Look at captions, diagrams, and illustrations.
- Keep your eyes moving consistently over the page.
- Don't use a dictionary.
- Don't spend time reading the details.

Which of these strategies do you use when you want to read quickly for general comprehension? Are there other strategies that you use? What are they?

**1.** Skim paragraphs 1–6 of the text "From Eyes on the Street to Safe Cities" to find the main idea.

**Key Words**

**corridor** *n* a long, narrow passage with doors leading off of it

**sprinkled** *adj* scattered small drops of water or small pieces of something

**subtle** *adj* not easy to notice unless you pay careful attention

**volatile** *adj* likely to change suddenly and without warning

#### From Eyes on the Street to Safe Cities

By Gerda Wekerle (from *Places*)

1   Many people quote the phrase from Jane Jacobs that "there must be eyes on the street" to emphasize the relationship between urban safety and design. Jacobs's views on urban safety were, in truth, far more complex than this phrase suggests, and they were widely attacked and dismissed when her book *The Death and Life of Great American Cities* was published. Still, they have become the basis of a worldwide movement to foster safer cities.

2   Jacobs made an important contribution to our understanding of cities by emphasizing the link between the *fear* of crime and urban design. Jacobs was visionary in arguing that we should be concerned about the everyday experiences of city inhabitants, instead of focusing on

---

#### Preparing for Lectures in Order to Improve Comprehension

Before going to a lecture, it is helpful to think about what to expect. If you have thought about the content in advance, you will probably find listening easier. To improve your listening skills, you can do the following:

- Consider what you already know about the lecture topic.
- Review your notes from previous lectures on related topics.
- Read the textbook chapter that matches the lecture topic. Look for main points and details that support each of the points.
- Make a short list of key vocabulary words that you will likely hear. If words are long or hard to spell, develop short forms for them to make note taking easier.

**2.** To improve your comprehension of the lecture, use information from the readings to answer the questions.

1. What do you think the topic of this lecture will be?
2. What are some specific things you already know about this topic?
3. What are some things you'd like to learn about this topic?

### Global Listening

#### Listening for a Speaker's Main Point(s)

To understand the main point(s) of a lecture, you can do the following:

- Listen carefully right at the beginning of a lecture because main points are often stated first. Don't wait to focus your attention.
- Listen for ideas that are repeated throughout the lecture.
- Listen for information about points that the professor has written on the board.
- Listen at the end of the lecture for concluding comments.

If you understand the professor's main point(s), it will help you understand the lecture details, take notes efficiently, and hear vocabulary words that are related to the topic.

**Key Words**

**boulevard** *n* a wide, main street

**grid** *n* a pattern of straight lines that cross, used to organize streets

**impoverished** *adj* very poor

**industry** *n* business that provides goods or services

**radical** *adj* extreme, very different

**1.** 🎧 Listen to the introduction of the lecture to discover the main point(s). Then discuss the questions with the class.

1. Why did urban planners develop new visions for the "modern" city?
2. What will the professor probably talk about in the rest of the lecture?

**2.** 🎧 Now listen to the entire lecture and complete the chart on the next page. As you listen, write the name of each Modern City Vision next to the name of the urban planner who created the vision. Write down the main point about each of the city visions.

In **Focused Reading/Listening**, students begin to explore the complexities of the selection. Comprehension, critical thinking, and/or inference activities in this section test students' detailed understanding of the text and lecture. This section might introduce another academic skill related to reading/listening and offer practice of the skill.

At the end of Sections 2 and 3, students are prompted to take an online test on **MyAcademicConnectionsLab**. These section tests (Checkpoints) monitor student progress and allow the teacher to assign individualized exercises focused on students' specific needs.

---

### Focused Reading

**Gathering Information to Make Inferences**

As you know, drawing inferences is deciding what is likely to be true based on the information you have. To make your inference, gather as much information as you can from pictures, diagrams, titles, headings, and subheadings, as well as the full text.

**1.** To help you answer inference questions about the text, first review the information from the reading by making an outline of the text. Then compare your outline with a classmate's. Create a shared outline on the board with the whole class.

- **(Paragraph 1)** As children's stories have many shared characteristics, children's literature can be considered a genre separate from adult genres of literature.
- **(Paragraph 2)** Stories for children reflect adult authors' ideas about childhood: that children are limited/vulnerable and must be protected and educated.
- **(Paragraphs 3–6)** Examples of children's stories that follow the generic schema.
- **(Paragraph 7)**

- **(Paragraph 8)**

- **(Paragraph 9)**

- **(Paragraph 10)**

- **(Paragraph 11)**

**2.** Work with a partner. Discuss the questions.

1. Why does the author of the text provide so many examples of children's stories?

2. Why does most children's literature present children's characters who are limited and need to be protected and educated?

3. Do you think this generic schema applies only to modern children's stories, or only to children's stories from a single culture? Why?

**3.** The reading on pages 167–168 does not have a formal academic conclusion. Work with a partner to make inferences about which pieces of information are most likely to be in the conclusion of this reading. For each one, explain why you believe it is appropriate to include it. Then confirm your answers with the class.

1. Examples of another variation on the generic schema.

---

**3.** Listen to the lecture. As you listen, number the points in the Actual Order column in the chart on pages 85–86 as you hear them presented. Where were the major points located in the lecture? Where were the important details? Where were the non-essential points?

**4.** After listening to the lecture, write out the major points on another piece of paper. Orally summarize the lecture by repeating the major points. Paraphrase as much as possible. After you practice, present your oral summary to a classmate.

### Focused Listening

**Recognizing Digressions or Asides**

Essential information is the information you need to understand the lecture. A digression, also called an aside, has little or no connection to the main points and supporting details, and does not help you understand the lecture. In some cases, an instructor will begin a digression with expressions such as:

- *By the way, . . .*
- *As an aside, . . .*
- *Incidentally, . . .*

Sometimes the instructor will say, *Let's get back to the lecture* to show that the aside is finished, but sometimes the end of the aside is not obvious. Listen carefully for pauses that may show the instructor is finished with the aside and is returning to the main lecture.

**1.** Listen to the lecture again. There are two digressions during the lecture. What does the lecturer say in each digression? Complete the sentences.

1. By the way, I should mention that there will be _____

2. Incidentally, you may have seen _____

**2.** Why are these digressions not essential information?

**Checkpoint 2** myacademicconnectionslab

# 4

## Building Academic Writing/ Speaking Skills

This section emphasizes development of productive skills for writing or speaking. It presents language and academic skills needed for the integrated task. Students also read or listen to another selection that expands on or otherwise complements the earlier selections.

Each unit concludes with an integrated writing or speaking task based on the authentic needs of the academic classroom. Units alternate between focusing on writing and speaking.

**Before You Write/Speak** introduces the language skill that students will need in the integrated task.

---

### 4

#### Building Academic Writing Skills

In this section, you will learn how to elaborate on information you present and how to select and present information from various sources. Then you will write a short report about an innovation of your choice and how information about that innovation was diffused. You will synthesize information from the readings and the lectures in this unit. You will also use the vocabulary you have learned.

For online assignments, go to

myacademicconnectionslab

#### Before You Write

**1.** Your sociology professor has given you a diagram to help explain the content of the next lecture. Look at the diagram and predict what your professor is going to say about individuals as channels of innovation diffusion.

Individuals as channels of diffusion → Cosmopolitan leaders ——→ Broad diffusion of new information
Local leaders ——→ Deep diffusion of new information

**2.** Listen to your professor's short lecture about individuals as channels of innovation diffusion. Then complete the tasks.

1. Was your prediction you made in Exercise 1 about the lecture content correct? Explain.

2. Place the characteristics of cosmopolitan and local leaders into the appropriate columns in the chart. Some characteristics fit into both columns.

- have large numbers of friends and acquaintances
- have a wide variety of interests
- are members of many groups that have different goals
- are members of many groups with similar goals
- have a deep reach into a single community
- have a wide reach into many communities

| Cosmopolitan Leaders | Local Opinion Leaders |
|---|---|
|  |  |

3. Does this short lecture contain abstract concepts or concrete information? Explain.

---

### 4

#### Building Academic Speaking Skills

In this section, you will learn how to consider audience needs when preparing oral presentations. Then you will prepare and give an oral presentation about how people can fight the spread of infectious diseases and antibiotic resistance.

For online assignments, go to

myacademicconnectionslab

#### Before You Speak

##### Taking into Account Audience Needs

When you are asked to give a presentation, you may be very nervous. You may be so nervous that you give your presentation and sit down as quickly as possible. While it is normal to be nervous, you must realize that you have a primary purpose for giving your presentation (to inform, to persuade, or to entertain), and your audience has specific needs. The planning of every excellent presentation begins with a careful consideration of your purpose and the audience's needs.

An audience looks for most of the following things from a presenter:

- An entertaining or dramatic beginning
- Understandable content
  - definitions of key vocabulary
  - a presentation outline
  - clear explanations of basic concepts
  - content geared to the audience's level of understanding
  - a clear voice (loud enough and with clear pronunciation)
- Interesting content
- Visual support to help the audience understand the content
- A definite ending
- Recognition from the presenter
  - eye contact

Remember that in almost all cases, your audience wants you to succeed, so they are hoping you will do well.

**1.** Work with a partner to discuss how your presentation would change depending on your purpose and audience. Take short notes about these factors in the chart.

- use of technical terms
- time spent on explaining basic concepts
- need for visuals
- how to achieve your primary purpose

| Presentation Topic: **How Can People Combat the Spread of Infectious Diseases and Antibiotic Resistance?** | | |
|---|---|---|
| Your Primary Purpose | Your Audience | Your Presentation |
| To inform | A group of children | • *don't use technical terms* <br> • *spend more time explaining basic concepts* <br> • *keep it short* <br> • *achieve your primary purpose (to inform) by entertaining—maybe tell a story with a moral* |

---

## Focused Writing

Innovations generally fall into two categories: social and technological.

*1. Look at the social and technological innovations in the chart. With the class, brainstorm some extra ideas to add to each category. You will select one of these innovations as the subject of your report.*

| Social Innovations: Ideas That Are Popular or Have Become Laws | Technological Innovations: Things That Have Become Popular |
|---|---|
| • women's right to vote<br>• child labor laws<br>• recycling<br>• bicycle sharing<br>• car sharing<br>• others: | • vaccinations<br>• computers<br>• cell phones<br>• others: |

### Selecting and Presenting Related Information from a Variety of Sources

When you write in an academic context, you need to combine different pieces of information into whatever you are writing—an essay, a report, a response paper, etc. This is called synthesizing information. To synthesize well, you need to identify your pieces of information, discover the relationships among the pieces of information, and express this clearly in writing.

One writer used the chart on page 109 to organize information about the innovation of car sharing. She found this information in her course textbook, on the Internet, and in her sociology lectures. Then she constructed the chart to make sure she synthesized information from this wide variety of sources and so that she could see the relationships among the pieces of information.

*2. Examine the chart on page 109 and then read the example student report on page 110. As you read the report, check off (✓) each source of information in the chart. Did the author succeed in synthesizing information from all of the sources?*

---

**Focused Writing/Speaking** explains the skill that will be used in the integrated task. Students use the additional reading or listening selection in this section to practice the skill and prepare for the integrated task activity.

---

1. What is the source of this information? Do you believe this is accurate information, or are you skeptical? Why?

2. Why are nanotubes compared to asbestos fibers?

3. Do you believe it is dangerous to inhale nanotubes? Use an expression that shows your degree of certainty.

4. Why is it unlikely that the results of this study will prevent the further development of nanotechnology?

5. What is required in the immediate future?

## Focused Speaking

### Expressing and Supporting Opinions

At the university level, you will often have to participate in discussions in which you will need to express your opinions about an issue. When you express your opinions, it is important to support them with details and evidence. Strong support will help people believe your opinion.

Strong support of your opinions should include facts, such as statistics and research results. It should also include explanations and reasons that are clear, logical, and based on facts. In expressing your opinions, you should use words that show a strong level of certainty.

In contrast, you should avoid support that includes facts people can't check easily and opinions of people who are not experts in the area you are discussing.

*1. Work in small groups. To help you form an opinion about and discuss the precautionary principle, talk about how it would affect:*

    a. An elementary school that is planning to build a climbing structure in the schoolyard for its students.

    b. A shipping company that wants to ship oil through an aquatic preserve.

    c. A medical research proposal to find a cure for cancer by testing a new drug on human subjects immediately.

    d. A company that wants to import a cheaper product from a foreign country.

*Then discuss with the class whether or not you think the precautionary principle should be applied to the development of nanotechnology.*

*2. Once you have defined your position on whether the precautionary principle should be applied to the development of nanotechnology, work with a partner who has a similar opinion to your own. Together, complete the chart. State your opinion and then search for facts in the readings and in your answers to the lecture questions that support your opinion(s).*

---

The **Integrated Writing/Speaking Task** challenges students to organize and synthesize information from the reading and listening selections in a meaningful way. Students follow clear steps that require them to use the vocabulary and academic skills they have learned in the unit. Completing the task is a productive achievement that gives students the tools and the confidence needed for academic success.

## Integrated Writing Task

Here is your report assignment: **Select a significant innovation and write a report about how information about that innovation was diffused.** Reports are divided into sections; unlike academic essays, each report section has its own heading.

*Follow the steps to write your report.*

**Step 1:** Select a social or technological innovation that interests you from the chart on page 94. Use your general knowledge about that innovation, or find reliable information sources about the innovation. Add the information, in point form, to the first row of the chart.

**INFORMATION ABOUT** _____

| Information source | Piece of information | Relationship to _____ | Included in the report? (✓ or ✗) |
|---|---|---|---|
| **Textbook reading:** Social Conditions that Encourage Innovation | 1. internal social inconsistencies that create stress | | |
| | 2. problems adapting to the physical environment | | |
| | 3. broadly defined social norms | | |
| | 4. high rates of succession or replacement | | |
| | 5. close contact between/among cultures | | |
| | 6. growth in population size and density | | |
| | 7. social catastrophe or natural disaster | | |
| **Lecture:** Mass Media and Diffusion of Innovation | mass media has limits • dependent on literacy • no human interaction • can't convert people to new opinions | | |
| **Lecture:** Individuals as Channels of Innovation Diffusion | individuals can have direct effects • cosmopolitan leaders • local opinion leaders | | |

**2.** *Complete the sentences to help you summarize Picasso's quotations. Be sure to use your own words. Then discuss your completed sentences with the class.*

1. Main idea for quotes 1, 2, and 3:

   Picasso did not care about _____

2. Main idea for quotes 4, 5, and 6:

   When Picasso considered whether his work was either representational or

   abstract, he _____

3. Main idea for quote 7:

   To develop cubism, Picasso _____

**3.** *The three sentences you wrote in Exercise 2 together should form a summary of Picasso's quotations. Write your summary.*

_____

_____

_____

## Integrated Speaking Task

Your debate statement is **Cubism, in its various forms, is fashion art.**

Here are some more examples of cubist works to use as examples in your debate.

Georges Braque. *Houses at L'Estaque.* 1908. Oil on canvas.

Pablo Picasso. *Glass of Absinthe.* 1914. Painted bronze with perforated silver absinthe spoon.

Pablo Picasso. *Violin.* 1915. Construction of painted metal.

# MyAcademicConnectionsLab

**MyAcademicConnectionsLab**, an integral part of the *Academic Connections* series, is an easy-to-use online program that delivers personalized instruction and practice to students and rich resources to teachers.

- Students can access reading and listening selections, do practice activities, and prepare for tests anytime they go online.
- Teachers can take advantage of many resources including online assessments, a flexible gradebook, and tools for monitoring student progress.

The **MyAcademicConnectionsLab** WELCOME page organizes assignments and grades, and facilitates communication between students and teachers. It also allows the teacher to monitor student progress.

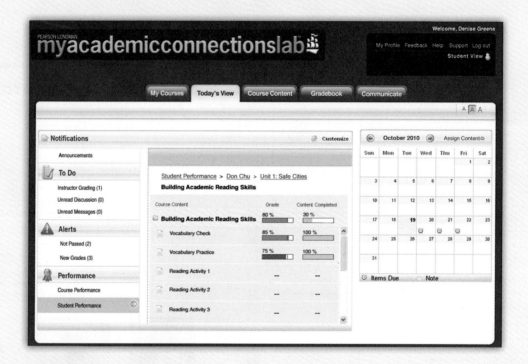

For Sections 1–3, MyAcademicConnectionsLab provides Vocabulary Check activities. These activities assess students' knowledge of the vocabulary needed for comprehension of the content and follow up with individualized instruction.

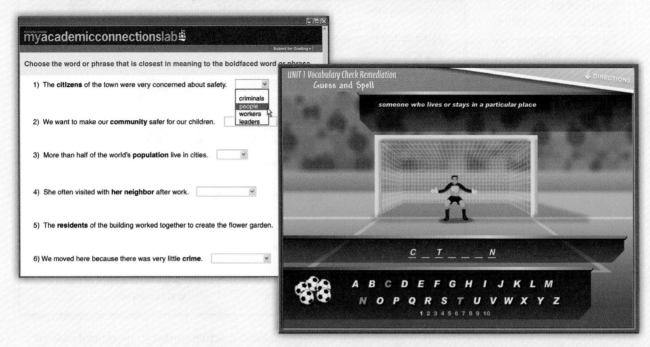

Reading and listening selections from the student book and additional practice activities are available to students online. Students benefit from virtually unlimited practice anywhere, anytime.

- Reading-based activities allow students to further engage with the unit's reading selection. Students practice comprehension, academic skills, grammar, and content vocabulary.

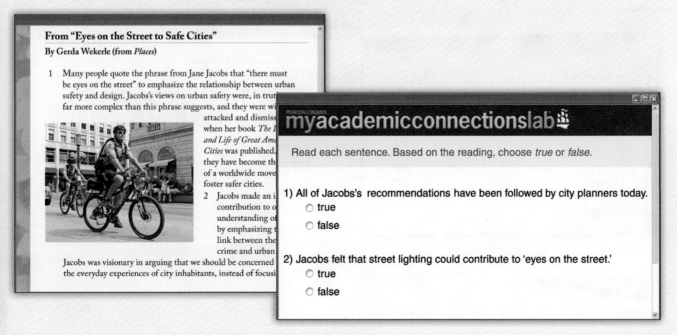

- Listening-based activities allow students to further engage with the unit's listening selection. Students practice comprehension, listening skills, and note-taking skills.

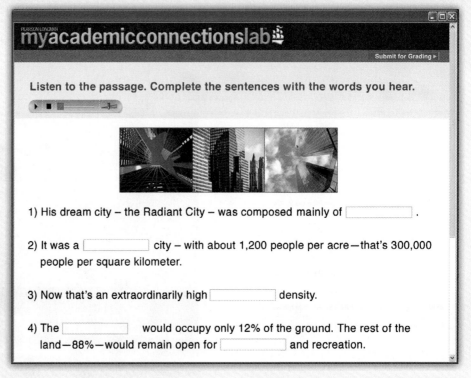

MyAcademicConnectionsLab offers additional activities that support the *Academic Connections* program.
- Fun, interactive games reinforce academic vocabulary and skills.
- Internet-based and discussion-board activities expand students' knowledge of the topic and help them practice new vocabulary.

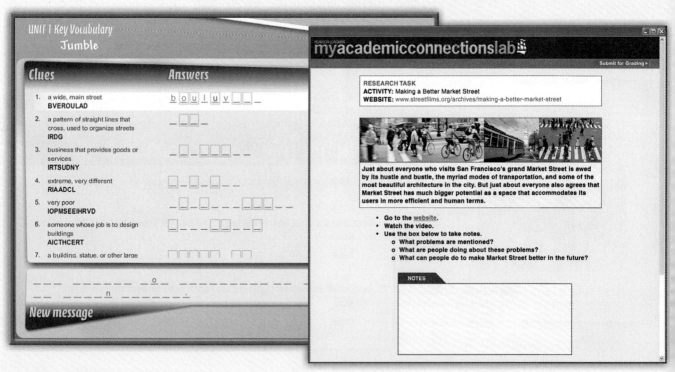

The MyAcademicConnectionsLab ASSESSMENT tools allow instructors to customize and deliver tests online.

- A placement test situates students in the appropriate level (also available in the paper format).
- Pre-course and post-course tests allow teachers to target instruction.
- Section tests monitor student progress.

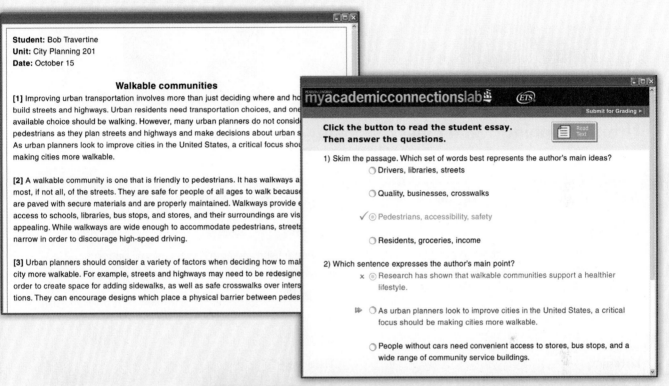

**Student:** Bob Travertine
**Unit:** City Planning 201
**Date:** October 15

### Walkable communities

[1] Improving urban transportation involves more than just deciding where and ho... build streets and highways. Urban residents need transportation choices, and one... available choice should be walking. However, many urban planners do not consid... pedestrians as they plan streets and highways and make decisions about urban s... As urban planners look to improve cities in the United States, a critical focus shou... making cities more walkable.

[2] A walkable community is one that is friendly to pedestrians. It has walkways a... most, if not all, of the streets. They are safe for people of all ages to walk becaus... are paved with secure materials and are properly maintained. Walkways provide e... access to schools, libraries, bus stops, and stores, and their surroundings are vis... appealing. While walkways are wide enough to accommodate pedestrians, streets... narrow in order to discourage high-speed driving.

[3] Urban planners should consider a variety of factors when deciding how to mak... city more walkable. For example, streets and highways may need to be redesigne... order to create space for adding sidewalks, as well as safe crosswalks over inters... tions. They can encourage designs which place a physical barrier between pedes...

**myacademicconnectionslab** (ETS)

Submit for Grading ▶

**Click the button to read the student essay. Then answer the questions.**

Read Text

1) Skim the passage. Which set of words best represents the author's main ideas?
   ○ Drivers, libraries, streets

   ○ Quality, businesses, crosswalks

   ✓ ◉ Pedestrians, accessibility, safety

   ○ Residents, groceries, income

2) Which sentence expresses the author's main point?
   x ◉ Research has shown that walkable communities support a healthier lifestyle.

   ▷▷ ○ As urban planners look to improve cities in the United States, a critical focus should be making cities more walkable.

   ○ People without cars need convenient access to stores, bus stops, and a wide range of community service buildings.

Teacher support materials in MyAcademic ConnectionsLab offer tips and suggestions for teaching the *Academic Connections* material and makes lesson planning easier.

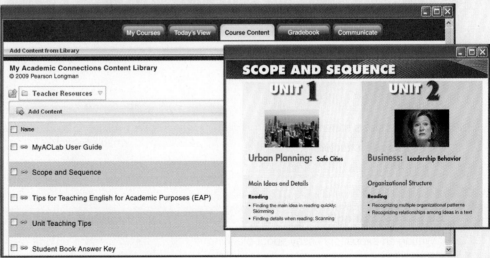

My Courses | Today's View | Course Content | Gradebook | Communicate

Add Content from Library

**My Academic Connections Content Library**
© 2009 Pearson Longman

📁 Teacher Resources ▽

📄 Add Content

☐ Name

☐ ∞ MyACLab User Guide

☐ ∞ Scope and Sequence

☐ ∞ Tips for Teaching English for Academic Purposes (EAP)

☐ ∞ Unit Teaching Tips

☐ ∞ Student Book Answer Key

**SCOPE AND SEQUENCE**

**UNIT 1**

**Urban Planning:** Safe Cities

Main Ideas and Details

**Reading**
- Finding the main idea in reading quickly: Skimming
- Finding details when reading: Scanning

**UNIT 2**

**Business:** Leadership Behavior

Organizational Structure

**Reading**
- Recognizing multiple organizational patterns
- Recognizing relationships among ideas in a text

# UNIT 1

## Urban Planning: Safe Cities

## Main Ideas and Supporting Details

### Reading

- Finding the main idea in reading quickly: Skimming
- Finding details when reading: Scanning

### Listening

- Preparing for lectures to improve comprehension
- Listening for a speaker's main point(s)
- Listening for supporting details

### Writing

- Writing a thesis statement
- Using parallel structure

### Integrated Writing Task

- Writing an expository essay about planning safe cities

# UNIT 2

## Business: Leadership Behavior

## Organizational Structure

### Reading

- Recognizing multiple organizational patterns
- Recognizing relationships among ideas in a text

### Listening

- Organizing information
- Recognizing relationships among parts of a lecture

### Speaking

- Presenting relationships among ideas clearly when speaking

### Integrated Speaking Task

- Presenting an oral response to a case study about a company having leadership problems

# UNIT 3

## Environmental Science: Forest Fires

### Coherence and Cohesion

**Listening**
- Using sentence structure to create coherence
- Recognizing speech markers

**Reading**
- Creating cohesion in a paragraph
- Recognizing cohesion in a text
- Creating special emphasis by starting a sentence with a negative expression

**Writing**
- Persuading your reader
- Using pronoun agreement

**Integrated Writing Task**
- Writing a persuasive essay about allowing people to live near forested areas

# UNIT 4

## Art History: Defining Cubism

### Summarizing

**Reading**
- Paraphrasing: The first step to summarizing
- Using synonyms
- Recognizing summary statements and conclusions when reading
- Summarizing information

**Listening**
- Distinguishing essential from non-essential information in a lecture
- Recognizing digressions or asides

**Speaking**
- Participating in a debate

**Integrated Speaking Task**
- Preparing and presenting a pair debate about cubism as fashion art

# UNIT 5

## Sociology: Innovation

### Synthesizing Information

#### Reading

- Recognizing the relationship between abstract concepts and concrete information

#### Listening

- Recognizing the relationship between two spoken sources

#### Writing

- Elaborating on information
- Selecting and presenting related information from a variety of sources

#### Integrated Writing Task

- Writing a short report about an innovation and how it was diffused

# UNIT 6

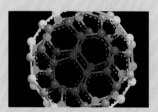

## Physical Science: Nanotechnology

### Fact and Opinion

#### Listening

- Identifying and evaluating information presented to support a position
- Recognizing a speaker's degree of certainty

#### Reading

- Distinguishing between facts and opinions

#### Speaking

- Expressing and supporting opinions

#### Integrated Speaking Task

- Preparing and delivering a short oral report about applying precautionary principle to nanotechnology

# UNIT 7

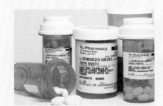

## Microbiology: Fighting Infectious Diseases

### Purpose

**Listening**

- Recognizing a speaker's purpose
- Understanding thought groups
- Using intonation
- Understanding sentence stress (rhythm)
- Recognizing how thought groups, intonation, and stress express a speaker's attitude

**Reading**

- Recognizing a writer's purpose
- Recognizing a writer's secondary purpose

**Speaking**

- Taking into account audience needs

**Integrated Speaking Task**

- Preparing and delivering an oral presentation about combating the spread of infectious diseases and antibiotic resistance

# UNIT 8

## Children's Literature: Characteristics of the Genre

### Inference

**Reading**

- Gathering information to make inferences

**Listening**

- Making inferences about a speaker's intention

**Writing**

- Introducing a specific book in an essay or oral presentation
- Identifying and using rhetorical devices

**Integrated Writing Task**

- Writing an analytical essay about a children's story

# ACKNOWLEDGMENTS

Thank you to the following people, who have greatly influenced the direction of this book in these ways.

To Judi Jewinski who creates opportunities for those around her.

To Carolyn Williams who found the reading on nanotechnology.

To Ron Williams whose interest in art defined the cubism topic.

To Pat Skinner who pointed out the infectious disease metaphor before I saw it.

To Keely Cook and Tanya Missere-Mihas who provided insight into issues of pronunciation.

To Nan Clarke whose sharp eyes smoothed many wrinkles.

To Debbie Sistino who coordinated the project.

To Stefan Rehm, Elizabeth Matthews, Dara Lane, and Andrea Brandt who consistently set a high bar.

To Wayne Parker who referenced the precautionary principle and who provides my foundation.

To Samuel and Scott Parker who both allowed me to write and helped me find a balance.

*Julia Williams*

The publisher would like to thank the following people.

**Matthew Chametzky**, R&D Capability Manager at ETS, who coordinated all assessment work for this project, bringing order when chaos seemed imminent.

**Terry Cryan**, Assessment Specialist at ETS who helped us all better understand (and appreciate) the many differences between testing and teaching.

**Kate Kazin**, Director of Client Management at ETS, whose clear vision kept the project true to its objective of evidence-based design.

## REVIEWERS

For the comments and insights they graciously offered to help shape the direction of *Academic Connections*, the publisher would like to thank the following reviewers and institutions.

**Donette Artenie**, Georgetown University; **Jennifer Castello**, Cañada College; **Carol A. Chapelle**, Iowa State University; **JoAnn (Jodi) Crandall**, University of Maryland; **Wendy Crockett**, J. W. North High School; **Lois Darlington**, Columbia University; **Christopher Davis**, John Jay College; **Robert Dickey**, Gyeongju University, Gyeongju, Korea; **Deborah B. Gordon**, Santa Barbara City College; **Mike Hammond**, University of California, San Diego; **Ian Hosack**, Ritsumeikan University, Kyoto; **Sylvie Huneault-Schultze**, Fresno City College; **Barbara Inerfeld**, Rutgers University; **Joan Jamieson**, Northern Arizona University; **Scott Jenison**, Antelope Valley College; **Mandy Kama**, Georgetown University; **Dr. Jose Lai**, The Chinese University of Hong Kong; **Rama Mathew**, Delhi University, Delhi, India; **Mitchell Mirkin**, Baltimore City Community College; **Carla Billings Nyssen**, California State University, Long Beach; **Yannick O'Neill**, Gyeongnam Education Board, Changwon, South Korea; **Gretchen Owens**, San Francisco State University; **Angela Parrino**, Hunter College; **Sarah C. Saxer**, Howard Community College; **Diane Schmitt**, Nottingham Trent University, Nottingham U.K.; **Gail Schmitt**, Montgomery College; **Fred Servito**, University of Washington; **Janet Shanks Van Suntum**, Fordham University, Pace University; **Karen Shimoda**, Freelance ESL Development Editor; **Dean E. Stafford**, Sanho Elementary School, Mason, South Korea; **Fredricka L. Stoller**, Northern Arizona University; **Richmond Stroupe**, Soka University, Tokyo; **Jessica Williams**, University of Illinois; **Kirsten Windahl**, Cuyahoga Community College

# UNIT 1

## Urban Planning
# Safe Cities

## Unit Description

**Content:**   This course is designed to familiarize the student with concepts in urban planning and design.

**Skills:**   Main Ideas and Supporting Details

- Finding the main idea when reading quickly: skimming
- Finding details when reading: scanning
- Preparing for lectures in order to improve comprehension
- Listening for a speaker's main point(s)
- Listening for supporting details
- Writing a thesis statement
- Using parallel structure

## Unit Requirements

**Readings:**   "From Eyes on the Street to Safe Cities" (from *Places*, G. Wekerle)

"Reducing Neighborhood Crime through Urban Design" (model expository essay)

**Lecture:**   "Visions of the Modern City"

**Integrated Writing Task:**   Writing an expository essay about planning safe cities

**Assignments:**   www.MyAcademicConnectionsLab.com

# 1

## Preview

For online assignments, go to

**PEARSON LONGMAN**
**myacademicconnectionslab**

### Key Words

**metropolitan** *adj* relating to a big city; **metropolis** *n*

**rural** *adj* relating to the countryside

**suburban** *adj* relating to the area immediately around a city

**urban** *adj* relating to cities

## Previewing the Academic Content

More than half the world's people live in large cities, forming a growing urban population. Almost all future population growth is expected to occur in these urban areas. With large numbers of people living closely together, personal safety is a concern. In the cities we know best, there are places where we feel safe and places where we fear for our safety. How can urban planners—the people who design cities—reduce, modify, or eliminate unsafe areas?

**1.** *Label the illustrations with the key words. Two of the adjectives apply to one of the illustrations. Compare your answers with a classmate's.*

_____ area

_____ area

_____ area

**2.** *Look at the table on the next page. It compares the rates at which victims experience property and violent crime in urban, suburban, and rural areas of the United States. This rate is called the victimization rate. What can you say about the victimization rates in urban, suburban, and rural areas?*

**Victimization Rates per 1,000 Residents by Type of Community, 1980, 2000, 2004**

| | Property Crime | | | Violent Crime | | |
|---|---|---|---|---|---|---|
| Year | 1980 | 2000 | 2004 | 1980 | 2000 | 2004 |
| U.S. Total | 53 | 36 | 35 | 5.8 | 5.1 | 4.7 |
| Urban Areas | 61 | 39 | 37 | 7.0 | 5.6 | 5.1 |
| Suburban Areas | 50 | 41 | 41 | 3.5 | 4.0 | 3.8 |
| Rural Areas | 21 | 17 | 17 | 1.8 | 2.1 | 2.0 |

Source: Federal Bureau of Investigation in Crime in the United States (2004)
(Retrieved from http://www.fbi.gov/ucr/cius_04/documents/CIUS2004.pdf?file)

**3.** *Work in small groups. Discuss the questions and share your ideas with the class.*

1. Why do you think crime rates are higher in urban areas?

2. Think of areas in your city (or a large city you know) where you feel unsafe. What are some specific reasons why you do not feel safe?

3. What kinds of things might urban planners do to help lower crime rates?

## Previewing the Academic Skills Focus

In this unit, you will learn strategies for identifying main ideas and details in readings and in lectures. You will also learn how to develop main ideas and use supporting details in your writing.

*Read the paragraph. Then complete the tasks.*

**Safe Cities**

If a city's residents feel safe, then the city will be an economic, social, and cultural success. A city is different from a town in that its inhabitants are essentially strangers to each other. In an urban setting, it is most likely that individuals are surrounded by more strangers than friends. Even neighbors living closely together may be strangers. The metropolis is successful only to the extent that these strangers feel secure on the streets and in their homes. Those residents who do not feel protected will not do business, socialize, or participate in the city. A city that does not provide a safe environment for its citizens will fail in many ways.

Source: Adapted from Jacobs, J. (1961). *The death and life of great american cities.* New York: Random House.

1. What is the main point in this paragraph? Write the main idea on a separate piece of paper. Then compare your answer with a partner's.

2. Discuss your answer to these questions with the class.
   - Do you agree or disagree with the main idea of this paragraph? Why?
   - What happens to a city if people do not feel safe there?

3. Read the last two sentences of the paragraph again. What are some specific ways in which a city might fail because its citizens don't feel safe?

The main idea is the writer or speaker's most important idea or point. A detail is a single fact or piece of information that supports a larger idea. A detail might be an example, explanation, elaboration, reason, solution, opinion, or exception.

When reading, use these strategies to find the main idea of a text:

- Read the title, headings, and subheadings if there are any.
- Find the topic sentence of a paragraph or the thesis statement of an essay.
- Read the first and last sentences of each paragraph.
- Look for repeated key words and synonyms of key words.

When you become skilled at identifying the main idea of a text, you will be able to understand the overall meaning quickly. This ability is important in situations where you have a limited amount of time to read a long text, or you need to get a general idea of what the text is about before you focus on the details.

Which of the strategies in the box did you use to find the main idea of the paragraph on page 3? What other strategies did you use?

## Before You Read

*1. Work in groups of three and write your names at the tops of the columns. Read the questions in the first column and write your answers in your own column. Then take brief notes as you listen to your partners' answers.*

| Students' Names: | | | |
|---|---|---|---|
| 1. Are large crowds of people safe or dangerous? Why? | | | |
| 2. Do you feel more comfortable walking down a busy street or a deserted one? Why? | | | |

## 2

## Building Academic Reading Skills

In this section, you will learn strategies to identify main ideas and supporting details in textbook readings. For online assignments, go to

PEARSON LONGMAN
myacademicconnectionslab

| Students' Names: | | | |
|---|---|---|---|
| 3. Does having a bar or late-night restaurant on your street make the street safer or more dangerous? Why? | | | |
| 4. Is it safer to have homes and stores on the same street or in separate areas of the city? Why? | | | |
| 5. Is it safe to have a park on your street? Why? | | | |

## Key Words

**foster** *v* to help develop over a period of time

**internship** *n* a short-term job that a student does to gain experience, often without pay

**prevailing** *adj* accepted at a particular time

**public housing** *n* houses or apartments built by the government for low income people

**slum** *n* an area of the city that is in very bad condition where low income people live

**2.** Based on your group's answers, describe the safest and the most dangerous places to live.

**3.** Collocations are words that are frequently used together. Form collocations by matching the words in the blue box with the words in the exercise. Use the indicated parts of speech to help. Some words in the blue box appear in more than one collocation. Confirm your answers with the class. Then write one sentence for each collocation and share your sentences in small groups.

| area | idea | project |
|---|---|---|
| busy/thriving | program | ~~provide~~ |

1. (*v*) ___provide___ public housing
2. public housing _____ (*n*)
3. suburban _____ (*n*)
4. rural _____ (*n*)
5. (*adj*) _____ metropolis
6. urban _____ (*n*)
7. prevailing _____ (*n*)
8. internship _____ (*n*)

# Global Reading

When you skim a text, you read it strategically to understand its general meaning or main idea. Here are some strategies you can use to skim a reading. Notice that some of these strategies were listed on page 4.

- Read the title, headings, and subheadings of a text.
- Read the first and last sentence of each paragraph.
- Look at captions, diagrams, and illustrations.
- Keep your eyes moving consistently over the page.
- Don't use a dictionary.
- Don't spend time reading the details.

Which of these strategies do you use when you want to read quickly for general comprehension? Are there other strategies that you use? What are they?

**1.** Skim paragraphs 1–6 of the text "From Eyes on the Street to Safe Cities" to find the main idea.

## Key Words

**corridor** *n* a long, narrow passage with doors leading off of it

**sprinkled** *adj* scattered small drops of water or small pieces of something

**subtle** *adj* not easy to notice unless you pay careful attention

**volatile** *adj* likely to change suddenly and without warning

## From Eyes on the Street to Safe Cities

### By Gerda Wekerle (from *Places*)

1   Many people quote the phrase from Jane Jacobs that "there must be eyes on the street" to emphasize the relationship between urban safety and design. Jacobs's views on urban safety were, in truth, far more complex than this phrase suggests, and they were widely attacked and dismissed when her book *The Death and Life of Great American Cities* was published. Still, they have become the basis of a worldwide movement to foster safer cities.

2   Jacobs made an important contribution to our understanding of cities by emphasizing the link between the *fear* of crime and urban design. Jacobs was visionary in arguing that we should be concerned about the everyday experiences of city inhabitants, instead of focusing on

crimes against property or the criminals themselves. Jacobs writes about the ways in which planning and design diminish or enhance people's sense of safety.

[ . . . ] The bedrock attribute of a successful city district is that a person must feel personally safe and secure on the street among all these strangers. It does not take many incidents of violence on a city street or in a city district to make people fear the streets. And as they fear them, they use them less, which makes the streets still more unsafe.

3   Although Jacobs's comment about the need for eyes on the street is still broadly quoted, her many other recommendations, based on close observation of public spaces, have received little attention. For Jacobs, eyes on the street came from stores and public places, including bars and restaurants "sprinkled along the sidewalks," street vendors, and pedestrians. She recommended the installation of bright street lights to "augment every pair of eyes."

4   But Jacobs widened her attention to urban safety in general, including parks and public housing projects. She discredited the prevailing myths about good design and expected behaviors. While most planners have great respect for neighborhood open spaces focusing on the green benefits of parks, she argued against open space in cities if it meant parks that were underused and dangerous. She argued that parks could be "volatile places." She observed that parks are successful when they encourage a range of activities and users.

5   Jacobs's views on public housing were equally controversial. She noted that slum clearance projects that created high-rise towers with concentrations of poor people were often dangerous places that people with other choices avoided at all cost. Her critique of public housing design included long, unwatched corridors, unguarded elevators, stairwells, and courtyards that became settings for rape, theft, and vandalism. She also observed that too often, public housing managers were more concerned with vandalism—the destruction of property—than danger to human beings.

6   Her recommendations to increase safety at public housing sites emphasized design and management policies to encourage interaction and commitment. She suggested integrating public housing communities into existing street patterns and cultivating street activity by including businesses in the buildings. She opposed fencing and security guards, which created a sense of territory and insulated public housing residents from the wider community. She suggested that women tenants could be elevator attendants to provide eyes on the vertical streets.

**2.** *Circle the choice that best represents the main idea of paragraphs 1–6.*

    a.  Jacobs wrote a book called *The Death and Life of Great American Cities.*

    b.  Jacobs examined the relationship between safety and urban planning.

    c.  Jacobs felt that including businesses in public housing projects would improve safety.

**3.** *Now skim paragraphs 7–12 to find the main idea.*

7    In the 1970s, Oscar Newman and others built on Jacobs's insights into the relationship between urban design and crime. They launched the new field of crime prevention through environmental design (CPTED). But they simplified Jacobs's vision, focusing on an approach that relied on experts (either design or security professionals) to define the issues and to provide standardized solutions.

8    CPTED programs often ignored a key aspect of Jacobs's argument—the importance of fear of crime. CPTED programs tended to ignore crimes against people and focused more on crimes against property and crime rates. Programs also ignored differences in fear of crime between men and women and between white and minority urban residents.

9    CPTED programs promoted hardware and design changes, rather than encouraging the presence of people and varied activities. Fences, buzzers, gates, and traffic barriers were proposed to keep people out and to define territory, particularly in residential areas—despite Jacobs's warnings to the contrary. CPTED largely ignored the more subtle elements of urban safety that Jacobs had suggested: a mix of activities and land uses that could attract diverse populations to streets, neighborhoods, housing projects, parks, and civic centers.

10    The evolution of high-security shopping malls illustrates CPTED principles. Shopping malls in high-crime areas in California have installed motion sensors and other high-tech security equipment around the mall that allow security forces to observe the entire mall, and security patrols are more visible.

11    In contrast, Dufferin Mall, in a working- and middle-class, ethnically diverse neighborhood in Toronto, took a community development approach to reduce crime rates and enhance profitability. The mall provides funding to youth theater, basketball, and soccer organizations; merchants participate in a youth internship program; it provides rent-free space for youth services, a teen drop-in center, a program for high-school dropouts, and a clothing exchange. As Jacobs suggested, these have brought a range of activities and users into the mall and reduced crime rates.

12    Jacobs wrote about her experience of daily life in the city and urged planners to pay attention to how ordinary people actually use urban space. From her experience as a wife, mother, and resident of Greenwich Village in New York City, she arrived at a more human vision of the city than the experts of the day did. Her concern about urban safety was visionary, and her manner of looking at the city still offers a critical viewpoint for evaluating crime prevention and community safety strategies today.

Source: Wekerle, G. (2000). From eyes on the streets to safe cities. *Places, 13* (1), 44–49.

**4.** *Circle the choice that best represents the main idea of paragraphs 7–12.*
     a. The CPTED movement was built on Jacobs's views of urban planning to encourage urban safety.
     b. The CPTED movement misinterpreted Jacobs's views of how to achieve urban safety.
     c. The Dufferin Mall is an example of a CPTED project.

**5.** *Now compare your answers with a partner's and talk about the strategies you used to find the main ideas of the text. Which strategies were most useful for you? Why?*

# Focused Reading

Scanning is reading strategically to find the answers to specific questions. It can be especially valuable when you need to answer a set of questions in a short amount of time. Here are some strategies you can use to scan readings for answers:

A. Find a key word in the question and search for the key word, or a synonym of it, in the text.

B. Look for capitalized letters if you are looking for an answer to a *where* or *who* question.

C. Read quotes. Authors usually quote only the most important information from another author.

D. Look for numbers if you are looking for an answer to a numerical question.

E. Read the first and last sentence of each paragraph to find the paragraph in which you will most likely find the answer.

F. Look for key transition words such as *in contrast*, *however*, and *therefore*. These indicate that a new point of view will be introduced.

**1.** *Read the questions. Then scan the text on pages 6 to 8 and write answers to the questions. Write the letter of the strategy you used to find the answer and a brief description of the strategy.*

1. Who is the author who wrote *The Death and Life of Great American Cities*?

   Answer: _Jane Jacobs_

   Strategy: _B—Look for capitalized letters to answer a "who" question_

2. According to Jacobs, what was the key to a successful city?

   Answer: _____

   Strategy: _____

3. What did Jacobs recommend to increase the eyes on the streets?

   Answer: _____

   Strategy: _____

4. What were Jacobs's views on public residential projects?

   Answer: _____

   Strategy: _____

5. When did Oscar Newman and others create the crime prevention through environmental design (CPTED) movement?

   Answer: _____

   Strategy: _____

6. What did CPTED programs promote to increase safety?

   Answer: _____

   Strategy: _____

7. Name and describe the shopping mall that exemplifies Jacobs's views of urban design to promote safety.

Answer: _____

Strategy: _____

8. How are Jacobs's views regarded today?

Answer: _____

Strategy: _____

*2.* *Work in groups of three and compare your answers. Discuss the strategies you used.*

---

**Checkpoint 1**    PEARSON LONGMAN myacademicconnectionslab

---

In this section, you will learn strategies that will help you to identify main ideas and details in lectures. You will also get some tips on how to prepare for lectures in order to maximize your understanding.
For online assignments, go to

PEARSON LONGMAN
myacademicconnectionslab

## Before You Listen

*1.* *Your professor has asked you to do some reading before you attend the lecture. Read the paragraph. Then answer the questions.*

From roughly 1820 to 1940, most urban criticism was premised on the physical hardships that resulted from the obvious overcrowding of city inhabitants. Men and women living in cities seemed unable to live the comparatively long and healthy lives of their rural counterparts. Similarly, urban critics were troubled by the inability of city families to raise healthy children. Concerns related to lack of sanitation, substandard housing, access to alcohol, high death rates, and low birth rates suggested that cities threatened prevailing religious and moral attitudes and worked against the traditional family unit. Cities were places of vice, crime, and revolt. A less immediate but still serious concern was that most cities were so ugly they seemed to produce men and women who were ignorant of the beauty of nature and incapable of creativity.

1. Write the main idea of the paragraph.

   _____

   _____

2. Make a list of the concerns urban critics had about cities. These concerns are the details that support the main idea.

   _____

   _____

3. Work in small groups. Brainstorm some solutions to these problems.

   _____

   _____

Before going to a lecture, it is helpful to think about what to expect. If you have thought about the content in advance, you will probably find listening easier. To improve your listening skills, you can do the following:

- Consider what you already know about the lecture topic.
- Review your notes from previous lectures on related topics.
- Read the textbook chapter that matches the lecture topic. Look for main points and details that support each of the points.
- Make a short list of key vocabulary words that you will likely hear. If words are long or hard to spell, develop short forms for them to make note taking easier.

**2.** *To improve your comprehension of the lecture, use information from the readings to answer the questions.*

1. What do you think the topic of this lecture will be?

2. What are some specific things you already know about this topic?

3. What are some things you'd like to learn about this topic?

# Global Listening

## Listening for a Speaker's Main Point(s)

To understand the main point(s) of a lecture, you can do the following:

- Listen carefully right at the beginning of a lecture because main points are often stated first. Don't wait to focus your attention.
- Listen for ideas that are repeated throughout the lecture.
- Listen for information about points that the professor has written on the board.
- Listen at the end of the lecture for concluding comments.

If you understand the professor's main point(s), it will help you understand the lecture details, take notes efficiently, and hear vocabulary words that are related to the topic.

## Key Words

**boulevard** *n* a wide, main street

**grid** *n* a pattern of straight lines that cross, used to organize streets

**impoverished** *adj* very poor

**industry** *n* business that provides goods or services

**radical** *adj* extreme, very different

**1.** ∩ *Listen to the introduction of the lecture to discover the main point(s). Then discuss the questions with the class.*

1. Why did urban planners develop new visions for the "modern" city?

2. What will the professor probably talk about in the rest of the lecture?

**2.** ∩ *Now listen to the entire lecture and complete the chart on the next page. As you listen, write the name of each Modern City Vision next to the name of the urban planner who created the vision. Write down the main point about each of the city visions.*

| Urban Planner | Name of Modern City Vision | Main Point |
|---|---|---|
| Ebenezer Howard | | |
| Le Corbusier | | |
| Daniel Burnham | | |

**3.** *Work in groups of three. Each of you will select an urban plan shown in one of the photos (A, B, or C) and examine it for the characteristics in the chart. Take notes in the appropriate column. Then discuss your observations with your group. Complete the chart with information you get from your partners.*

A

B

C

| Characteristics | Plan A | Plan B | Plan C |
|---|---|---|---|
| How are the streets organized? (in a grid, in a wavy pattern, or in a curved pattern?) Could people walk along the streets? | | | |
| What are the size and shape of the buildings? | | | |
| Are the places where people live, work, and play close together or far apart? | | | |
| What is the correct name of each Modern City Vision? | | | |

# Focused Listening

In most lectures, professors will state a main point and follow it with supporting details. Supporting details can be examples, explanations, elaborations, reasons, solutions, opinions, or exceptions. Most often supporting details simply follow the main point, without any key words to indicate that they are details. This is the case with the paragraph about the physical hardships of living in early cities on page 10.

Sometimes key words are used to show that the speaker has moved from a main point to a supporting detail.

| Type of detail | Sometimes introduced by these expressions |
| --- | --- |
| examples | *for example, for instance, such as* |
| explanations | *this means that, that is, in other words* |
| elaborations | *in addition, moreover, furthermore, also* |
| reasons | *because, in order to, as a result, therefore* |
| solutions | *one solution/approach/idea/answer* |
| opinions | *in his/her opinion, from his/her point of view* |
| exceptions | *except for, apart from, other than* |

Supporting details provide essential information that will help you understand the main point more fully.

Often, professors will post course notes or PowerPoint slides on their course websites. You can download these notes or slides and bring them to the lecture or use them to study for exams. Generally, course notes contain the main points the professor will cover during a lecture. Students must add the details.

*1.* 🎧 *Listen again to the introduction of the lecture. While you listen, look at the first slide, which indicates the main idea of the lecture. Notice the details that a student has added. These details support the main point.*

| Main Lecture Points | Details |
| --- | --- |
| • **Urban life (late 1800s) was dangerous and unhealthy** | **Problem:** *Dirty, noisy, smelly* |
| | • *Poverty and poor health* |
| | • *Cities seen as evil and offensive to nature* |
| • **20th century city planners' reaction** | **Reaction to problem:** *New ideas emerged about what a city could/should look like* |

SLIDE ONE   ◀ ▶

**2.** 🎧 *Listen again to the entire lecture. While you listen, look at each slide and add more details to develop a complete and personalized set of study notes.*

**Vision One:**
**Howard's Garden City**

- Move the city into the country
- Functions separated— work from residential, cultural from industrial

**Details about the Garden City:**

_____

_____

_____

**Problem:**

_____

_____

_____

_____

SLIDE TWO ◄ ►

**Vision Two:**
**Le Corbusier's Radiant City**

- Bring the country into the city

**Details about the Radiant City:**

_____

_____

_____

**Problem:**

_____

_____

_____

_____

SLIDE THREE ◄ ►

**Vision Three:**
**Burnham's City Beautiful**

- All important buildings built along a central boulevard

**Details about the City Beautiful:**

_____

_____

_____

**Problem:**

_____

_____

_____

_____

SLIDE FOUR ◄ ►

**Conclusion:**

**When city functions are separated, cities become unsafe**

**More Details:**

_____

_____

_____

_____

_____

_____

_____

_____

SLIDE FIVE ◀ ▶

**3.** *Work with a partner. Discuss the details you added. Do you have the same details? Combine what you heard to include as many details as possible. You can listen to the lecture again if you wish. Discuss your notes with the class.*

**Checkpoint 2** PEARSON LONGMAN myacademicconnectionslab

# 4

## Building Academic Writing Skills

In this section, you will practice writing thesis statements and using parallel structure. Then you will write an expository essay about planning safe cities. You will use information from the readings and the lecture in this unit to complete the writing assignment.

For online assignments, go to

PEARSON LONGMAN
myacademicconnectionslab

## Before You Write

An expository essay gives information about a topic. Classification, cause-effect, compare-contrast, process, and definition essays are all expository essays. Details are essential in expository essays, as they provide the information about a topic that you want your reader to know.

**1.** *To help you write your essay, read the model expository essay on page 16. Follow the steps as you read:*
- Label the introduction, body, and conclusion of the essay.
- Underline the sentence in the introduction that is the thesis statement.
- Underline the topic sentence of each paragraph in the body.
- In the conclusion, underline the sentence that is the concluding statement.

**2.** *When you have finished reading, make sure your class agrees on the sentences you underlined. Then discuss the questions with the class.*

1. What is the main point of each paragraph?

2. In each paragraph, which sentence(s) contain(s) the main point? Which sentences contain the details?

**Essay Question: What design factors reduce neighborhood crime?**

**Model Expository Essay:** Reducing Neighborhood Crime through Urban Design

As crime statistics clearly show, crime rates in urban areas are decreasing. However, concern about crime is still a major public issue. Every day, newspapers print stories abot personal violations, property damage, and school invasions. There are regular calls for increased police presence on the streets and longer prison sentences for convicted criminals. But rarely does the public stop to consider what design features might reduce neighborhood crime. In fact, urban planners can significantly reduce neighborhood crime through the use of target hardening, access control, and offender deflection.

Target hardening is a term that describes measures taken to make a "target" (for example, a home) more difficult to break into. Research indicates, not surprisingly, that criminals planning to break into a house consider how likely they are to be seen breaking in. If home owners have made some effort to make their homes look like "hard targets," criminals may decide to pass them by. Some methods of target hardening include making the front door visible to neighbors and drivers, fencing backyards and locking the gates, and installing a burglar alarm that is police monitored. Even the presence of a dog can make burglars think twice about breaking in. Target hardening is a practical method to reduce the chances that criminals will be active in your neighborhood.

Some neighborhoods use access control to keep criminals out. These communities are often called "gated communities," and the people who live there are generally wealthy. Gated communities can be identified by pillars or gates at the entryway to the neighborhood. Even though the gates are not closed or locked, they provide a visible separation, discouraging non-owners from entering. These communities may also have a security guard patrolling the neighborhood, as well as fenced exteriors. People who choose to live in gated communities rely on these measures of access control to prevent criminals from entering.

Other neighborhoods may try to reduce crime by planning land use that deflects, or turns away, potential offenders. For example, bus stops may be moved away from the main entry into a neighborhood. While this makes accessing public transit more difficult for people living in the community, it means that potential criminals who might linger at a bus stop to identify possible targets will be farther away from the neighborhood. Similarly, some communities will fight the establishment of a bar or restaurant that may bring more traffic or encourage strangers to enter their neighborhoods late at night. Criminal deflection reduces crime by discouraging possible burglars from entering the neighborhood.

Despite crime statistics that indicate urban crime is falling, fear of crime is as prevalent as ever. When neighbors come together to discuss what they can do to help reduce crime, there are certain measures they can take. The "hardening" of targets, controlling access, and offender deflection are a few approaches home owners and communities can use to reduce criminal activity. Hopefully, urban planners will keep these methods in mind as they plan the communities of the future.

# Focused Writing

Writing effective thesis statements is key to becoming a strong writer. An effective thesis statement will identify the following essential information for your reader:

- the topic of the essay
- your opinion about the topic (without saying "I think" or "In my opinion")
- the main points of the essay written in parallel structure

**1.** *Look closely at the thesis statement from the model expository essay. Identify the three features of an effective thesis statement.*

In fact, urban planners can significantly reduce neighborhood crime through the use of target hardening, access control, and offender deflection.

| |
|---|
| Essay topic: |
| Author's opinion: |
| Main points: |

## Using Parallel Structure

Notice that the thesis statement uses parallel structure, which allows the reader to easily see the similarity of the listed items. Parallel structure, or parallelism, is the listing of similar items using similar grammatical forms.

It is a good idea to use parallel structure in your writing whenever you can as it helps your reader to understand, creates a pleasing rhythm, and shows you have good language control.

**2.** *Read the sentences. How is the structure of these sentences similar? Discuss with the class.*

- Methods used in the field of crime prevention through environmental design (CPTED) include security guards, buzzer gates, and traffic barriers.
- For Jacobs, safe streets meant a mix of residential, commercial, and recreational buildings.
- Howard designed the Garden City to eliminate the ills of larger cities, such as high crime rates, short life expectancy, and small family size.

*Look at each underlined item in this sentence. Each underlined item consists of two words: a noun used as an adjective, followed by a noun.*

- Methods used in the field of crime prevention through environmental design (CPTED) include <u>security guards</u>, <u>buzzer gates</u>, and <u>traffic barriers</u>.

*Look at each underlined item in this sentence. Each of these items is an adjective, and each adjective ends in -al.*

- For Jacobs, safe streets meant a mix of <u>residential</u>, <u>commercial</u>, and <u>recreational</u> buildings.

*Look at each underlined item in this sentence. Each of these items is a three-word combination of adjective, noun (used as an adjective), noun.*

- Howard designed the Garden City to eliminate the ills of larger cities, such as <u>high crime rates</u>, <u>short life expectancy</u>, and <u>small family size</u>.

**3.** *Read the parallel sentences. Underline each listed item and identify the part of speech (adjective, noun, adverb, etc.) of each item.*

1. Personal safety depends on lifestyle, location, wealth, and awareness.

2. Parking barriers, fenced yards, and entry phones are used to discourage modern criminals.

3. Airport security planners use metal detector equipment, X-ray baggage screening, and explosive trace detection to control crime on airplanes.

**4.** *Each of the sentences lists items that are not in parallel structure. Underline the items and decide which item is not parallel with the other items. Then correct the non-parallel item.*

1. All public buildings—art galleries, museums, and hospitals—should be built with safety in mind.

2. City features that people enjoy, such as walking paths, public parks, and businesses, may encourage crime.

3. Improved street lighting, front doors that have high visibility, and increased traffic flow are factors that can decrease crime in neighborhoods.

**5.** *An ineffective thesis statement will not successfully inform the reader about the essay topic, the author's opinion, or the main points. Study these common thesis errors.*

1. Urban planning is a broad field of study.
   - Problem: There is no main focus. If the thesis statement is too general, the essay will have no clear topic.
   - Improved thesis: Urban planning combines urban design with safety considerations and building regulations.

2. Urban planning is the field of designing urban spaces.
   - Problem: There is no opinion. This thesis is a statement of fact. The thesis should express an opinion.
   - Improved thesis: Urban planning can use design to make urban spaces safer.

3. I believe that urban planners can help reduce crime rates.
   - Problem: There is no need to state "I believe," "I think," or "In my opinion." Leave these phrases out.
   - Improved thesis: Urban planners can help reduce crime rates.

4. What can urban planners do to reduce crime rates?
   - Problem: A thesis is a statement, not a question.
   - Improved thesis: Urban planners can use target hardening, access control, and offender deflection to reduce crime rates.

5. To prevent their homes from being broken into, home owners can trim their gardens to make their front doors visible from the street, build fences, and install a burglar alarm that is police monitored.
   - Problem: Main points in a thesis should be written in parallel structure so they are easy to understand.
   - Improved thesis: To prevent their homes from being broken into, home owners can trim bushy trees, build secure fences, and install burglar alarms.

**6.** *Most of these thesis statements are ineffective. Determine why they are ineffective and rewrite them so they are more effective. Which thesis statement is the most effective? Why?*

1. What factors contributed to the development of the modern suburb in the United States?

   Problem: _____

   Improved thesis: _____

2. The increasing use of the automobile, the car industry, the growing network of urban roads running out of the city, and the suburbs all developed together.

   Problem: _____

   Improved thesis: _____

3. I think urban planners do not have much influence on the crime rate simply through urban planning.

   Problem: _____

   Improved thesis: _____

4. There is much to be said about the building of "Levittowns" in the late 1940s and early 1950s.

   Problem: _____

   Improved thesis: _____

5. All countries need good highways.

   Problem: _____

   Improved thesis: _____

6. At the end of the Second World War, the growth in automobile use, the car industry, and the road network combined to create a demand for suburban housing.

   Problem: _____

   Improved thesis: _____

# Integrated Writing Task

You have read texts and listened to a lecture about how urban planners can help create safe environments for residents. Use your knowledge of the unit content, topic vocabulary, effective thesis statements, and parallel structure to write a short expository essay in response to this question: **What visions have urban planners proposed to design safe cities?**

Your essay will have an introduction, a body (with two or three paragraphs), and a concluding paragraph. Each paragraph will have a main point and supporting details. You will use vocabulary specific to urban planning, and parallel structure when necessary.

*Follow the steps to write your essay.*

**Step 1:** To prepare for writing, develop a set of key words that you will likely use in your essay. Work with a partner to brainstorm vocabulary words in each category in the chart.

| Words for Large Cities | Words For People Who Live in Large Cities | Words to Express Poverty | Words for Different Areas Within a City | Words to Describe Urban Safety |
|---|---|---|---|---|
| metropolis | residents | impoverished | residential areas | streets |
| | | | | |
| | | | | |
| | | | | |

**Step 2:** Think about the essay question. Then review the readings and the lecture. How many urban planners have you learned about? What were their visions? What details could you use to explain those visions? Fill in the chart on the next page to help you organize your ideas.

| Urban Planner | Vision | Details |
|---|---|---|
| Jane Jacobs | "eyes on the streets" | •<br><br>•<br><br>• |
| Oscar Newman | | "Hardware solutions" such as<br>• traffic barriers<br><br>• fences<br><br>• buzzer gates<br><br>• police patrols |
| Ebenezer Howard | The Garden City | •<br><br>•<br><br>• |
| Le Corbusier | | •<br><br>•<br><br>• |
| Daniel Burnham | | •<br><br>•<br><br>• |
| No specific planner | Urban design that reduces neighborhood crime | • Target hardening<br><br>•<br><br>• |

**Step 3:** Decide which urban planners and visions you would like to discuss in your essay. You don't need to use all six. Remember, you should have at least one urban planner from the reading and one from the lecture to demonstrate that you can integrate information from multiple sources.

**Step 4:** Write your thesis statement and analyze it. Does it include the three features of an effective thesis statement? Show it to a classmate. Ask him or her to identify the thesis topic, author's opinion, and main points stated in parallel structure.

**Step 5:** Write your introductory paragraph. Finish with your thesis statement.

**Step 6:** Write the body and conclusion of your essay.
- Include a paragraph for each main point of your essay.
- Make sure that each paragraph includes a topic sentence that states the main point of that paragraph clearly.
- Complete each paragraph with supporting details.
- Finish with a concluding paragraph. The final sentence should restate your thesis.

**Step 7:** Ask your teacher or a classmate to review your essay based on the features listed in the checklist.

| Essay Feature Checklist | Yes | No |
|---|---|---|
| Introductory paragraph | | |
| Effective thesis | | |
| Main points of thesis in parallel structure | | |
| One main point per paragraph | | |
| Topic sentences clearly state the main point of each paragraph. | | |
| Supporting details complete the paragraph. | | |
| Concluding paragraph | | |
| Thesis restated in the concluding paragraph | | |
| Vocabulary is specific to the topic. | | |

**Step 8:** Based on the information in the checklist, rewrite your essay and hand it in.

# UNIT 2

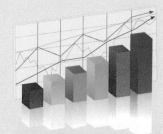

## Business

# Leadership Behavior

## Unit Description

**Content:** This course is designed to familiarize the student with concepts in business management.

**Skills:** Organizational Structure
- Recognizing multiple organizational patterns
- Recognizing relationships among ideas in a text
- Organizing information
- Recognizing relationships among parts of a lecture
- Presenting relationships among ideas clearly when speaking

## Unit Requirements

**Reading:** "The Search for Leadership Traits" (from *Organizational Behavior: Understanding and Managing Life at Work*, 6th Edition, G. Johns & A.M. Saks, Pearson Prentice Hall)

**Lecture:** "Behavioral Theories of Leadership"

**Listening:** "Three Contrasting Managerial Styles" (a student presentation)

**Integrated Speaking Task:** Presenting an oral response to a case study about a company that is having leadership problems

**Assignments:** www.MyAcademicConnectionsLab.com

# 1

## Preview

For online assignments, go to

**PEARSON LONGMAN**
**myacademicconnectionslab**

Bill Gates

## Previewing the Academic Content

What characteristics make Bill Gates, the founder of Microsoft, so successful? Successful businesspeople have always fascinated the public and researchers alike. Researchers have studied successful business leaders to develop theories that explain their successes. What qualities do they have, how do they behave, and does their behavior change depending on the work situation?

*1. Here is a list of qualities that might be valuable in a leader. Rate them from most important (1) to least important (11). Then compare your ranking with another student's. Are there differences in your rankings? Explain why you ranked these qualities in the order you did by giving examples from your own experience.*

\_\_\_\_\_ Charismatic—motivates people by inspiring them

\_\_\_\_\_ Directive—gives direction to others

\_\_\_\_\_ Ruthless—demonstrates determination when making unpleasant decisions

\_\_\_\_\_ Sensitive—understands others' problems

\_\_\_\_\_ Communicative—communicates key information

\_\_\_\_\_ Cunning—uses clever but possibly dishonest means to achieve a goal

\_\_\_\_\_ Team builder—facilitates groups of employees working together to achieve a goal

\_\_\_\_\_ Intelligent—thinks clearly and understands quickly

\_\_\_\_\_ Organized—plans ahead to ensure needs are met

\_\_\_\_\_ Self-monitoring—considers how to work more efficiently

\_\_\_\_\_ Persevering—continuing in spite of difficulties

*What other qualities can you add to this list?*

> Linda Cook, former chief executive officer (CEO) of a large oil company, is one of very few female leaders in the male-dominated oil industry. She has been recognized as one of the world's leading female entrepreneurs and was named the 44th most powerful woman in the world by *Forbes Magazine* in September 2007. She is a member of the board of directors of the Boeing Company.

*2. Read the paragraph on page 25. Then decide which of the valuable leadership qualities listed in Exercise 1 Linda Cook demonstrates. Discuss your answers with the class.*

## Linda Cook, former CEO of Shell Canada

In July 2003, Linda Cook arrived in Calgary to begin her new job as CEO of Shell Canada Ltd. The new job made her the first woman ever to head a major integrated oil-and-gas company, and at the age of 45, she was the youngest CEO ever to lead Shell Canada. She has been **a rising star** since she joined the Shell Oil Company in 1980 as a reservoir engineer after graduating with a degree in petroleum engineering from the University of Kansas. She has been described by colleagues as "personable" and as a "great communicator." She is also known for her efficiency. Within the oil-and-gas industry, she is known for her high energy and **sound business judgment**. She has a reputation for dealing well with customers, **extracting value** by **offloading faltering assets,** and persevering on complex projects. She describes herself as a team player, saying, "I like in the end to move forward as a team with important decisions we have made and expect people to stand behind them. I have high standards and expectations in terms of performance and **delivery against targets**, including for myself."

Source: Johns, G., & Saks, A.M. (2005). *Organizational behavior: Understanding and managing life at work* (6th ed.). Toronto: Pearson Prentice Hall.

---

## Key Words

a. delivery against targets

b. extracting value

c. faltering assets

d. offloading

e. a rising star

f. sound business judgment

**3.** *The paragraph you just read contains many business-related expressions. Write the letter of each key word next to its definition. Use a dictionary if you need to. Compare your answers with a partner's.*

_____ 1. Things that used to make money that are now losing money

_____ 2. The ability to make logical decisions about business

_____ 3. Selling off financially weak companies or divisions of companies

_____ 4. Someone who is doing well at work and being promoted

_____ 5. The ability to get things done after you said you would do them

_____ 6. Finding the financially strong elements in a weak company

This unit will help you recognize organizational patterns in readings and lectures, and develop and effectively use organizational patterns in speaking.

## Previewing the Academic Skills Focus

Most academic texts are expository in nature, that is, they are written to provide information. As you read books and articles and listen to lectures, you will discover that the texts are often organized in similar patterns. Recognizing patterns of organization can help you predict and anticipate what you will read or hear next, which can make your reading faster and your listening easier.

What are patterns of organization? You may be familiar with some of them already. Typical patterns of text organization are description, definition, process, cause-effect, advantage-disadvantage, problem-solution, and compare-contrast. These patterns are closely linked to an author's purpose.

| Patterns of Organization | Author's Purpose |
|---|---|
| Description text | Describe someone or something |
| Definition text | Define a term and give an example |
| Process text | Explain how to do something |
| Cause-effect text | Explain what caused something |
| Advantages-disadvantages text | List the strengths and weaknesses of something |
| Problem-solution text | Describe a problem and explain a solution |
| Compare and/or contrast text | Show similarities or differences between two or more items |

**1.** *Work with a partner. Read the text outlines. Label each outline with the correct pattern of organization: description, definition, process, cause-effect, advantages-disadvantages, problem-solution, or compare-contrast. Then check your answers with the class. What might explain any differences you have?*

**A. Organizational Pattern:** *Description text*

Introduce the person or thing you want to describe

↓

Provide details that describe the person or thing

1. _____ 2. _____ 3. _____ 4. _____

↓

Summarize

**B. Organizational Pattern:** _____

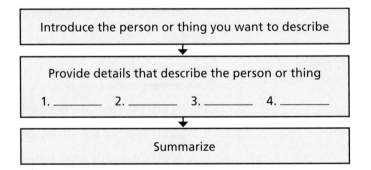

Describe the situation → Explain the problem → Describe the solution → Explain the results

**C. Organizational Pattern:** _____

| Block-Style Organization | |
|---|---|
| Introduce two items | |
| Describe item 1<br>1. | Describe item 2<br>1. |
| 2. | 2. |
| 3. | 3. |
| Conclusion | |

| Point-by-Point Organization | |
|---|---|
| Introduce two items | |
| Point 1 | Describe item 1<br>Describe item 2 |
| Point 2 | Describe item 1<br>Describe item 2 |
| Point 3 | Describe item 1<br>Describe item 2 |
| Conclusion | |

**D. Organizational Pattern:** _____

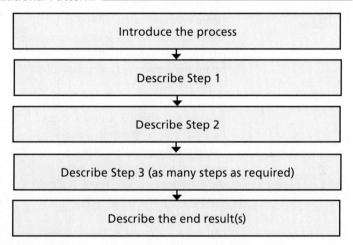

Introduce the term to be defined   is a   Classify the term   that   Provide a definition

**E. Organizational Pattern:** _____

Introduce the process
↓
Describe Step 1
↓
Describe Step 2
↓
Describe Step 3 (as many steps as required)
↓
Describe the end result(s)

**F. Organizational Pattern:** _____

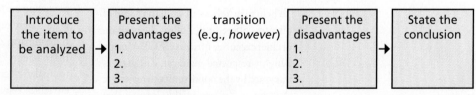

Introduce the item to be analyzed → Present the advantages 1. 2. 3.   transition (e.g., *however*)   Present the disadvantages 1. 2. 3. → State the conclusion

**G. Organizational Pattern:** _____

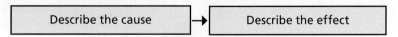

Describe the cause → Describe the effect

What was the organizational pattern of the text about Linda Cook on page 25? How do you know?

**2.** *Read the text about a trucking company called Yellow Corporation. As you read, think about how the text is organized. Then answer the questions.*

## The Turnaround at Yellow Corporation

1  Since its founding in 1923, Yellow Corporation has been a leader in the transportation industry, using trucks to haul goods between points in Canada, the United States, and Mexico. For decades, Yellow achieved success by concentrating virtually all of its attention on increasing efficiency at every turn. Yellow has long been a master at ensuring that trucks are full before they leave a warehouse, and it has also developed precisely timed delivery schedules.

2  Unfortunately, Yellow eventually fell victim to its own success. As operational efficiency increased, customer service received less and less attention, and before long, newer and more responsive companies were taking away the firm's customers. Compounding this problem was the fact that the customers most likely to seek a more service-oriented transportation provider were also the ones willing to pay high prices for the extra service. As a result, Yellow's financial performance began to decline, slowly at first, but then more dramatically. Naturally, the decline in revenue led to even worse across-the-board service.

3  To help turn Yellow around, the board of directors offered Bill Zollars the position of chief executive officer (CEO). Already a highly respected manager, Zollars was intrigued by the opportunity to revitalize the carrier. Zollars quickly learned that organizational change at Yellow would have to be profound. Over a period of decades, people throughout the company had come to accept mediocrity and were often willing to do only the minimal amount necessary to get their jobs done. Zollars knew that he had to alter the attitudes, behavior, and performance of 30,000 employees. He began by improving communication. The CEO spent 18 months traveling to several hundred locations, and at each site, he talked face-to-face with customers and with employees at all levels. He asked for opinions and consistently provided his own message—namely, that enhanced customer service was to become the firm's new focus.

4  Zollars's plan consisted of more than promises and motivational speeches. Whereas previous leaders often didn't focus on problems and refused to divulge information about the firm's performance, Zollars openly acknowledged the company's defect rate—the percentage of shipments that were late, wrong, or damaged. Employees were stunned to find that the rate was a whopping 40 percent, but that knowledge was necessary to enhance motivation and set a benchmark for improvement. Zollars also instituted the company's first ongoing program for surveying customer satisfaction, and the results were reported openly throughout the company. Zollars made a real effort to listen to employees, gave them authority to make decisions, and developed an enviable reputation for honesty and commitment. "If people doing the work don't believe what's coming from the leadership," says Zollars, "it doesn't get implemented. Period."

Source: Adapted from Griffin, R.W., Ebert R.J., & Starke, F.A. (2005). Concluding case: Yellow delivers the goods. *Business*, (8th ed.). Upper Saddle River, NJ: Pearson Prentice Hall.

1. Which pattern of organization does the author use in this text?

2. If you looked only at the first two paragraphs of this text, what might you think the author's purpose was?

3. There are four paragraphs in this text. What is the function of each paragraph? Choose from these four possibilities: problem, results, solution, situation.

Paragraph 1: _____

Paragraph 2: _____

Paragraph 3: _____

Paragraph 4: _____

4. What leadership characteristics did Zollars demonstrate? You can refer to the list of characteristics on p. 24 if you wish.

## Before You Read

*1.* Work in small groups. Read the paragraphs and answer the questions.

**2**

**Building Academic Reading Skills**

In this section, you will learn more about identifying organizational patterns in longer texts and recognizing the relationships among parts of a text.

For online assignments, go to

PEARSON LONGMAN
myacademicconnectionslab

**Boss A:**

You have just been hired by a small company that sells computer parts. You will be the receptionist for the company, directing phone calls to the appropriate salespeople, taking phone messages, greeting visitors, and so on. This is your first job, and you are very nervous. Your boss meets you a little early on your first day and shows you your desk and phone. You admit to being nervous. Your boss is encouraging and says, "Don't worry, you'll be fine. It's good to be nervous on the first day. In a few days, you'll feel right at home." She then wishes you good luck and leaves. The phone starts to ring, and the first visitors come through the door. You realize you don't know the names or phone extensions of the salespeople, or how to work the complicated phone system.

**Boss B:**

You have just been hired by a small photocopying company. As you don't have much customer service experience, you will spend most of your time photocopying the orders that the customer service representatives take. Your boss meets you a little early on the first day. He shows you the photocopier you will be using, how to change the paper and the copy settings, and where the ink cartridges are located. He has three large photocopy jobs for you this morning. He says you must finish the three large jobs before lunch or you will be fired, and he goes away.

**Key Words**

personal quality =
characteristic =
trait

1. List the traits each boss demonstrates. Then discuss which boss you would rather work for and why.

2. Do you think that knowing the boss's traits will tell you if he or she is someone you would want to work for? What other things about a boss or the company might help you decide if you would want to work there?

*2.* With your group, discuss each vocabulary item and its meaning in the chart on page 30. Then complete the third column to link the new vocabulary to your own experience.

| Vocabulary Item | Meaning | Link to Your Own Experience |
|---|---|---|
| 1. implicit assumption | Something that is understood without being stated | Give an example of an implicit assumption. *Education is good.* Can you think of others? |
| 2. stable personality | A personality that is steady, reliable, and not changeable | Name someone famous who has a stable personality. |
| 3. orchestrate a turnaround | To organize, arrange, and manage a complete change in fortune or outcome | Name a politician who has orchestrated a turnaround of a country. |
| 4. ailing company/ ailing person | A company that is not doing well  A person in poor health | Give an example of an ailing company or an ailing person. |
| 5. extroversion | A personality characteristic of someone who is confident and enjoys the company of others | Name someone you know who has an extroverted personality. |
| 6. prominent firm | A company that is doing well in business | Name five prominent firms. |
| 7. the former . . . the latter | *The former* refers to the idea or point that comes first in a sentence, and *the latter* refers to the idea or point that comes second in a sentence. | In the sentence below, which idea is the former, and which one is the latter? *While motivational leaders inspire their employees to do well, directive leaders risk annoying their employees by sounding bossy.*  Which type of leader would you rather work for, the former or the latter? |

## Global Reading

### Recognizing Multiple Organizational Patterns

Short texts, like the ones you have looked at so far in this unit, usually demonstrate only a single pattern of organization. However, when you read or listen to longer texts, you may notice that longer texts are often divided into sections, and each section may have its own organizational pattern. This is the case with the textbook excerpt you will read in this section.

*1.* Read the text. Work alone to determine the pattern of organization for each section of the text. Write it in the space provided. Then discuss your answers with the class.

## The Search for Leadership Traits

1  Throughout history, social observers have been fascinated by obvious demonstrations of successful interpersonal influence, whether the consequences of this influence were good, bad, or mixed. Individuals such as Henry Ford, Martin Luther King, Jr., Barbara Jordan, Ralph Nader, and Joan of Arc have been analyzed and reanalyzed to discover what made them leaders and what set them apart from less successful leaders. The implicit assumption here is that those who become leaders and do a good job of it possess a special set of traits that distinguishes them from the masses of followers. While philosophers and the popular media have advocated such a position for centuries, trait theories of leadership did not receive serious scientific attention until the 1900s.

2  During World War I the U.S. military recognized that it had a leadership problem. Never before had the country mounted such a massive war effort, and able officers were in short supply. Thus, the search for leadership traits that might be useful in identifying potential officers began. Following the war, and continuing through World War II, this interest expanded to include searching for leadership traits in populations as diverse as schoolchildren and business executives. Some studies tried to differentiate traits of leaders and followers, while others searched for traits that predicted leader effectiveness or distinguished lower-level leaders from higher-level leaders.

**Organizational pattern for paragraphs 1 and 2:** *cause-effect or a short* *problem-solution text*

Paul Tellier

3  Just what is a trait, anyway? **Traits** are personal characteristics of an individual that include physical characteristics, intellectual ability, and personality. Research has shown that many traits are not associated with whether people become leaders or how effective they are. However, research also shows that some traits are associated with leadership. Exhibit 2.1 on page 32 provides a list of these traits. As you might expect, leaders (or more successful leaders) tend to be higher than average on these dimensions, although the connections are not very strong. Notice that the list portrays a high-energy person who really wants to have an impact on others but at the same time is smart and stable enough not to abuse his or her power. Interestingly, this is a very accurate summary description of Bombardier CEO Paul Tellier, who, while CEO of Canadian National Railways, orchestrated a turnaround that transformed the ailing company into the best run and most efficient railroad in North America.

> **Exhibit 2.1**
> Traits associated with leadership effectiveness.
>
> **Traits.**   Individual characteristics such as physical attributes, intellectual ability, and personality
>
> Intelligence
> Energy
> Self-confidence
> Dominance
> Motivation to lead
> Emotional stability
> Honesty and integrity
> Need for achievement

**Organizational pattern for paragraph 3:** _____

4   In recent years, there has been a renewed interest in the study of leadership traits, and a number of studies have shown that certain traits are more closely linked to leadership. For example, one study found that three of the "Big Five" dimensions of personality (agreeableness, extraversion, and openness to experience) are related to leadership behaviors. In addition, research that compared top performers with average performers in senior leadership positions found that the most effective leaders have high levels of emotional intelligence. The emotional intelligence of leaders has also been found to be positively related to the job satisfaction and organizational citizenship behavior of employees. Many prominent firms use personality tests and assessment centers to measure leadership traits when making hiring and promotion decisions. However, there are some aspects of the trait approach that limit its ultimate usefulness.

5   Even though some traits appear to be related to leadership, there are several reasons why the trait approach is not the best means of understanding and improving leadership. In many cases, it is difficult to determine whether traits make the leader or whether the opportunity for leadership produces the traits. For example, do dominant individuals tend to become leaders, or do employees become more dominant *after* they successfully occupy leadership roles? This distinction is important. If the former is true, we might wish to seek out dominant people and appoint them to leadership roles. If the latter is true, this strategy will not work. Secondly, even if we know that dominance, intelligence, or tallness is associated with effective leadership, we have few clues about what dominant or intelligent or tall people *do* to influence others successfully. As a result, we have little information about how to train and develop leaders and no way to diagnose failures of leadership. And finally, the most crucial problem of the trait approach to leadership is its failure to take into account the *situation* in which leadership occurs. Intuitively, it seems reasonable that top executives and first-level supervisors might require different traits to be successful. Similarly, physical prowess might be useful in directing a logging crew but irrelevant to managing a team of scientists.

6   In summary, although there are some traits that are associated with leadership success, traits alone are not sufficient for successful leadership. Traits are only a pre-condition for certain actions that a leader must take in order to be successful. In other words, possessing the appropriate traits for leadership makes it possible—and even more likely—that certain actions will be taken and will be successful.

Source: Johns, G. & Saks, A.M. (2005). *Organizational behavior: Understanding and managing life at work* (6th ed.). Toronto: Pearson Prentice Hall.

**Organizational pattern for paragraphs 4, 5, and 6:** _____

**2.** *Complete the graphic organizers to show the organization of the content of this reading.*

**Paragraphs 1 and 2**

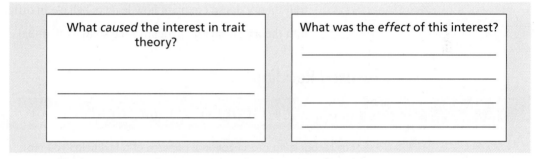

**Paragraph 3**

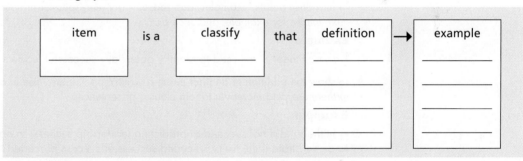

**Paragraphs 4, 5, and 6**

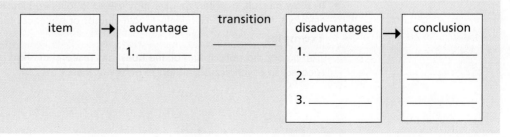

**3.** *Work with a partner to answer the questions.*

1. What is the assumption about why some people become leaders and others do not?

2. Why did researchers begin to study leadership traits, and why was it important at that time?

3. What is a trait?

4. What are some traits that are associated with successful leaders?

5. What are the three weaknesses of the trait theory *that the author writes about*? Check (✓) your answers.

   _____ trait theory doesn't reflect a modern way of thinking

   _____ trait theory doesn't explain which comes first, the leadership traits or the leadership position

   _____ trait theory doesn't explain why some people with leadership traits aren't leaders

   _____ trait theory doesn't explain how leaders behave or what they do

   _____ trait theory doesn't explain how leaders behave in different situations

   _____ trait theory doesn't help identify the soldiers that make good leaders

# Focused Reading

## Recognizing Relationships among Ideas in a Text

Just as recognizing organizational patterns of a text helps you read faster or listen better, recognizing connecting words in a text can help you understand the relationships among ideas. Here are some key connecting words.

- **To introduce points, examples,** and **reasons,** a writer/speaker may use *first, second, next, finally, for example,* and *such as.*

  **Example**

  *First,* trait theory was used to identify potentially successful leaders.

- **To show the addition of another point,** a writer/speaker may use *in addition, furthermore,* and *moreover* to join clauses or sentences.

  **Examples**

  Trait theory did not succeed at predicting leadership success; *in addition,* it failed to demonstrate if the traits preceded success or success preceded the traits.

  Trait theory did not succeed at predicting leadership success. *Moreover,* it failed to demonstrate if the traits preceded success or success preceded the traits.

- **To show a result,** a writer/speaker may use *so* to join two clauses and *as a result, therefore, thus,* and *consequently* to join clauses or sentences together.

  **Examples**

  Trait theory did not explain all the questions researchers had about leader success, *so* psychologists turned to behavior theory.

Behavior theory did not take into account how the work situation affected the leader's behavior; *as a result*, researchers began to consider situational theory.

Behavior theory did not take into account how the work situation affected the leader's behavior. *Therefore*, researchers began to consider situational theory.

- **To show contrast,** a writer/speaker may use *while, although, even though,* or *whereas* to join an adverb clause and an independent clause. *However* or *on the other hand* may be used to join clauses or sentences.

**Examples**

*While* trait theory identified potential leaders, behavioral theory explained how leaders behaved when they were in a job.

Some traits are associated with leadership success; *however*, some traits are obviously not.

- A writer/speaker may also **show contrast** by using *but* to join two independent clauses.

**Example**

Trait theory showed promise to explain leadership success, *but* the theory also had weaknesses that could not be overcome.

- **To show similarity,** a writer/speaker may use *similarly* or *likewise* to join clauses or sentences.

**Example**

Some leaders are noted for their charisma; *similarly*, these leaders are often skillful communicators.

- **To conclude** a text, a writer/speaker may use *in conclusion, in summary,* or *in closing.*

**Example**

*In summary*, both trait and behavioral theory have their limitations.

---

*The words that show the relationships among the ideas in the text have been omitted. Fill in each blank with an appropriate word to show the relationships (in parentheses) between the ideas. Use the information in the box on pages 34–35 to help you. Compare your answers with a classmate's, and then check the answers against the original reading. Your answers may be different from those in the reading.*

1. Throughout history, social observers have been fascinated by obvious demonstrations of successful interpersonal influence, whether the consequences of this influence were good, bad, or mixed. Individuals _____ (give examples) Henry Ford, Martin Luther King, Jr., Barbara Jordan, Ralph Nader, and Joan of Arc have been analyzed and reanalyzed to discover what made them leaders and what set them apart from less successful leaders.

2. _____ (show contrast) philosophers and the popular media have advocated such a position for centuries, trait theories of leadership did not receive serious scientific attention until the 1900s.

3. During World War I the U.S. military recognized that it had a leadership problem. Never before had the country mounted such a massive war effort, and able officers were in short supply. _____, (show a result) the search for leadership traits that might be useful in identifying potential officers began.

4. Research has shown that many traits are not associated with whether people become leaders or how effective they are. _____, (show contrast) research also shows that some traits are associated with leadership.

5. As you might expect, leaders (or more successful leaders) tend to be higher than average on these dimensions, _____ (show contrast) the connections are not very strong.

6. For example, one study found that three of the "Big Five" dimensions of personality (agreeableness, extraversion, and openness to experience) are related to leadership behaviors. _____, (add a point) research that compared top performers with average performers in senior leadership positions found that the most effective leaders have high levels of emotional intelligence.

7. Secondly, even if we know that dominance, intelligence, or tallness is associated with effective leadership, we have few clues about what dominant or intelligent or tall people do to influence others successfully. _____, (show a result) we have little information about how to train and develop leaders and no way to diagnose failures of leadership.

8. _____, (conclude) although there are some traits that are associated with leadership success, traits alone are not sufficient for successful leadership.

Checkpoint 1    PEARSON LONGMAN myacademicconnectionslab

# 3

## Building Academic Listening Skills

In this section, you will listen to a lecture and a conversation and learn how to recognize the organization of what you are listening to.
For online assignments, go to

PEARSON LONGMAN
myacademicconnectionslab

### Key Words

**consideration behavior** *exp* leadership behavior that builds trust, respect, and good relationships with employees

**initiation behavior** *exp* leadership behavior that makes employees work efficiently

## Before You Listen

*Work with a partner. Check the correct column to show whether a leader's behavior is an example of consideration behavior or initiation behavior. Then discuss your answers with the class.*

| Leader's Behavior | Consideration Behaviors | Initiation Behaviors |
|---|---|---|
| 1. assigning an employee a task to complete | | ✓ |
| 2. celebrating the birthdays of employees | ✓ | |
| 3. complimenting an employee who has performed well | | |
| 4. setting short-term productivity goals for a team | | |
| 5. calculating the number of unhappy customers to show employees where customer service needs to improve | | |
| 6. giving a lunch for employees and their families | | |
| 7. spending a few minutes each day to find out how employees are doing | | |
| 8. setting long-term goals for company productivity | | |
| 9. asking employees for their opinions before beginning a new project | | |
| 10. making a controversial decision without asking employees for their opinions | | |

# Global Listening

Organizing information can help you in a number of ways. It can help you
- see the relationships between/among ideas
- reduce large amounts of information into smaller chunks
- remember the information
- prepare to present information

**Organizational tools**

When you organize information, you can use a variety of tools to help you. You can use these three common tools:
- graphic organizers (such as those you have used in the Reading section of this unit)
- charts (such as those you have used in the Listening section of Unit 1)
- outlines (like the ones you will use in this section)

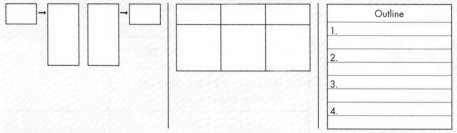

**Lecture organization**

When you are thinking about the organization of a lecture, remember that most academic lectures have an introduction, a body, and a conclusion. The introduction can be very short but is key to understanding the organization of the lecture. In the *introduction*, the instructor may
- review information from a previous lecture or reading
- introduce a new broad topic
- narrow the broader topic to a specific topic

In the *body* of the lecture, the instructor will continue by providing information about the topic. This information may be organized into patterns with which you are already familiar:
- description—to describe someone or something
- definition—to define a term
- process—to explain how to do something
- cause and effect—to explain what caused something
- advantages-disadvantages—to list the strengths and weaknesses of something
- problem-solution—to describe a problem and explain a solution
- compare and/or contrast—to show similarities and/or differences

The *conclusion* can be very short but is key to knowing what to do before the next lecture. In the conclusion of the lecture, the instructor may
- mention the topic of the next lecture
- tell students the homework for the next day

**1.** *These 10 key pieces of information from the lecture are listed out of order. Place each piece of information in the appropriate place in the lecture outline.*

**Key Pieces of Lecture Information**

~~1. Review of trait theory~~

2. Homework: to read about situational theories of leadership

3. Introduction to behavioral theory

4. An example of consideration versus initiation behavior

~~5. Research on behavioral theory~~

6. Weakness of behavioral theory

7. Weakness of trait theory

8. Research on the influence of work situations

9. Two main orientations of behavioral theory: consideration and initiation behaviors—definitions

10. Work situations and their impact on leadership behavior

---

### Leadership Behavior

Date: _____

Lecture Outline for Behavioral Theories of Leadership

Introduction:

1. *Review of trait theory* _____

2. _____

Body:

3. _____

4. *Research on behavioral theory* _____

5. _____

6. _____

7. _____

8. _____

9. _____

Conclusion:

10. _____

---

**2.** 🎧 *Listen to the lecture to check the order of the information. Then confirm the order with the class.*

**3.** *Use your notes in the outline on page 39 and your memory of the content of the lecture to answer the questions. If necessary, listen to the lecture again. Then compare your answers with a classmate's.*

1. What were the two orientations of the behavioral theory of leadership discovered by researchers at Ohio State University? Give an example of each.

2. What was the weakness of the behavioral theory of leadership?

3. Classify the characteristics of a work situation (shown in the box) into two categories: characteristics that create stress and characteristics that don't create stress. When you have finished, decide which leader behavior (consideration or initiation) is best for each situation. Discuss your answers with the class.

| | |
|---|---|
| clearly defined task | long lead time (lots of time before a deadline) |
| experienced employees | tight deadlines |
| inexperienced employees | unclear task |

| Characteristics of Work Situations that Create Stress | Characteristics of Work Situations that Don't Create Stress |
|---|---|
| | |
| | |
| | |
| Most effective leader behavior for these situations: | Most effective leader behavior for these situations: |

## Focused Listening

**Recognizing Relationships among Parts of a Lecture**

You may remember from the Reading section that brief reading texts usually demonstrate one pattern of organization, and longer readings may demonstrate multiple patterns of organization. Similarly, brief lectures usually demonstrate only one pattern of organization, and longer lectures may demonstrate multiple patterns of organization. For a longer lecture, listen for the same kinds of connecting words that you see in a longer reading text to help identify the patterns of organization within the lecture.

**1.** *Classify the words from the box into the appropriate columns to help you remember the words that indicate relationships among parts of a lecture.*

| although | however | on the other hand |
| as a result | in addition | second |
| but | in closing | similarly |
| consequently | in conclusion | so |
| even though | in contrast | such as |
| finally | in summary | therefore |
| ~~first~~ | likewise | thus |
| for example | moreover | whereas |
| furthermore | next | ~~while~~ |

| To Introduce Points, Examples, Reasons | To Add a Point | To Show a Result | To Show a Contrast | To Show a Similarity | To Conclude |
|---|---|---|---|---|---|
| *first* | | | *while* | | |

The lecture is a good example of a problem-solution text that repeats itself. Remember that a traditional problem-solution text consists of four parts: situation, problem, solution, and results.

**2.** 🎧 *Listen again to the lecture. In the first column of the chart, write the connecting words that indicate the relationships among the parts of the lecture.*

| Words that Show Relationships among Ideas | Content | Pattern of Organization |
|---|---|---|
| *To start,* | Review of trait theory | Stage one: situation |
| | Trait theory was useful to describe leaders, but which came first, the traits or the leader? | Stage two: problem |
| | Behavioral theory | Stage three: solution |
| | Consideration and initiating behaviors | Short definition text |

*(continued on next page)*

| Words Showing Relationships among Ideas | Content | Pattern of Organization |
|---|---|---|
| | Example of David Pottruck | Stage one: situation |
| | Employees didn't like working with Pottruck | Stage two: problem |
| | Pottruck changed his leadership style | Stage three: solution |
| | Employees began to like working with Pottruck and now cooperate with him | Stage four: results |
| | Behavior theory weakness—the situation often affects the behavior of the leader | Stage two: problem |
| | Researchers began to consider the impact of work situation | Stage three: solution |
| | Work situation is important, so leaders should consider it, too | Stage four: not revealed |

# 4

## Building Academic Speaking Skills

In this section, you will listen to a classmate present three different management styles. You will then respond orally to a case study about a company that is having leadership problems. For online assignments, go to

PEARSON LONGMAN
myacademicconnectionslab

## Before You Speak

As the midterm exam approaches, you have formed a group with two of your classmates to help prepare for the exam. To divide up the work, each of you has prepared notes on a different theory of leadership. Your study group has just finished reviewing trait and behavior theories of leadership. Your classmate is about to give an oral presentation about three contrasting managerial styles. It is important that you know the difference among these three styles.

**1.** *Predict the method of organization your classmate will use to present this information.*

**2.** ∩ *Listen to your classmate's presentation about the three contrasting managerial styles. Take notes in the chart as you listen. Then compare your notes with a classmate's. Fill in any gaps you have.*

| Management Style | Details |
|---|---|
| Autocratic | |
| Democratic | |
| Free-reign | |

Was your prediction about your classmate's method of organization correct? Why or why not?

## Focused Speaking

*1. Make a list of specific vocabulary items that you might like to use to show your mastery of the vocabulary and content of the unit.*

| Trait Theory Vocabulary |
|---|
| List as many leadership traits as you can: |
| List synonyms for *trait*: |
| Write expressions that mean<br>  a. to change the fortune of a company—<br><br>  b. a company that is not doing well—<br><br>  c. a company that is well known— |

| Behavior Theory Vocabulary |
|---|
| List the two behavioral orientations covered in the lecture: |

| Management Style Vocabulary |
|---|
| Write the management style that is reflected in these decisions:<br>  a. An industry leader asks for opinions about product pricing and then sets a price.<br><br>  b. An industry leader gives his employees total control over a new project.<br><br>  c. An industry leader tells her employees to write a report by tomorrow morning. |
| Write synonyms for *employees*: |

**2.** *Work with a partner and take turns using the vocabulary words from the chart on page 43 in sentences.*

## Integrated Speaking Task

Translate IT is a software company that has developed a product that translates text from one language to another. You will read about a leadership problem at Translate IT and discuss the problem with a small group of students. You will then develop and present an oral response to the problem on your own.

**1.** *Read the explanation of the work situation at Translate IT. Then work in small groups to answer the questions.*

### The Leadership Problem at Translate IT

You are the founding entrepreneur and CEO of Translate IT, a fast-growing digital software company that specializes in translation software. Customer demand to license your software has boomed so much that in just two years you have added over 50 new software programmers to help develop a new range of software products. These people are young and inexperienced but are highly skilled and used to putting in long hours to see their ideas succeed. The growth of the company has been so swift that you still operate informally. As CEO, you have been so absorbed in your own work that you have paid little attention to the issue of leading your growing company. You have allowed your programmers to find solutions to problems as they go. They have also been allowed to form their own work groups, but there are signs that problems are arising.

There have been increasing complaints from employees that you do not recognize or reward good performance and that they do not feel equitably treated. Moreover, there have been growing concerns that top managers are either too busy or not willing to listen to the employees' new ideas and act on them. A bad atmosphere seems to be developing in the company, and recently several talented programmers have left.

As the CEO, you realize that you have done a poor job of leading your employees and that you need to develop a leadership approach to encourage workers to perform well and to stay with your company.

Source: Based on George, J.M., & Jones, G.R. (2005). *Understanding and managing organizational behavior* (4th ed.). Upper Saddle River, NJ: Pearson Prentice Hall.

1. What advantages does Translate IT have?

2. What challenges does Translate IT have?

3. As the CEO, what traits do you need in order to orchestrate a company turnaround? Why?

4. What leader behavior orientation would work best at Translate IT? Why?

5. What management style have you been using? What management style might work best now?

6. What solutions will you try to orchestrate a turnaround at Translate IT?

**2.** *Prepare a short oral presentation in which you explain how you will orchestrate a turnaround at Translate IT. Follow the steps to prepare your presentation.*

**Step 1:** Before you give an oral presentation, it is best to plan the information you will present. Use the connecting words you learned in the Reading and the Listening sections to signal the relationships between (or among) the pieces of information. To prepare, organize the information you will need to present in the chart. Most of the information you need is found in the answers to questions 1–6 on page 44. Start your response with an introduction to the leadership problem, and conclude with the solutions you will use to orchestrate the company's turnaround.

| Organizational Chart | |
| --- | --- |
| Introduction to the leadership problems at Translate IT | |
| The advantages of Translate IT | |
| Key sentence or connecting word | |
| The challenges of Translate IT | |
| Necessary leadership traits | |
| Most effective behavior orientation | |
| Key sentence or connecting word | |
| Best managerial style | |
| Key sentence or connecting word | |
| Solutions | |

**Step 2:** Use your notes to present your response to a partner. Then listen as your partner presents his or her response to you. As you listen to your partner's response, fill in the checklist on page 46. It will help you identify if his or her response has the characteristics of a good oral response.

| The oral response has . . . | Yes | No |
| --- | --- | --- |
| an introduction about the leadership problem at Translate IT. | | |
| an analysis of the advantages and challenges of the company. | | |
| information about trait theories of leadership. | | |
| information about behavior theories of leadership. | | |
| information about managerial styles. | | |
| a reasonable solution to the problem at Translate IT. | | |
| key sentences and/or transition words that signal the organization of the response. | | |
| **The speaker . . .** | **Yes** | **No** |
| seems well prepared. | | |
| is easy to understand. | | |
| is not too nervous. | | |

**Step 3:** If, based on your partner's checklist, you are not satisfied with your response, work to improve it and try again. Have a partner listen and complete another checklist.

**Step 4:** Present your response to the class or a group of students in the class. As you speak, each member of your audience will fill out the checklist. These checklists will provide you with feedback that you can use to improve your next speaking task.

# UNIT 3

# Environmental Science
# Forest Fires

## Unit Description

**Content:** This course is designed to familiarize the student with concepts in forest management.

**Skills:** Coherence and Cohesion
- Using sentence structure to create coherence
- Creating cohesion in a paragraph
- Recognizing speech markers
- Recognizing cohesion in a text
- Creating special emphasis by starting a sentence with a negative expression
- Persuading your reader
- Using pronoun agreement

## Unit Requirements

**Lecture:** "The Benefits of Forest Fires"

**Readings:** "Out of Control" (from, *Maclean's*, K. McQueen)

"Question of the Week" (from *Maclean's*)

**Integrated Writing Task:** Writing a persuasive essay about allowing people to live near forested areas

**Assignments:** 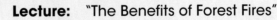www.MyAcademicConnectionsLab.com

# 1

## Preview

For online assignments, go to

myacademicconnectionslab

## Previewing the Academic Content

As the urban population increases, there are also increasing numbers of people looking for a country retreat, where they can live closer to nature. Many of these people build homes, cabins, or cottages close to forests to enjoy the peace and solitude that nature can provide. The human presence in or near these forests has changed forest management practices in these areas. Instead of letting wildfires, which are caused by lightning, naturally clear the forest overgrowth and regenerate soil and seeds, forest managers prevent fires at all costs in an attempt to protect homes. This constant prevention of naturally occurring forest fires creates a dangerous buildup of forest fuels that can erupt into explosive forest fires that are difficult and expensive to control. These fires are called interface fires because they occur in places where urban development and forests overlap, or interface.

**1.** *Work in groups of three to discuss the questions.*

1. Are forest fires beneficial or detrimental? List as many beneficial and detrimental effects your group can think of in the chart. At the end of this section, you will be asked to fill in this chart again.

| Beneficial (positive) Effects | Detrimental (negative) Effects |
|---|---|
|  |  |

2. If you could, would you build a home in a beautiful forested area knowing that there might be a forest fire at some time in the future? Why or why not?

3. Should societies or governments allow people to live in or near forested areas? Why or why not?

**2.** *Discuss the information in your group's chart with the class. Then survey the class by asking the questions in Exercise 1. Take notes. Work with the class to complete the sentences based on the results of your survey.*

If they could, _____ percent of our classmates would build a home in a forested

area because _____.

If they could, _____ percent of our class would not build a home in a forested area

because _____.

Should governments allow people to live in or near forested areas?

Yes _____ percent

No _____ percent

**Key Words**

**branch** *n* part of a tree that grows out from the trunk

**canopy** *n* the leaves and branches of trees that make a kind of "roof" over the forest

**cone** *n* the hard, brown fruit that contains the seed of a tree

**crown** *n* the highest part of a tree

**herb** *n* a grass or other plant that grows close to the ground

**leaves** *n* flat green parts of a plant that are joined to its stem or branches (*sing.* **leaf**)

**overstory** *n* the tallest trees that grow in a forest

**shrub** *n* a small bush with several woody stems

**soil** *n* the top layer of earth in which plants grow

**stand of trees** *n* a group of trees growing close together

**twig** *n* a small, very thin stem of wood that grows from a branch

**understory** *n* short trees that grow below taller trees in a forest

**3.** *Write the key words in the appropriate blanks on the diagram. Then compare your answers with your classmates'. You will not use all the words.*

1. _____

2. _____

3. _____

4. _____

5. _____

6. _____

7. _____

8. _____

9. _____

10. _____

This unit will help you recognize coherence and cohesion in readings and lectures. It will also show you how to create coherence and cohesion in your own writing.

# Previewing the Academic Skills Focus

In Units 1 and 2, you learned about expository essays and lectures, which provide information in an organized pattern. In this unit, you will learn about persuasive essays and lectures, which attempt to persuade the audience to agree with the author's main point.

## Coherence and Cohesion

There is coherence in a reading or lecture when all the paragraphs of the reading or lecture are connected in a clear and reasonable way. Coherence makes a reading or lecture easy to understand as a whole.

There is cohesion in a paragraph when all the sentences, clauses and parts, are connected in a clear and reasonable way. Cohesion is essential for readers and listeners to understand the text.

Coherence and cohesion are similar. However, coherence refers to how paragraphs are connected in a larger text, while cohesion refers to how sentences are connected in a paragraph or how clauses are connected within a sentence.

**1.** *Read the persuasive essay about the beneficial effects of forest fires. As you read, underline the thesis statement and the concluding statement, and consider how they create coherence by connecting the paragraphs. Remember, a thesis statement states the essay topic, the author's opinion, and the author's main points, often in a single sentence. The concluding statement is a restatement (not repetition) of the thesis.*

## The Beneficial Effects of Forest Fires

1   Forest fires are undoubtedly a menace. They ruin valuable stands of trees, destroy animal habitats, kill woodland creatures, pollute the air, and endanger human life, homes, and communities. In the mid-1900s, all forest burns were considered undesirable, and firefighters responded to all of these fires whether or not they were burning close to human habitation. This approach to forest fires was both expensive and risky. However, more recently, forest managers began to see that forest fires did have benefits. Foresters saw that forest fires were beneficial for trees, soil, and animals.

2   Previously, people believed that forest fires caused irreparable damage to trees; however, now forest managers know that trees are the major beneficiaries of fires. Many naturally occurring forest fires, often caused by lightning strikes, are surface fires that burn the understory—the shrubs and herbs from the forest—without damaging the trees in the overstory. In this way, the fire eliminates competition from the smaller trees, allowing the larger trees to flourish. Once the understory has been burned away, the forest is less likely to burn from high-temperature fires—the combined crown, surface, and ground fires that can do real damage to the tall trees. Burns are also a natural form of control for tree disease and insect pests. Furthermore, the heat from a fire can

stimulate seed growth required to regenerate a forest after a fire. All of these benefits are a result of natural forest fires.

3   In the past, it was not obvious how forest fires enriched the soil. Today, foresters understand that forest fires improve soil quality by converting the 'litter'—dead leaves, twigs, and branches on the forest floor—to nutrient-rich soil. Normally, litter decomposes very slowly. However, fire releases the nutrients in the litter immediately. This creates an increase in the amount of phosphorus and potassium which are key elements that promote tree growth. The resulting rich soil encourages seed growth. Furthermore, the heat from the fires stimulates soil microorganisms, which again promote growth. As a result, fires create improved soil conditions that benefit the plants in the forest.

4   Years ago, people saw only that woodland animals were trapped and burned in forest fires, and it seemed unlikely that animals could benefit from forest fires in any way. In fact, birds and other animals are often able to escape fires. In a large Siberian fire in 1915, both large and small mammals swam across a large river to avoid the smoke; in 1969, animals made no more than 'local adjustments' to their movements to avoid a large fire in Alaska. Furthermore, burns can 'thin out' the forest so larger animals can live in the forest. Animals like deer and moose, which need some open space to live, benefit from the thinning of the understory. As the enriched soil allows new herbs and shrubs to grow, there is new food for these animals as well. Consequently, forest fires contribute to the diversity of species living within the forest.

5   As forest managers have learned more about the long-term effects of forest fires, they have realized that forest fires can have beneficial effects and have changed their forest management practices to reflect this new opinion. It is now recognized that forest fires are a natural part of forest ecosystems and are beneficial to the trees, soil, and animals. As long as fires are no threat to homes and communities, foresters now often choose to let the fires burn.

**2.** *Answer the questions to show how* **coherence** *is created in this essay. Remember, coherence is the linking of paragraphs in a longer text.*

1. Work with a partner to see if you agree on which sentences are the thesis statement and the concluding statement. Are the main points of both statements in parallel structure?

2. For each main point you see in the thesis statement, draw an arrow from the point to the corresponding topic sentence in the body of the essay. Remember, a topic sentence is the first sentence of a paragraph in the body of an essay.

3. How do the thesis and concluding sentences create coherence in this essay?

4. Look at the topic sentence from the first body paragraph of the text.

*Previously, people believed that forest fires caused irreparable damage to trees; however, now forest managers know that trees are the major beneficiaries of fires.*

Are the words highlighted in yellow a statement about the past or the present? Are the other words a statement about the past or the present?

5. Can you see this past/present pattern in the other topic sentences? Why did the author choose to write topic sentences like this?

## Using Sentence Structure to Create Coherence

In an essay, coherence is created with the use of a thesis statment and topic sentences. As you can see in this essay, sometimes there is also a similarity of topic sentence structure, although the topic sentences should not be repetitive.

**3.** *Read the first paragraph of the persuasive essay again. Then answer the questions to see how* **cohesion** *is created in this paragraph. Remember, cohesion is the linking of sentences within a paragraph or of clauses within a sentence.*

Forest fires are undoubtedly a menace. They ruin valuable stands of trees, destroy animal habitat, kill woodland creatures, pollute the air, and endanger human life, homes, and communities. In the mid-1900s, all forest burns were considered undesirable, and firefighters responded to all of these fires whether or not they were burning close to human habitation. This approach to forest fires was both expensive and risky. However, more recently, forest managers began to see that wildfires did have benefits. Foresters saw that forest fires were beneficial for trees, soil, and animals.

1. What do the words highlighted in pink have in common? Why did the author use a variety of synonyms rather than repeat the same word many times? How do these words create cohesion?

2. The words highlighted in yellow are pronouns. A pronoun is a word that replaces a noun in the sentence. A pronoun always refers to a noun that comes before it. How do the pronouns create cohesion? Draw arrows from the pronouns to the nouns they replace.

3. The words highlighted in green demonstrate another useful way to connect ideas together in a paragraph; these are summary phrases. Draw arrows from the summary phrases to the ideas they represent.

A forest fire: beneficial or detrimental?

PEARSON LONGMAN
myacademicconnectionslab

## 2

## Building Academic Listening Skills

In this section, you will learn more about the tools that effective speakers use to create coherence and cohesion. For online assignments, go to

4. The word *however* is highlighted in gray because it is a connecting word. What does the connecting word do to create a connection between the first part of the paragraph and the last part of the paragraph?

### Creating Cohesion in a Paragraph

In a paragraph, cohesion is created with the use of synonyms, pronouns, summary phrases (such as *this/these* + summary word), and connecting words.

**4.** Using information from the essay, list other beneficial or detrimental effects of forest fires in the chart on page 48.

## Before You Listen

These are some of the significant wildfires that have occurred all over the world.

| Place | Year | Details |
|---|---|---|
| Kursha-2, Soviet Union | 1936 | killed 1,200 people |
| Lüneburg Heath, Germany | 1975 | destroyed over 74 km$^2$ (29 sq mi)[1] and killed 5 firefighters |
| Yellowstone National Park, U.S. | 1988 | burned 3,200 km$^2$ (1,235 sq mi). Finally suppressed by winter snow |
| Kuznia Raciborska, Poland | 1992 | burned over 90 km$^2$ (35 sq mi) and killed 3 people |
| France, Corsica, and Italy | 2000 | caused by 40–45 °C (104–113°F)[2] heat wave in southern Europe |
| Canberra, Australia | 2003 | damaged or destroyed 431 homes in Australia's capital city |
| British Columbia, Canada | 2003 | started by lightning and burned over 250 km$^2$ (96.5 sq mi). You will read more about this fire later in this unit. |
| Kalimantan and Sumatra, Indonesia | 1999–2005 | burned 1,345 km$^2$ (519 sq mi) |
| Guadalajara, Spain | 2005 | burned 130 km$^2$ (50 sq mi) and killed 11 people |
| Peloponnese, Greece | 2007 | killed 64 people |
| | | |
| | | |

---

[1] km$^2$ = square kilometer; sq mi = square mile
[2] °C = degree Celsius; °F = degree Fahrenheit

Source: Based on "List of wildfires" from http://en.wikipedia.org./wiki/List_of_wildfires.

**1.** Which wildfire in the chart caused the greatest loss of life? Which one burned the largest area of land?

**2.** Work in small groups and discuss any wildfires or forest fires that you know of or have heard about. Add them to the chart on page 53. Have the effects of these wildfires been beneficial or detrimental? When you hear news reports about forest fires (on television, in newspapers, or on the Internet), are they presented positively or negatively? Why?

## Global Listening

**1.** ⌒ The five points you will hear the professor talk about in the lecture are listed out of order. Read the points and then listen to the lecture about the benefits of forest fires. As you listen, number the points in the order in which they are presented.

**Points: Benefits of Forest Fires**

\_\_\_\_\_ encourage seed growth          \_\_\_\_\_ improve soil quality

\_\_\_\_\_ increase animal and plant diversity          \_\_\_\_\_ reduce disease and pests

\_\_\_\_\_ reduce the risk of big forest fires

**2.** What are some words that the professor uses to create coherence in the lecture? List them in your notebook.

**3.** Read the statements. Circle **T** (true) or **F** (false). Correct the false statements. Then check your answers with a classmate's.

1. This lecture is about the positive and negative effects of forest fires.          **T** **(F)**

   *This lecture is about the positive effects of forest fires.*

2. Wildfires started by lightning strikes are usually isolated and don't produce enough heat to create a large-scale forest fire.          **T** **F**

   _____

3. The bark on larger trees can protect them from fires that burn at relatively low temperatures.          **T** **F**

   _____

4. Small forest fires increase the chances of a large forest fire occurring later.          **T** **F**

   _____

5. Burning the litter on the forest floor releases phosphorus and potassium, which are dangerous to plants.          **T** **F**

   _____

6. Forest fires eliminate old and diseased trees, which improves tree quality in the forest.          **T** **F**

   _____

7. Heat from forest fires kills all the seeds on the forest floor.     **T   F**

8. If a fire burns a hole in the forest canopy, it encourages biodiversity within the forest.     **T   F**

9. Foresters try to prevent all forest fires from burning.     **T   F**

## Focused Listening

### Recognizing Speech Markers

Effective speakers use speech markers to show clear relationships between their ideas. Selecting appropriate speech markers creates coherence and cohesion because the markers show how pieces of information are related. This helps the listener understand how content is organized. If you learn to listen for these speech markers, you will more easily understand what you are hearing. Professors may use speech markers when they

- **begin a lecture:** *Today we will talk about . . . Let's discuss . . . We will begin by . . . Let's get started . . .*
- **list points:** *First . . . Second . . . Third . . . Next . . . Finally . . . Another point . . . Also . . . As well . . .*
- **give an example:** *For example . . . Such as . . . To demonstrate . . .*
- **change the topic:** *Now let's turn to another matter (issue, problem) . . . However, we must also consider . . . Here's another problem to think about . . .*
- **end a lecture:** *To summarize (In summary) . . . To conclude (In conclusion) . . . We are almost out of time for today . . . To wrap up . . . To finish off . . .*

***1.*** 🎧 *Listen again to the lecture. As it progresses from introduction to body to conclusion, listen for the speech markers the professor uses to create coherence. In the chart, circle the speech markers you hear. Check with a classmate to see if you heard the same ones.*

| Speech Markers to Build Coherence in the Lecture **Introduction** | Speech Markers to Build Coherence in the Lecture **Body** | Speech Markers to Build Coherence in the Lecture **Conclusion** | Speech Markers to Build Coherence by Showing **Examples** | Speech Markers to Build Coherence by Signaling a **Change in Topic** |
|---|---|---|---|---|
| Today we will talk about . . . | First . . . | To wrap up . . . | Such as . . . | Now let's turn to another matter . . . |
| We will begin by . . . | Another point . . . | To summarize . . . | To demonstrate . . . | However, we must also consider . . . |
| Let's get started . . . | Third . . . | To conclude . . . | For example . . . | Here's another problem to think about . . . |

*(continued on next page)*

| Speech Markers to Build Coherence in the Lecture **Introduction** | Speech Markers to Build Coherence in the Lecture **Body** | Speech Markers to Build Coherence in the Lecture **Conclusion** | Speech Markers to Build Coherence by Showing **Examples** | Speech Markers to Build Coherence by Signaling a **Change in Topic** |
|---|---|---|---|---|
| Let's discuss . . . | As well . . . | To finish off . . . | For instance . . . | Now let's look at another problem . . . |
| | Finally . . . | We are out of time for today . . . | | |
| | Second . . . | | | |
| | Also/In addition . . . | | | |
| | Next . . . | | | |
| | Similarly . . . | | | |

**2.** With your partner, take turns using appropriate speech markers from the chart to introduce the key phrases from the lecture or to link two of the phrases together. Use as many of the speech markers and phrases as possible. The speech markers are italicized in the examples.

**Examples**

- *Today we will talk about* the beneficial effects of forest fires.
- Forest fires have destroyed many woodland areas and human lives. *However, we also must consider* the beneficial effects of forest fires.
- Forest fires improve soil quality. *For example,* heat from forest fires releases phosphorus and potassium into the soil.

**Key Phrases from the Lecture**

. . . beneficial effects of forest fires . . .

. . . naturally occurring forest fires . . .

. . . destroyed many woodland areas and human lives . . .

. . . reduce the likelihood of larger fires . . .

. . . improves soil quality . . .

. . . releases phosphorus and potassium into the soil . . .

. . . eliminate tree disease . . .

. . . eliminate destructive pests . . .

. . . encourage seed growth . . .

. . . open up the forest canopy . . .

. . . sun's heat reaches the forest floor . . .

. . . enhances biodiversity in the forest . . .

. . . suppress forest fires near human homes . . .

. . . allow some forest fires to burn . . .

# 3

## Building Academic Reading Skills

In this section, you will learn more about the tools effective writers use to create coherence and cohesion.

For online assignments, go to

PEARSON LONGMAN
myacademicconnectionslab

## Key Words

**fire exclusion** *exp* an approach to forest fires that tries to prevent all forest fires

**fire suppression** *exp* an approach to forest fires that tries to prevent forest fires near human habitation

**prescribed fire/ prescribed burn** *exp* a fire that is planned and set by forest managers. Usually done in wet conditions, prescribed fires burn away the litter on the forest floor to reduce the probability of larger fires. Use the verb *start*, *set*, or *light* with the noun *fire* to mean a planned fire.

## Before You Read

Despite the recognition that forest fires can be beneficial, forest managers have been practicing fire exclusion to prevent naturally occurring forest fires. Look at the graph to see how effective foresters have been at fire exclusion.

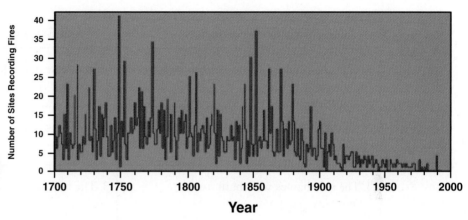

Source: Swetnam, T.W., & Betancourt, J.L. (2003, April 10). Mesoscale ecological responses to climactic variability in the American Southwest. Retrieved from http://geochange.er.usgs.gov/sw/impacts/biology/fires_SOI.

**1.** *Work with a partner. Use the numbers in the box to complete the sentence that explains the meaning of the graph. Then check your answers with the class.*

| 0 | 40 | 300 | 1750 | 2000 |

According to the graph, over the last _____ years, the number of sites recording forest fires has decreased from a high of _____ in _____ to a low of _____ in _____.

**2.** *With the class, discuss why foresters are now practicing fire exclusion.*

**3.** *What is the danger of practicing fire exclusion?*

## Global Reading

In the article you will read, you will encounter some "extreme vocabulary." These words show very strong feeling. For example, you could say (or write) that the view of the forest was *beautiful*. But if you wanted to express that the view was extremely beautiful, you could say (or write) that the view of the forest was *stunning*. The word *stunning* expresses how extremely beautiful the view was.

**1.** *Read the sentences in the left column of the chart and match an extreme word or expression from the box to make the sentence express a stronger meaning. Write the extreme words on the blanks in the sentences in the right-hand column of the chart.*

| benign *adj* | ominous *adj* | sobering *adj* | waging a battle against *exp* |
|---|---|---|---|
| mitigated *v* | on the fringe of *n* | spared by *adj* | |
| naïvely *adv* | riveting *adj* | ~~stunning *adj*~~ | |

| Sentence (not extreme) | Add Extreme Word or Expression |
|---|---|
| 1. The view of the forest was *beautiful*. | 1. The view of the forest was _stunning_. |
| 2. The smoke from the forest fires looked *threatening*. | 2. The smoke from the forest fires looked _____. |
| 3. The new homes were built *on the outskirts of* town. | 3. The new homes were built _____ town. |
| 4. Nature is *kind* when the weather is calm. | 4. Nature is _____ when the weather is calm. |
| 5. People *innocently* think that living near or in a forest will always be safe. | 5. People _____ think that living near or in a forest will always be safe. |
| 6. Their home was *safe from* the fire. | 6. Their home was _____ the fire. |
| 7. It can be *interesting* to watch trained firefighters fight a forest fire. | 7. It can be _____ to watch trained firefighters fight a forest fire. |
| 8. The death of a firefighter is a *serious* reminder of the danger of forest fires. | 8. The death of a firefighter is a _____ reminder of the danger of forest fires. |
| 9. *Fighting* a forest fire can be dangerous. | 9. _____ a forest fire can be dangerous. |
| 10. Forest managers *reduced* the risk of a large forest fire by setting a prescribed burn. | 10. Forest managers _____ the risk of a large forest fire by setting a prescribed burn. |

**2.** *Complete each sentence with the correct extreme word from the box on page 58. Some sentences require a different form of the extreme word you learned.*

1. Forestry crews, contractors, hundreds of soldiers, and urban firefighters—more than 3,500 in all—are _____ tough odds.

2. "Things are things," he says later, after a hectic night that saw their home _____ the fire. "As long as everyone is OK, that's the important stuff."

3. It's the potential for massive loss of property and life that sets this year's fire season apart—and causes some to ask if the B.C. government could have _____ the risk.

4. Never before have so many fires threatened those living on the wilderness _____ of B.C.

5. Three pilots have died in two crashes in the aerial fire fights that are a _____ spectacle of skill and courage.

6. The _____ natural setting that attracted Dina and Mel Kotler to their home on the edge of Gallagher's Canyon in Kelowna's southeast is the very thing that rose up against them last Thursday.

7. Many discovered to their alarm that nature isn't as _____ as it may seem.

8. The treed view of canyon, lake, and city turned _____, as it has in so many places across British Columbia in this summer of flames.

9. "To lose three people this year is a very _____ reminder of the dangers and the risks that these people face on a daily basis," says provincial fire information officer Steve Bachop.

10. "I have to admit," says Mel, a retired executive, "to being very _____ about the implications of that danger."

**3.** *Compare your answers with a classmate's. Then work together to predict what you will read about based on the sentences you just completed. Discuss your predictions with the class.*

**4.** *Read the article and answer the questions that follow it on page 61.*

In July and August of 2003, British Columbia (B.C.), Canada's most westerly province, experienced 825 forest fires, forcing the evacuation of thousands of residents from their homes.

by Ken MacQueen (from *Mclean's*)

# OUT OF CONTROL

**Thousands flee their homes as British Columbia endures its most destructive summer of forest fires**

## Key Words

**canyon** *n* a deep valley with steep rock sides that usually has a river running through it

**deploy** *v* to organize and move people or equipment so they are in the right place and ready to be used

**evacuation** *n* sending people away from a dangerous place to a safe place

**flammable** *adj* highly likely to burn

**high stakes** *exp* the risks (dangers) are high

**to raise the stakes** *exp* to increase the risks (dangers)

1  The stunning natural setting that attracted Dina and Mel Kotler to their home on the edge of Gallagher's Canyon in Kelowna's southeast is the very thing that rose up against them last Thursday. The treed view of canyon, lake, and city turned ominous, as it has in so many places across British Columbia in this summer of flames. Never before have so many fires threatened those living on the wilderness fringe of B.C. Many discovered to their alarm that nature isn't as benign as it may seem. "I have to admit," says Mel, a retired executive, "to being very naïve about the implications of that danger."

2  With the sky glowing red as wildfires consumed Okanagan Mountain Provincial Park to the south, he packed to leave home Thursday night, just ahead of an evacuation order that moved 10,000 people out by early Friday. Overnight, 15 homes burned. Dina was away visiting family. It was left to Mel to gather papers, jewelry, the works of his wife and her father who are both artists, and their cat. "Things are things," he says later, after a hectic night that saw their home spared by the fire. "As long as everyone is OK, that's the important stuff."

3  Across the province, 825 fires have forced the evacuation of thousands from the Okanagan Valley, Kamloops, and the mountainous Kootenay region of southeastern B.C. By Friday, more than 170,000 hectares (420,000 acres) of forest had been destroyed by these fires in the most devastating and expensive fire year in provincial history. Consequently, as of Friday, the provincial government had burned through more than $156.7 million—three times its annual fire suppression budget.

4  Nowhere are the stakes higher than the populous Okanagan region, where the fate of homes, orchards, wineries, and the peak of the tourist season depend on the variability of wind and weather. "It's tough to imagine that 10,000 of our citizens have now been evacuated," says Kelowna mayor Walter Gray. Some have gone to stay with family members, others at community centers that have been hastily converted into evacuation refuges.

5  Three pilots have died in two crashes in the aerial fire fights that are a riveting spectacle of skill and courage. "To lose three people this year is a very sobering reminder of the dangers and the risks that these people face on a daily basis," says provincial fire information officer Steve Bachop. Forestry crews, contractors, hundreds of soldiers, and urban firefighters—more than 3,500 in all—are waging the battle against tough odds.

6 The risk on the ground, too, is enormous. At their peak, flames in the McLure-Barriere and Okanagan Mountain park fires
5 climbed more than 60 meters into the forest canopy, and spread at more than 90 meters a minute, says Bachop. "You can drop all the water you've got access to
10 and in most cases it's not going to do anything to slow it down," he says. The latter fire, started on August 16 by lightning, became a "double-headed monster," as one
15 official put it, as winds pushed it north to Kelowna and south toward the postcard-perfect village of Naramata.

7 It's the potential for massive loss of property and life that sets this year's fire season apart—and causes some to ask if the B.C. government could have mitigated the risk. An independent report
5 warned two years ago of the growing threat of "interface fires," where human development is close to the natural forest—already seen claiming communities and lives in California, New Mexico, and Australia. Ironically, the near-mythical love
10 of British Columbians for their forests seems to be a contributing factor. Not only are they building

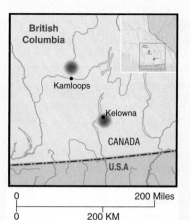

British Columbia

Kamloops

Kelowna

CANADA

U.S.A

0                    200 Miles
0        200 KM

flammable little pieces of suburbia among the trees, but a case can be made that the province's woods
15 are being killed with kindness. Logging provincial parks to remove dead and bug-infested trees, and expanding prescribed burns to clear forest underbrush,
20 have been controversial. Decades of suppressing the natural cycle of fires also added to a "significant buildup of forest fuels."

8 Forests Minister Mike de Jong has signaled a willingness to consider reinstituting such remedies as controlled burns to limit further disasters for forest fires. As a
5 result, last week, the province hurriedly created a special fire department with the power to instantly deploy equipment and people to fight interface fires. Kamloops forester Gary Barber is part of the ongoing battle, running a crew of 75 on the fires
10 across the B.C. interior in the worst conditions he's seen in his 23 years in the woods. That there are homes amid the trees only raises the stakes. "You never heard much about these fires until there were houses out there," he says. "When it's just
15 trees getting burned, and no one sees it, it's not a big deal."

Source: McQueen, K. (2004, September 1). Out of Control. Maclean's, 116 (35), 24–26.

1. What clues in the text indicate that this is an article from a magazine and not an excerpt from a textbook?

2. What was it that initially attracted the Kotlers to their home that is now a danger to them? Were they prepared for that danger? How do you know?

3. Describe the detrimental effects of this forest fire in terms of land burned, personal action required, and cost (in money and human lives).

4. What are interface fires and why are they a threat in forested areas?

5. What does the author mean when he writes that the woods are being "killed by kindness"?

6. What has the province done recently to help fight forest fires in the future?

7. According to Gary Barber, why do we hear more about the fires now than in the past?

# Focused Reading

Writers use various tools to create cohesion in their texts:

- **Repetition** of important words focuses the reader's attention on the main topic of the paragraph.
- **Synonyms** show that the author is writing about the same topic without being repetitive.
- **Pronouns** can show connections to nouns that were mentioned earlier in the paragraph or sentence. There are many different pronouns—for example, *he, she, which, who, that, it, they, them.*
- **Demonstrative adjectives** (such as *this/these*) + summary word can create a connection among sentences because they refer to things, ideas, or people in previous sentences.
- ***The former/the latter*** can create a connection among sentences because they refer to things, ideas, or people in the previous sentences.
- **Connecting words** show the relationships between parts of a paragraph or a sentence—*however, therefore, as a result, consequently,* and so on.

Of course, not all of these tools are used in every paragraph. Writers choose the tools that work best for their texts.

---

**1.** *Work in groups of three. Each of you will be responsible for looking for elements of cohesion in several paragraphs. (Note: The symbol ¶ means paragraph.)*

- Write your name in the chart next to the numbers of the paragraphs you will look at. All students will answer question 1. Then individually answer the questions for your paragraphs.
- When you have finished, check your answers with a student from another group who completed the same questions you did.
- Return to your group of three students and exchange information about cohesion in your paragraphs.

| Student | Read Paragraphs | Answer Questions |
|---------|-----------------|------------------|
| A. | 1–2 | 2–5 |
| B. | 3–4 | 6–9 |
| C. | 5–8 | 10–13 |

**Question for All Students**

1. Scan your paragraphs. How many times can you see the words *fire, wildfire,* and *flames*? What tool of cohesion is the author using?

**Student A**

Scan paragraphs 1 and 2 and answer the questions.

2. What does the expression *the very thing* (¶ 1, line 5) refer to? Draw an arrow to connect this expression to the idea it refers to.

3. What does *it* (¶ 1, line 8) refer to? Draw an arrow to connect *it* to what it refers to. What tool of cohesion is this?

4. What does *it* (¶ 1, line 14) refer to? Draw an arrow to connect *it* to what it refers to. What tool of cohesion is this?

5. What does *who* (¶ 2, line 11) refer to? Draw an arrow to connect *who* to what it refers to. What tool of cohesion is this?

**Student B**

Scan paragraphs 3 and 4 and answer the questions.

6. What does the expression *these fires* (¶ 3, line 8) refer to? Draw an arrow to connect the expression to what it refers to. What tool of cohesion is this?

7. Why did the author write *consequently* (¶ 3, line 10)? What tool of cohesion is the author using here?

8. What does *where* (¶ 4, line 3) refer to? Draw an arrow to connect *where* to what it refers to. What tool of cohesion is this?

9. What do *some* (¶ 4, line 9) and *others* (¶ 4, line 11) refer to? Draw an arrow to connect these words with the word(s) they are replacing. What tool of cohesion is this?

**Student C**

Scan paragraphs 5, 6, 7, and 8 and answer the questions.

10. What does the expression *these people* (¶ 5, line 7) refer to? Draw an arrow to connect the expression to what it refers to. What tool of cohesion is this?

11. Which fire does *the latter fire* (¶ 6, line 12) refer to? Draw an arrow to connect *the latter fire* to the fire it refers to. What tool of cohesion is this?

12. What does *they* (¶ 7, line 11) refer to? Draw an arrow to connect *they* with what it refers to. What tool of cohesion is this?

13. Why did the author write *as a result* (¶ 8, lines 4–5)? What tool of cohesion is the author using here?

**2.** *With your group, use your knowledge of cohesion to complete the paragraph. Share your group's answers with the class. What elements of cohesion did you use?*

If you live in or near a forested region, sooner or later you may have to contend with the spread of a wildfire. The best protection against loss, damage, or injury due to (1) _____ is prevention. Your home contains many flammable items. Properly preparing (2) _____ home doesn't guarantee that (3) _____ won't incur fire damage, but preparation does reduce the risks. Mature trees, shrubs, litter, and even your woodpile are all flammable. (4) _____ first clear the 10 meters around your home of all vegetation. (5) _____ keep your grass short and watered. A (6) _____ without a good fuel-free space around it can make firefighting difficult, if not impossible. Second, keep all trees within 20 (7) _____ of your home spaced out and trimmed. Space trees so that the crowns of individual (8) _____ are 3 to 6 meters apart. (9) _____, use fire-resistant materials when you are building your home. Materials such as metal, clay, or asphalt roof tiles are the best. Wood shingles are not recommended. The (10) _____ materials offer superior fire resistance to wildfire; the (11) _____ are perfect fuels for a roaring wildfire. These (12) _____ can reduce the risk that a wildfire will damage or destroy your home.

**3.** *Look at the sentences from the reading. What do they have in common?*
   a. *Never before* <u>have</u> so many fires <u>threatened</u> those living on the wilderness fringe of B.C.
   b. *Nowhere* <u>are</u> the stakes higher than in the populous Okanagan region, where the fate of homes, orchards, wineries, and the peak of the tourist season depend on the variability of wind and weather.
   c. *Not only* <u>are</u> they <u>building</u> flammable little pieces of suburbia among the trees, but a case can be made that the province's woods are being killed with kindness.

## Creating Special Emphasis by Starting a Sentence with a Negative Expression

In a situation where there has been a natural disaster, like a forest fire, it is possible to show how unusual the situation is by starting your sentence with a negative expression. After the negative expression, the verb comes before the subject.

**4.** *Work with a partner to complete the sentences that begin with a negative expression. Invert the normal subject-verb order to give special emphasis to your sentences. Check your sentences with the class.*

   1. Never before (with this expression, use the present perfect)

   _____.

   2. Never again (with this expression, use the future)

   _____.

   3. Nowhere _____.

   4. Not only _____.

   5. Under no circumstances _____.

# 4

## Building Academic Writing Skills

In this section, you will write a persuasive essay about whether people should be allowed to live in or near forested areas. The goal of a persuasive essay is to convince the reader that the author's opinion is correct.

You will use ideas and vocabulary from the lecture and the reading in this unit to write your essay.

For online assignments, go to

PEARSON LONGMAN
myacademicconnectionslab

## Before You Write

Before you begin, it's a good idea to have an opinion about your essay topic.

Here is your essay topic: **Should there be a law preventing people from living in or near a forested area?**

**1.** *At the beginning of the unit, you were asked to survey the class. The question was, "Should governments allow people to live in or near a forested area?" Look back at the results of the class survey on page 49. Survey the class again. Should there be a law preventing people from living in or near a forested area?*

Yes _____ percent          No _____ percent

**2.** *Have the results changed since you began the unit? Why? Has your own opinion changed since then? Do you agree with the majority of your class?*

**3.** *It may help you to read about the opinions other people have on this subject. Read these opinion statements. Then, in your notebook, write one of your own. Be sure that you clearly express an answer to the question and the reason(s) why you feel the way you do.*

---

### Question of the week

*Should laws be passed to discourage people from building homes adjacent to open forests?*

| SURVEY OF RESPONDENTS: | |
| --- | --- |
| ■ **YES** | 32 percent |
| ■ **NO** | 68 percent |

Building subdivisions adjacent to forested areas is risky, especially in our world today. Climate change is a reality. Places like Alberta and the interior of B.C. are going to get drier and drier, so houses built close to large stands of timber are going to be subject to a steadily increasing risk of destruction. Besides the danger to the homes, placing houses right up against forests is disruptive to the area's wildlife, and thus the area's entire ecological system. A buffer between houses and forests would be best for both.
—David, Sherwood Park, Alta.

To not build near a forest would be rather silly, especially here in Canada. Why should people not live in the country? As for the B.C. fires, acts of nature are a fact of life. Of course, there is some loss, and I feel sorry for the people who built homes and have lost them, but life is a risk. People who build on riverbanks risk loss by flooding, and people who build on ravines risk loss by erosion. People who build in inner cities risk loss by crime, yet they all do it.
—Peter Duchesne, Ottawa, Ont.

*(continued on next page)*

The lives of our firefighters should not be put in danger because people want a nice view and fresh air. Property can be replaced, a human being can never be. It's just not worth it.

—Jennifer, Calgary, Alta.

I think that is just ridiculous! How many homes are built adjacent to forests and are not causing any problems? Should people be discouraged from owning homes in earthquake zones or tornado belts? Where does it end?

—Tracy, St. Adolphe, Man.

The closer we get to the forests, the more trees and wildlife we lose. It's time to leave the forests as they are. There is enough land without destroying our natural resources.

—L. Lalonde, Cornwall, Ont.

Yes, yes, yes. The loss of all those expensive homes built so close to the forests is going to cost taxpayers millions. [People's] desire to live a grandiose lifestyle, by ignoring nature, has resulted in this needless tragedy.

—John Fertile

Laws to stop people from building near forested land . . . where will it stop? Will there be laws against building near a lake, a mountain, or a roadside? Use common sense for a change! Yes, people have lost their homes because of the fires, but you can't protect people from nature. Don't be ridiculous. Next, you will want people to stop planting trees.

—D. Deyo, London, Ont.

Fires happen naturally in these ecosystems. Specific tree species, such as the jack pine, rely heavily on fire to regerminate. Without these fires, we are subjecting these species to extinction. Houses should not be built in these areas. If you do, do not be surprised when fires do occur and get out of control.

—Joanne Parsons, Newmarket, Ont.

Source: Question of the week. (2004, September 8). *Maclean's.* Retrieved from www.macleans.ca/article.

**4.** *Work in small groups. Share your opinion statements. As you listen to the opinion statements, write down the good reasons you hear in support of or against the question. This information will help you to write your persuasive essay.*

| Yes, there should be a law preventing people from living in or near a forested area. | No, there should not be a law preventing people from living in or near a forested area. |
|---|---|
| Reasons why: | Reasons why: |

As a writer developing a persuasive essay, it is important to know who your audience is. If you know your audience is likely to disagree with your opinion, then you will write differently from the way you would write if you think your audience might agree with you. This consideration of audience is basic to persuasive essay writing as well as to oral presentations and even informal discussions with friends. To give you an example of how we intuitively consider audience, ask yourself whether you would tell your friend about asking your parents for money if you knew your friend was working at two jobs to be independent from his or her parents. You probably wouldn't mention your request for money because you know your friend (your audience) would disagree with your actions.

For most academic writing, your audience will likely be your instructor or professor. In an academic setting, your instructor probably doesn't care which opinion you have, as long as you present your opinion in a persuasive way. It is your ability to persuade—to present the reasons why you believe what you do—that most instructors are evaluating, not the opinion itself.

Authors can use a number of methods to persuade their readers. Authors may state

- the opposing view and then contradict it
- facts or statistics
- logical arguments
- quotations from an expert

**5.** *To help you prepare to write your own persuasive essay, reread the example persuasive essay on pages 50–51 and answer the questions.*

1. What essay question did the author answer in this essay? Based on this question, how did the author write the title of the essay?

2. What methods of persuasion did the author use in the essay? Write the approach used in each paragraph of the essay.

3. Prepare to write your own persuasive essay by filling in the chart. You may or may not complete all the rows in the chart.

| My Opinion | The Reasons for My Opinion | My Methods of Persuasion |
|---|---|---|
| | | |
| | | |
| | | |
| | | |

# Focused Writing

There are many different kinds of pronouns in English. All pronouns, no matter which kind, take the place of a noun that came before them.

- All pronouns must match the *number* of the noun that came before them. This means that if the noun that came before the pronoun is singular, the pronoun must also be in the singular form. If the noun that came before the pronoun is plural, the pronoun must also be in the plural form.

**Examples**

*A crown fire* moves quickly through the tops of the trees. *It* can be more destructive than a surface fire.

*Wildfires* are naturally occurring events in the vast majority of forests. *They* can have beneficial effects on plant and animal diversity.

- All pronouns must match the *gender* of the noun that came before them. This means that if the noun that came before the pronoun is feminine, the pronoun must also be feminine. If the noun that came before the pronoun is masculine, the pronoun must also be masculine.

**Examples**

*My son David* is working as a forest manager. *He* is trying to enhance soil quality through careful use of prescribed fires.

*Susan* has won a number of awards for her work in plant diversity. *She* is one of a group of researchers working in Thailand.

*1.* *Use the correct pronoun to match the boldfaced noun in each sentence.*

1. In British Columbia, Canada, there are often **serious forest fires** in the summertime. _____ can cause damage and destruction to forests and homes.

2. If a **forest fire** is burning near human habitation, firefighters will try to extinguish _____.

3. **Mel Kotler** had to evacuate his home. _____ was worried that his home would be burned, but _____ was more concerned about personal safety.

4. **Mel's wife Dina** was away at the time of the fire. _____ was not able to help with the evacuation of their home.

5. There are **new chemicals** used to fight forest fires today. _____ suppress the fire without damaging forest ecology.

People learning English often make the mistake of using a plural pronoun (*their*) when the noun that came before is singular. The sentences below are examples of pronoun agreement errors.

**Example 1**

✗ A **parent** can be proud if **their** child becomes a forest manager.

This sentence is incorrect because the noun that came before is the singular noun *parent*. The pronoun must also be singular.

Here is the corrected sentence.

✓ A **parent** can be proud if **his or her** child becomes a forest manager.

**Example 2**

✗ Once an evacuation order has been issued, **everyone** will have to evacuate **their homes**.

This sentence is incorrect because *everyone* is singular (not plural) and does not match the pronoun *their*.

Here is the corrected sentence.

✓ Once an evacuation order has been issued, **everyone** will have to evacuate **his or her home**.

---

Remember that all of these words are singular:

- everyone, everybody, everything
- someone, somebody, something
- anyone, anybody, anything
- no one, nobody, nothing
- each, either, neither

---

You may find that using "his or her" is awkward. You could write this instead:

✓ Once an evacuation order has been issued, **everyone** will have to evacuate **her** home.

However, this excludes males. The solution to this problem is to switch to a third-person, plural subject.

✓ Once an evacuation order has been issued, **all people** must evacuate **their** homes.

**2.** *Complete each sentence with the correct pronoun that agrees with the noun that came before. Then check your answers with the class.*

1. Forest managers must use _____ best judgment when deciding whether to issue an evacuation order.

2. A forest manager must use _____ best judgment when deciding whether to issue an evacuation order.

3. Now everyone knows that building _____ home near a forested region is a risk.

4. People know that building _____ homes near a forested region is a risk.

5. While there are some precautions that can reduce the risk of forest fires, people can't protect _____ homes from every risk.

6. While there are some precautions that can reduce the risk of forest fires, no one can protect _____ home from every risk.

## Integrated Writing Task

You have now listened to a lecture and read texts about the benefits and dangers of wildfires. Use your knowledge of the content, vocabulary, and parallel structure (from Unit 1) to write a short persuasive essay in response to this question: **Should there be a law preventing people from living in or near a forested area?**

Your essay will have an introduction (with a thesis statement), a body (with two or three paragraphs), and a concluding paragraph. Each paragraph will have a main point and supporting details. You will use vocabulary specific to forest fires and parallel structure when necessary (for example, in your thesis statement).

*Follow the steps to write your essay.*

**Step 1**: In this unit, you have surveyed the class twice, and you have written a short opinion statement in answer to the essay question. What is your opinion about this question?

**Step 2**: From the chart on page 66, select the best reasons that support your opinion. You will write one body paragraph about each of these reasons.

**Step 3**: From the chart on page 67, which method would be best to persuade your reader that your reason is good? (Note: You probably will not be able to use quotations or statistics here unless you do some extra research.)

**Step 4**: Write your thesis statement and analyze it. Show it to a classmate. Can your classmate identify the thesis statement, author's opinion, and main points stated in parallel form?

**Step 5**: Write your introductory paragraph. Finish with your thesis statement.

**Step 6**: Write the body and conclusion of your essay.
- For each reason for your opinion, write a paragraph in your essay.
- The topic sentence of each paragraph should state its reason clearly.
- In each paragraph, persuade the reader that your opinion is correct.
- Finish with a concluding paragraph. The concluding paragraph should have a concluding sentence that restates your thesis statement.

**Step 7**: Ask your teacher or a classmate to review your essay based on the checklist.

| Features of an Effective Essay | Yes | No |
| --- | --- | --- |
| Introductory paragraph | | |
| Effective thesis statement that clearly states the author's opinion | | |
| Main points of thesis statement in parallel structure | | |
| One main point per paragraph | | |
| Clearly stated topic sentence in each paragraph | | |
| Each paragraph effectively persuades the reader. | | |
| Concluding paragraph | | |
| Thesis is restated in the concluding paragraph. | | |
| Vocabulary is specific to the topic of forest fires. | | |
| There is cohesion among the essay paragraphs. | | |
| There is coherence in each paragraph. | | |

**Step 8**: Based on the information in the checklist, revise your essay and hand it in.

# UNIT 4

## Art History
# Defining Cubism

## Unit Description

**Content:**  This course is designed to familiarize the student with concepts of cubism and its connection to modern art.

**Skills:**  Summarizing

- Paraphrasing: The first step to summarizing
- Using synonyms
- Recognizing summary statements and conclusions when reading
- Summarizing information
- Distinguishing essential from non-essential information in a lecture
- Recognizing digressions or asides
- Participating in a debate

## Unit Requirements

**Readings:**  "The Influence of Cubism" (from "Cubism" in *History of Modern Art*, 5th Edition, H. Arnason & P. Kalb, Pearson Prentice Hall)

"Quotations from Picasso" (from *Picasso dit . . .*, H. Parmelin, Allen & Unwin)

**Lecture:**  "Cubism as Fashion Art"

**Integrated Speaking Task:**  Preparing and presenting a pair debate about cubism as fashion art

**Assignments:**
www.MyAcademicConnectionsLab.com

Pablo Picasso.
*Portrait of Daniel-Henry Kahnweiler.*
1910. Oil on canvas.

# 1

## Preview

For online assignments, go to

## Previewing the Academic Content

Pablo Picasso (1881–1973) and his friend Georges Braque (1882–1963) were the artists who created cubism, one of the most influential art movements of the early 20th century. Cubism changed the way artists and their audiences viewed art and the world around them. However, cubism is controversial, with some critics calling Picasso a genius while others suggest his cubist works lack skill. How did cubism lead to abstract art, and are cubist works skillful?

*Four very different approaches to painting the human face are demonstrated in the paintings below. Work with a partner to complete the tasks.*

1. Put the paintings in order from the most representational (showing things as they actually appear in real life) to the most abstract (showing shapes and patterns that do not look like real things or people).

2. Identify which painting is the work of a cubist. What characteristics of this painting suggest that it is a cubist painting?

3. Put the paintings in order from the most skillful to the least skillful. What characteristics of a painting make it skillful?

4. Match the paintings to these painters: *Bronzino, van Gogh, Munch, Picasso*

Artist _____

Artist _____

Artist _____

Artist _____

This unit will provide you with techniques that will develop your skill of summarizing both written and spoken information. This skill is essential for success in an academic setting.

# Previewing the Academic Skills Focus

## Paraphrasing: The First Step to Summarizing

Paraphrasing is expressing other people's ideas in your own words. This is an essential skill in an English language academic context because it is not permissible to present another person's ideas as your own or to copy another person's words. A paraphrase is usually about the same length as the original spoken or written source, while a summary is always shorter than the original source. This is important because a key distinction between a paraphrase and a summary is the length of each compared to the original source. It is helpful to know paraphrasing techniques before you learn how to summarize.

Paraphrasing can be hard work, especially if you are working in a language that is different from your first language. Here are a few techniques you can use to help you paraphrase well:

- Use synonyms for the key words in a sentence.
- Change the form of the key words in a sentence (change nouns to verbs, verbs to adjectives, adjectives to nouns, and so on).
- Change the structure of a sentence (change the organization of the clauses).
- Change the voice of a sentence (from active to passive, or passive to active).

Usually, you have to use more than one of these techniques to paraphrase well.

*What is Picasso saying in this quotation? Select the best paraphrase from the choices. Then answer the questions on page 76.*

Art does not evolve by itself. The ideas of people change, and art changes in order to express these ideas. If an artist changes his way of expressing himself, it means that his way of thinking and seeing reality has changed. If the change is consistent with the changing ideas of his time, then his work has improved; if not, then it has deteriorated or failed.

**Paraphrase 1**
Picasso felt that art reflects ideas. At the time an artwork is created, it reflects the artist's way of thinking. The art will be considered good when the artist's ideas are similar to society's ideas. The art will be considered bad when the artist's ideas are different from society's ideas.

**Paraphrase 2**
Picasso believed that art evolves with time and reflects people's changing ideas. If an artist's work expresses society's ideas, then his work is accepted; if not, then his work is rejected.

**Paraphrase 3**
Art does not change by itself. People's thoughts evolve, and art evolves in order to reflect these thoughts. If a painter expresses himself differently, it means that he is thinking differently. If his thoughts are the same as the thoughts of his time, then his work is better; if not, then his work is worse.

1. Compare your answer with another student's. Do you agree on which paraphrase is best? Why?

2. What are some of the paraphrasing techniques from the skills box on page 75 that the writer used to paraphrase?

3. What is similar about the first sentence in paraphrase 1 and 2? Why did the writer start these two paraphrases in this way?

## 2

**Building Academic Reading Skills**

In this section, you will learn more about paraphrasing techniques. These techniques will help you summarize information later in the unit. You will also learn how to recognize summary and concluding statements.

For online assignments, go to

PEARSON LONGMAN myacademicconnectionslab

## Before You Read

### Using Synonyms

Synonyms are words that have the same, or similar, meanings. Using synonyms is one key technique you can use to paraphrase—express in your own words—someone else's ideas. Using synonyms can also add variety to your speaking and writing.

**1.** *Write each synonym next to its definition in the chart. Pay attention to the forms of the words.*

| artist | far-reaching implications | impact | painter | subject |
| artwork | figure | (the) legacy of | painting | subtle clues |
| broken down | float | lingering influence | repercussion | work of art |
| creator | fragmented | monochromatic | single color/tone | |
| dissected | hover | object | small details | |

| Definition | Synonyms |
|---|---|
| Something created by an artist | *artwork (n), work of art (exp)* |
| Someone who creates art | |
| Something larger that has been reduced to smaller parts | |
| Not easy to see unless you pay careful attention | |

| Definition | Synonyms |
|---|---|
| Painted in just one color, usually mixed with grey | |
| A person or a thing in a painting | |
| To stay in one place in the air | |
| The effect or consequence of something | |

**2.** *Work in groups of three. Use some of the synonyms from the chart to discuss the questions about art.*

1. What characterizes abstract art?

2. What might abstract painters do to make their works of art easier to understand?

3. Who is an artist whose paintings have had a significant effect on other creators?

**3.** *Examine the examples and evaluations of paraphrases. Look for the specific techniques listed in the Previewing the Academic Skills section on page 75.*

**Example 1**

**Original text**
*Although cubism was never itself an abstract style, the many varieties of nonobjective art it helped usher in throughout Europe would have been unthinkable without it.*

**How to paraphrase by using synonyms**
Replace words from the original text with synonyms. There will be some words that have no synonyms, such as the names of people, places, religions, technical words, and public domain words such as *the*.

**Paraphrase**
*While cubism was not abstract, the large quantity of abstract art that followed would not have been possible in the absence of cubism.*

**Evaluation:** This is a good start, but because the sentence structure has remained the same, it is still too much like the original text. We need to keep working on it.

**How to paraphrase by changing the sentence structure**
Only when you understand the sentence structure of the original text can you change the sentence structure to paraphrase. In Example 1, the original text consists of a dependent clause followed by an independent clause.

**Paraphrase using synonyms and changing the sentence structure**
*Cubism, which was not abstract art, opened the door for a large quantity of abstract art that followed it.*

**Evaluation:** Now you have one independent clause, with an adjective clause after the subject. The sentence structure is very different from the original text. This, combined with synonyms, makes a good paraphrase.

### Example 2
**Original text**
*Cubism altered forever the Renaissance conception of painting as a window into a world where three-dimensional space is projected onto the flat picture plane by way of drawing and one-point perspective.*

**How to paraphrase by changing the voice from active to passive**
Consider whether the original source is in the active or passive voice. In Example 2, the original source is in the active voice. *Cubism* is the subject, and *altered*, an active-voice verb, is followed by a very long object: *the Renaissance conception of painting as a window into a world where three-dimensional space is projected onto the flat picture plane by way of drawing and one-point perspective.* When a subject is followed by an active-voice verb plus an object, you can change the sentence to the passive voice.

**Paraphrase**
*The Renaissance conception of painting as a window into a world where three-dimensional space is projected onto the flat picture plane by way of drawing and one-point perspective was altered forever by cubism.*

**Evaluation:** This is a good start, but clearly there is too much repetition of the original text to make this a good paraphrase. We need to add another technique.

**Paraphrase using changed voice and synonyms**
*The previous notion of a canvas as a view of reality where three-dimensional space is represented on a flat surface using skillful perspective was changed irrevocably by cubism.*

**Evaluation:** This is a better paraphrase.

### Example 3
**Original text**
*The cubists concluded that reality has many definitions, and that therefore, objects in space—and indeed space itself—have no fixed or absolute form.*

**How to paraphrase by changing the parts of speech**
Change nouns into verbs, adjectives into adverbs, verbs into adjectives, adjectives into nouns, and so on.

**Paraphrase**
*The cubist* (adj) *conclusion* (n) *that reality could be defined* (v) *in many ways meant that objects in space—and indeed space itself—have no fixed or absolute form.*

**Evaluation:** This is not bad, but the last part of the paraphrase is too similar to the original.

**Paraphrase using changed parts of speech and synonyms**

*The cubist conclusion that real life could be defined in a variety of ways meant that three-dimensional space could be represented through non-traditional methods.*

**Evaluation:** This is a reasonable paraphrase.

**4.** *Work with one or two partners to practice paraphrasing the sentences. Use the vocabulary from Exercise 1 on page 76 to help you. You may need to write several drafts of the paraphrase, as demonstrated in the examples in Exercise 3. Write the paraphrases in your notebook. Use the grid to help you keep track of the techniques you used to paraphrase.*

1. Cubism had far-reaching implications for modern art.

2. Cubist paintings show subjects that are broken down yet recognizable. They seem to float on the canvas.

3. Cubist painters did not use a wide range of color in their paintings; however, their paintings seem to radiate light.

4. Today, many works of modern art include written words, but in 1911, Braque was the first artist to use words in his paintings. Not surprisingly, the words he used in his cubist works are as fragmented as his subjects.

| | Sentences | | | |
|---|---|---|---|---|
| **Technique** | 1 | 2 | 3 | 4 |
| used synonyms | ___ | ___ | ___ | ___ |
| changed the sentence structure | ___ | ___ | ___ | ___ |
| changed from active to passive | ___ | ___ | ___ | ___ |
| changed the parts of speech | ___ | ___ | ___ | ___ |

**5.** *Now compare your paraphrases with other students'. Did you use the same techniques to paraphrase? Is one paraphrase better than another? Why?*

## Global Reading

*Read the questions. Then read the excerpt from an art history textbook on pages 80–81 and answer the questions based on the information in the text.*

1. How did cubism influence other kinds of art? List at least two other kinds of art that cubism influenced.

2. What are the characteristics of cubist paintings?

3. On the spectrum of representational to abstract art, place an *X* where you think cubist paintings belong. Explain why you think cubism belongs where you have placed it.

REPRESENTATIONAL                                                           ABSTRACT

**dissolve** *v* to gradually become smaller or weaker until disappearing completely

**fluctuate** *v* to change by becoming higher or lower

**obscure** *adj* difficult to see or understand

**plane** *n* a completely flat surface (from geometry)

**still life** *exp* a picture of an arrangement of objects, often fruit or flowers

**usher in** *v* to cause something new to start

## The Influence of Cubism

1   The various types of cubism that Pablo Picasso developed jointly with Georges Braque in France between 1908 and 1914 offered a radically new way of looking at the world. Their shared vision had an inestimable impact on the abstract art that followed it. Although cubism was never itself an abstract style, the many varieties of nonobjective art it helped usher in throughout Europe would have been unthinkable without it. From Italian futurism to Dutch neo-plasticism to Russian constructivism, the repercussions of the cubist experiment were thoroughly international in scope. But the legacy of cubism was not exhausted in the first quarter of the 20th century, when these movements took place. Its lingering influence can be felt in much art after World War II, in works as diverse as the paintings of Willem de Kooning, the sculpture of David Smith, the multimedia constructions of Robert Rauschenberg, the photographs of David Hockney, and the architecture of Frank Gehry.

4.1. Pablo Picasso. *Portrait of Daniel-Henry Kahnweiler.* 1910. Oil on canvas.

2   Cubism altered forever the Renaissance conception of painting as a window into a world where three-dimensional space is projected onto the flat picture plane by way of realistic drawing and one-point perspective. The cubists concluded that reality has many definitions, and that therefore objects in space—and indeed, space itself—have no fixed or absolute form. Together, Picasso and Braque translated those multiple readings of reality into a wide range of art forms. They began with analytic cubism, in which the object is analyzed, broken down, and dissected.

3   One of the masterpieces of analytic cubism is Picasso's *Portrait of Daniel-Henry Kahnweiler.* The painting belongs to a series of portraits of art dealers that Picasso made in 1910. In this portrait, for which Kahnweiler apparently sat 20 times, the figure seems merged with the background. Here the third dimension is stated entirely in terms of flat, slightly angled planes organized within a linear grid that hovers near the surface of the painting. Planes shift in front of and behind their neighbors, causing space to fluctuate and solid form to dissolve. Nevertheless, Picasso managed a likeness of his subject. In small details—a wave of hair, the sitter's carefully clasped hands, an identifiable still life at the lower left—the painter particularized his subject and helps us to reconstruct a figure seated in a chair. Though Picasso kept color to the bare minimum, his canvas emits a shimmering, mesmerizing light, which he achieved by applying paint in short strokes that contain generous amounts of white. The Italian critic

Ardengo Soffici referred to the "prismatic magic" of such works.

4 However indecipherable their images, Braque and Picasso never relinquished the natural world altogether, and they provided subtle clues that help us to understand their obscure subject matter. In *Accordionist* (which represents a young girl, according to Picasso, not a man, as critics have often presumed), curved lines near the bottom edge of the painting stand for the arms of a chair, while the small circles and stair-step patterns toward the center indicate the keys and bellows of an accordion.

4.2. Pablo Picasso. *Accordionist.* 1911. Oil on canvas.

5 *The Portuguese (The Emigrant)*, Braque said, shows "an emigrant on the bridge of a boat with a harbor in the background." This would explain the transparent traces of a docking post and sections of nautical rope at the upper right. In the lower portion are the strings and sound hole of the emigrant's guitar. Braque introduced a new element with the stenciled letters and numbers in the painting's upper zone. Like other forms in *The Portuguese*, the words are fragmentary. The letters *D BAL* at the upper right, for example, may refer to *Grand Bal*, probably a reference to a common dance-hall poster. While Braque had incorporated a word into a cubist painting as early as 1909, his letters there were painted freehand as descriptive local detail. For *The Portuguese* he borrowed a technique from commercial art and stenciled his letters. Because they are flat, the letters and numbers exist "outside of space," Braque said. And because they are on the surface of the painting, they underscore the nature of the painted canvas as a material object, a physical fact, rather than a site for the depiction of the real world.

4.3. Georges Braque. *The Portuguese (The Emigrant).* 1911. Oil on canvas.

6 In conclusion, cubism was the single most influential art movement of the early 20th century. Braque's introduction of words in his painting, a practice soon adopted by Picasso, was one of many cubist innovations that had far-reaching implications for modern art. Like so many of their inventions, the presence in the visual arts of letters, words, and even long texts is commonplace today. The cubists believed that reality was not absolute, so it could take on multiple forms. This opened the door to many kinds of nonobjective, or abstract, art that followed.

Source: Arnason, H.H., & Kalb, P. (2004). Cubism. In *History of modern art* (5th ed.). Upper Saddle River, NJ: Pearson Prentice Hall.

# Focused Reading

## Recognizing Summary Statements and Conclusions when Reading

Statements that summarize ideas in a text are easy to recognize because they often begin with similar expressions:

- *In summary . . .*
- *To summarize . . .*
- *In conclusion . . .*
- *To conclude . . .*
- *To finish . . .*
- *To wrap up . . .* (informal, used in lectures, not in readings)

They are often located at the beginning of the final paragraph of text, or the beginning of the final section of text.

**1.** *Highlight the conclusion of the text on pages 80–81. What expression does it start with?*

**2.** *Paraphrase the first sentence of the concluding paragraph. Use your knowledge of typical summary statements to help you.*

**Original text:**

*In conclusion, cubism was the single most influential art movement of the early 20th century.*

**Paraphrase:** _____

_____

_____

## Summarizing Information

When your original source is short—two or three sentences at the most—you can paraphrase the original. Remember that paraphrasing is presenting the ideas from an original source in your own words (see the skills box on page 75). However, when you have a longer source such as a reading from a textbook or a lecture, you need to summarize the source.

A summary presents the main ideas from an original source in your own words and is shorter than the original. To summarize:

- Find the major points and important details. Eliminate the minor points and non-essential information.
- Paraphrase the major points and important details from the original source.

Because you are summarizing, your spoken or written summary will be shorter than the original lecture or text. A summary might be one-quarter to one-third the length of the original lecture or text. However, the exact length of a summary is less important than summarizing the main points well.

One key to writing an effective summary is the ability to distinguish between major and minor points in a text. A summary should include all the major points, and any important details that are essential to understanding the main points. It should *not* include minor points or non-essential information.

**3.** *What techniques did you use to paraphrase this sentence?*

**4.** *On the line beside each of the points from the reading, write **I** (include) if the point is a major point or important detail. Write **E** (eliminate) if the point is a minor point or non-essential information. When you have finished, compare your answers with two other students'.*

_____ 1. Cubism was developed by Picasso and Braque together.

_____ 2. Cubism influenced many different forms of art.

_____ 3. Cubism was developed between 1908 and 1914.

_____ 4. The influence of cubism can still be felt in art created after World War II.

_____ 5. Cubist artists rejected the idea that art had to be representational.

_____ 6. Cubist artists believed that "reality has many definitions."

_____ 7. Analytic cubist paintings break down the object into planes and angles.

_____ 8. One of Picasso's major cubist works is the *Portrait of Daniel-Henry Kahnweiler.*

_____ 9. Kahnweiler sat for this painting 20 times.

_____ 10. Characteristics of cubist paintings include the merging of the background and the subject and a minimal use of color.

_____ 11. Cubist artists always provided some small details that revealed the reality of the subject.

_____ 12. In *The Portuguese* by Braque, there are a docking post and rope in the upper right-hand corner.

_____ 13. Braque was one of the first painters to use letters in his cubist paintings.

_____ 14. Today, letters are often used in abstract art.

_____ 15. Cubism, while not abstract itself, ushered in many kinds of abstract art.

**5.** *Paraphrase the major points you have selected in Exercise 4 to create a summary. Add transition words to create cohesion as required. Then, to avoid copying, check to make sure that the sentences are different from those in the original reading. Compare your summary with your classmates'. How are your summaries similar or different?*

**Checkpoint 1**    PEARSON LONGMAN myacademicconnectionslab

In this section, you
will learn more about
distinguishing major and
minor points in a lecture.
You will also learn about
distinguishing essential
from non-essential
information.
For online assignments,
go to

PEARSON LONGMAN
myacademicconnectionslab

# Before You Listen

From 1912 to 1914, Picasso continued to produce cubist works of art. He
experimented with sculpture—called cubist sculpture—and collage, which is the
gluing of objects onto the canvas—called cubist collage.

*Look at three of Picasso's works of art that represent his cubist experiments. Work in
small groups and decide which one is the most skillful. What are some qualities or
characteristics that make it skillful?*

| Analytic cubism | Collage cubism | Cubist construction |
|---|---|---|
| Pablo Picasso. *Portrait of Daniel-Henry Kahnweiler.* 1910. Oil on canvas. | Pablo Picasso. *Guitar, Sheet Music and Wine Glass.* 1912. Charcoal, gouache, and pasted paper. | Pablo Picasso. *Guitar.* 1912. Construction of sheet metal and wire. |

# Global Listening

### Distinguishing Essential from Non-essential Information in a Lecture

In order to summarize a lecture, you must be able to distinguish essential from non-
essential information. As you know, when you summarize, you include the major
ideas and important details in your summary, and you leave out the non-essential
information.

It may help you to think about main ideas, or major points, as the information that
the lecturer wants you to understand and remember. Before and while you are
listening, think about the purpose of the lecture. The major points will fulfill the
purpose of the lecture; the important details will support the major points. Both major
points and important details should be included in summaries.

While minor points elaborate important details, they are not included in summaries.
Similarly, non-essential information, or information that does not help you understand
the purpose of the lecture, is not included in a summary.

### Introduction of major points/main ideas

A lecturer might identify a major point by saying things like:

- *Here is an important point . . .*
- *I want you to think about this . . .*
- *I want to introduce a new term . . .*

However, a lecturer might not signal a major point in one of these ways. In such situations, you can use other clues to determine major points.

### Clues for determining major points

Anything that your lecturer writes down on the board is probably a major point. If the lecturer takes the time to write something on the board, it is likely information you should remember. Also, if the lecturer talks about the same point for a significant amount of time, or returns to the point more than once, it is likely to be a main point.

**1.** *Eleven of the points in the lecture you will hear are listed out of order in the chart. To help you prepare to summarize the lecture, identify whether you would include the point in a summary or not. If the point is a major point or an important detail, write* **I** *(include). If the point is a minor point or non-essential information, write* **E** *(eliminate). Check with the class to see if you all agree which are major points and important details, and which are the minor points or non-essential information. You will work with the Predicted Order and Actual Order columns later.*

| *include* = major points and important details<br>*eliminate* = minor points and non-essential information | Points | Predicted Order | Actual Order |
|---|---|---|---|
| | Is cubism skillful? | | |
| | *Still Life with Chair Canning* is an example of synthetic cubism. | | |
| | Fashion art displays too much novelty and not enough skill. | | |
| | Picasso's constructed guitar was used to advertise music groups in the 1920s. | | |
| | Great art is a combination of novelty and skill. | | |
| | *Portrait of Daniel-Henry Kahnweiler* is an example of analytical cubism. | | |
| | There is an exhibition of Picasso's sketches coming to town soon. | | |
| | Is cubism—especially the later forms of cubism—fashion art? | | |

*(continued on next page)*

| include = major points and important details<br>eliminate = minor points and non-essential information | Points | Predicted Order | Actual Order |
|---|---|---|---|
| | *The Guitar* is an example of cubist sculpture. | | |
| | *The Man with a Hat* is an example of cubist collage. | | |
| | Be ready to discuss whether you think the later forms of cubist art are fashion art. | | |

**2.** *Look at the chart again and predict the order in which you will hear the points. Write your answers in the Predicted Order column. Then work in small groups to compare your answers.*

Here are the artworks by Pablo Picasso that will be referred to in the lecture.

Portrait of Daniel-Henry Kahnweiler. 1910.

Woman's Head. 1909.

Still Life with Chair Canning. 1912.

Guitar. 1912.

Guitar, Sheet Music and Wine Glass. 1912.

Man with a Hat. 1912–1913.

**3.** 🎧 *Listen to the lecture. As you listen, number the points in the Actual Order column in the chart on pages 85–86 as you hear them presented. Where were the major points located in the lecture? Where were the important details? Where were the non-essential points?*

**4.** *After listening to the lecture, write out the major points on another piece of paper. Orally summarize the lecture by repeating the major points. Paraphrase as much as possible. After you practice, present your oral summary to a classmate.*

## Focused Listening

### Recognizing Digressions or Asides

Essential information is the information you need to understand the lecture. A digression, also called an aside, has little or no connection to the main points and supporting details, and does not help you understand the lecture. In some cases, an instructor will begin a digression with expressions such as:

- *By the way, . . .*
- *As an aside, . . .*
- *Incidentally, . . .*

Sometimes the instructor will say, *Let's get back to the lecture* to show that the aside is finished, but sometimes the end of the aside is not obvious. Listen carefully for pauses that may show the instructor is finished with the aside and is returning to the main lecture.

**1.** 🎧 *Listen to the lecture again. There are two digressions during the lecture. What does the lecturer say in each digression? Complete the sentences.*

1. By the way, I should mention that there will be _____

   _____

2. Incidentally, you may have seen _____

   _____

**2.** *Why are these digressions not essential information?*

**Checkpoint 2**   PEARSON LONGMAN myacademicconnectionslab

## Building Academic Speaking Skills

In this section, you will prepare and present a pair debate. As part of your pair debate, you will need to summarize the information from the readings and the lecture in this unit.
For online assignments, go to

PEARSON LONGMAN
myacademicconnectionslab

# Before You Speak

A pair debate is a semiformal presentation of two opposite opinions. The goal of each pair is to persuade a panel of judges of its opinion. Study the pair debate process.

- You and a partner will work with another pair of students that is arguing the opposite side of the statement. There should be four classmates in one group (one pair that agrees and one pair that disagrees with the debate statement). Four of your other classmates will be the panel of judges for your debate.
- The pair that agrees with the debate statement (Pair 1) speaks first for four minutes. Both members of the pair should speak in turn. All the information presented supports the debate statement. The pair should conclude its presentation with a concluding statement.
- The pair that opposes the debate statement (Pair 2) speaks second for four minutes. Members of the pair should speak in turn. All the information presented opposes the debate statement. The pair should conclude its presentation with a formal concluding statement.
- Pair 1 speaks one more time in favor of the debate statement for *two* minutes. Again, both members of the pair should speak. This is an opportunity for the pair to directly respond to any statements that Pair 2 made.
- Pair 2 speaks one more time to oppose the debate statement for *two* minutes. Again, both members of the pair should speak. This is an opportunity for the pair to directly respond to any statements that Pair 1 made.
- Once the required amount of time has passed, the debate is over. What is the opinion of the judges? The pair that has been the most persuasive has won the debate.

As you can see, a debate requires two sets of presentation skills. The first time a pair speaks, they present a prepared statement that is thoughtful and well organized. The second time a pair speaks, they try to directly respond to the points in the other pair's presentation. Since the pairs don't know exactly what the other pair will say, their second opportunity to speak is more spontaneous—in other words, less planned. Therefore, each pair must be able to think quickly while the other pair is speaking, decide what to say in response, and say it with very little preparation time.

*1.* Work with a partner to write a summary of the pair debate process.

_____

_____

_____

_____

_____

_____

_____

_____

*2.* Now compare your summary with the summary of another pair of students to make sure you have included all the main points.

# Focused Speaking

## Key Words

**approbation** *n* official praise or approval

**component** *n* one of several parts that make up a whole

**in vogue** *exp* popular as a fashion, style, activity, or method

**posterity** *n* all the people in the future who will be alive after you are dead

**1.** *Read the seven quotations from Pablo Picasso.\* They give you an idea about how Picasso saw his own art. Paraphrase each quotation.*

**1.**

*I do not care about the approbation of future generations. I have dedicated my life to freedom and I want to continue being free, which means that I do not worry what will be said about me. Those who are concerned with the judgments of posterity cannot be free.*

**Paraphrase:** _____

_____

_____

**2.**

*Cubism is no different from any other school of painting. The same principles and elements are found in every artistic experience. The fact that cubism was not accepted for such a long time and that still today there are people who refuse it, means nothing. I do not read English and because of this every English book is a blank page for me. This does not mean that the English language does not exist.*

**Paraphrase:** _____

_____

_____

**3.**

*I work exclusively for myself, I do not seek applause. I am not interested in the opinions of others, and I don't care about what is in vogue.*

**Paraphrase:** _____

_____

_____

\*Source: Parmelin, H. (1969). *Picasso dit. . .* (C. Trollope, Trans.). St. Leonard, U.K.: Allen & Unwin.

**4.**

> *My art is not at all abstract. Rather abstract art does not even exist and cannot exist. You can eliminate every aspect of realism and what remains is an idea which is just as real as the object which has disappeared. Art is always a representation of reality.*

**Paraphrase:** _____

_____

_____

**5.**

> *I attempt to reconstruct reality.*

**Paraphrase:** _____

_____

_____

**6.**

> *Action and reaction, realism and abstraction alternate in my art, just as in life. My art has always been connected to life. That is reality.*

**Paraphrase:** _____

_____

_____

**7.**

> *Mathematics, trigonometry, chemistry, psychoanalysis, music, and many other things have been cited as being components of cubism and have been taken out of context in order to explain cubism. But all this is pure literature, which is another way of saying pure nonsense. When we invented cubism we didn't have any intention of inventing cubism. We simply wanted to express what was inside us. Not one of us ever presented a project or a plan.*

**Paraphrase:** _____

_____

_____

**2.** Complete the sentences to help you summarize Picasso's quotations. Be sure to use your own words. Then discuss your completed sentences with the class.

1. Main idea for quotes 1, 2, and 3:

   Picasso did not care about _____

   _____

2. Main idea for quotes 4, 5, and 6:

   When Picasso considered whether his work was either representational or

   abstract, he _____

   _____

3. Main idea for quote 7:

   To develop cubism, Picasso _____

   _____

**3.** The three sentences you wrote in Exercise 2 together should form a summary of Picasso's quotations. Write your summary.

_____

_____

_____

## Integrated Speaking Task

Your debate statement is **Cubism, in its various forms, is fashion art.**

Here are some more examples of cubist works to use as examples in your debate.

Georges Braque. *Houses at L'Estaque*. 1908. Oil on canvas.

Pablo Picasso. *Glass of Absinthe*. 1914. Painted bronze with perforated silver absinthe spoon.

Pablo Picasso. *Violin*. 1915. Construction of painted metal.

*Follow the steps to prepare your debate.*

**Step 1:** Select a partner and decide whether your pair will agree (speak for) or oppose (speak against) the debate statement.

**Step 2:** In your pair, decide on your most persuasive points. You may use logic, statistics, and/or quotations to support your point, just like you did to write your persuasive essay in Unit 3. It is unlikely you will have statistics either for or against this debate statement, but you will be able to use information from the unit readings, the unit lecture, the examples of Picasso's work in this unit, and Picasso's quotations. Turn your most persuasive points into your first presentation. Decide who will present the information and how long each member will speak. Practice the presentation.

**Step 3:** With your partner, try to anticipate what the other pair will say in their first presentation. Decide what you might say in response to the other pair's statements. You can plan for this by thinking, "If the other pair says _____, then we can say _____." Plan as much as you can. Decide who will present this information and how long each of you will speak. Practice these responses.

Your goal in this step is to plan as much as possible. However, you must also realize that the other team may make a point that you have not anticipated, so you will have to be ready to think quickly and respond as best you can.

**Step 4:** Form a group of four students—one pair that agrees with the debate statement and one that opposes it. Keep to the time limits. After the debate, complete the checklist on page 92 to help you evaluate your presentations. The panel of judges (the rest of the class) will also complete the checklist.

| Checklist for a Debate | Pair 1 | Pair 2 |
| --- | --- | --- |
| The team's first presentation was persuasive—good use of logic (examples), quotations, or statistics to support their points. | | |
| The team finished their first presentation with a summary/concluding statement. | | |
| The team's second presentation was effective—it responded to the other team's points. | | |
| The team finished their second presentation with a summary/concluding statement. | | |
| The team used information from all (or many) of the unit sources—the unit readings, lectures, examples, and quotations. | | |
| The team's presentation skills are strong—good volume, effective eye contact, and easy-to-understand style. | | |

Based on the judges' evaluations, which was the most persuasive pair? Why was one pair more persuasive than the other?

# UNIT 5

## Sociology
# Innovation

## Unit Description

**Content:** This course is designed to familiarize the student with concepts of innovation and social change.

**Skills:** Synthesizing Information

- Recognizing the relationship between abstract concepts and concrete information
- Recognizing the relationship between two spoken sources
- Elaborating on information
- Selecting and presenting related information from a variety of sources

## Unit Requirements

**Readings:** "The Social Conditions That Encourage Innovation" (from "Sources of Innovation" in *Exploring Social Change: America and the World*, 5th Edition, C. Harper & K. Leicht, Pearson Prentice Hall)

"The Innovation of Car Sharing" (online publication)

**Lectures:** "Mass Media and Diffusion of Innovation" "Individuals as Channels of Innovation Diffusion"

**Integrated Writing Task:** Writing a short report about innovation and how it was diffused

**Assignments:** www.MyAcademicConnectionsLab.com

# 1

## Preview

For online assignments, go to

### Key Words

**innovate** *v* to start to use new ideas, methods, or inventions

**innovation** *n* a new idea, method, or invention

**innovative** *adj* a description of a person or thing that is new and different

**invent** *v* to make, design or produce something for the first time; **invention** *n*

## Previewing the Academic Content

We live in an age where technical and social innovations are almost commonplace. Daily, the mass media report improvements to technology and changes to the way we live. The rate of innovation, or the number of innovations per year, is very high. Why is that? What conditions exist today that encourage innovation? How do innovative ideas spread around the globe?

1. *Work with a partner and talk about the changes in society over the last ten years. List as many new ideas or technologies as you can. For example, you might think of wireless technologies, improvements in health care, changes to language testing practices, or the discovery of nanotechnology. Then share your ideas with the class and discuss the questions.*

- Which innovations are mentioned the most often?
- Which are the most unusual?
- Which have had the most impact on your lives?
- Which are the least significant?

2. *Look at the innovations of the first five years in each of the last five centuries. Then answer the questions on the next page.*

### Innovation over the Centuries

| YEARS | INVENTIONS |
|---|---|
| 1600–1605 | Electric insulator, magnetism, glass eye |
| 1700–1705 | Steam pump (used to drain water from mines) |
| 1800–1805 | Electric battery, hot-air heating, infrared radiation, Jacquard loom, niobium metal used in semiconductor research, welding with hydrogen and oxygen, coal stove, gas stove, amphibious vehicle (vehicle that travels over land and water) |
| 1900–1905 | Rigid airship (Zeppelin), quantum theory, 80 different types of optical glasses, radio receiver, hearing aid, internal combustion tractor, vacuum cleaner with 5-horsepower engine, aircraft engine with four cylinders, discovery of chromosomes (which carry genetic code), gyrocompass, hydraulic brakes, subway, milking machine |
| 2000–2005 | Cloning, animal to human bone marrow transplant, artificial heart and transplant, Braille glove, Scramjet, wireless headset, hybrid vehicle (powered by either gas or electricity), medication delivered by sound waves rather than injection |

Source: Adapted from Hjorth, L., Eichler, B., Khan A., & Morello J. (2008). *Technology and society: Issues for 21st century and beyond* (3rd ed.). Upper Saddle River, NJ: Pearson Prentice Hall.

1. What do you notice about the number of innovations as you move closer to the present time?

2. Why do you think there are more inventions as we move toward the present day?

3. What factors encourage invention and innovation?

**3.** *In English, people say, "Necessity is the mother of invention." Discuss what this means with the class. Do you believe that "necessity is the mother of invention?" Do you have a similar proverb in your own language? Compare the proverbs you know and their English translations with the proverbs of other students in the class.*

In this unit, you will learn how to recognize the relationships among pieces of information that come from a variety of sources and synthesize that information.

# Previewing the Academic Skills Focus

## Synthesizing Information

In an academic context, you will often need to find information about a single topic from a variety of sources. You will learn from textbooks, lectures, and academic journal articles; you will even learn from conversations you have with your classmates. It is the combination of all of this information that helps you develop your own ideas about the topic.

As you collect information about a topic from a variety of sources, you need to see the relationships among these various pieces of information. This will help you to understand the information more deeply and quickly.

There are common relationships among pieces of information. Pieces of information might be:

- similar
- contrasting
- concrete examples of an abstract concept
- solutions to a problem
- reasons why something is true
- unrelated

When you speak or write about multiple pieces of information from a variety of sources, the resulting combination of ideas is called a synthesis.

To explain why there seems to be more innovation and social change today than in the past, it is helpful to look at how innovative ideas begin. For the next activity, assume that your instructor has asked you to write an essay about how innovations develop. You begin to collect information from different sources, and you decide to list these pieces of information in a chart to help you see the relationships among the ideas. As you read the notes in the chart on page 96, think about the relationships among the pieces of information that you have found.

| Source | Piece of Information |
|---|---|
| 1. A reliable Internet source | Innovation is a result of a clever person who experiences an "aha moment" that allows her or him to solve complex problems with a sudden flash of insight, producing a solution that leads to a new product or significant social change. |
| 2. A classmate in math | Some mathematicians say they experience moments of clarity that allow them to solve mathematical problems. |
| 3. Your sociology textbook | Social conditions can encourage innovation. |
| 4. The lecture from your sociology class | When social tensions (such as large differences between rich and poor) or cultural interaction (such as that produced by significant immigration) occur, the rate of innovation will increase. |
| 5. A journal article | Innovation is not the result of any single person, but the result of planned or accidental collaboration among people. |

**1.** *Work with a partner. Select the relationship from the skills box on page 95 to identify the relationships among the sources of information in the chart.*

1. What is the relationship between sources 1 and 2?

   *Two is an example of one.*

2. What is the relationship between sources 3 and 4?

   _____

3. What is the relationship between sources 1 and 5?

   _____

4. What is the relationship among sources 1, 3, and 5?

   _____

5. What is the relationship between sources 1 and 4?

   _____

**2.** *Discuss your answers with the class. Explain any differences in your answers. What other sources of information can you think of?*

# 2
## Building Academic Reading Skills

In this section, you will learn about the relationship between abstract concepts and concrete information and some ways in which they can be connected.
For online assignments, go to

PEARSON LONGMAN myacademicconnectionslab

## Key Words

cascade *n*
conventional *adj*
elite *n*
inconsistency *n*
integrated *adj*
latitude *n*
norm *n*
peripheral *adj*

## Before You Read

**1.** *Match the words on the left to their definitions on the right. Then compare your answers with two other students'. If there are any definitions you are not sure about, check with other students, your teacher, or a dictionary.*

1. **cascade** ___d___     a. a change in reaction or behavior that confuses people

2. **conventional** _____     b. a generally accepted standard of social behavior

3. **elite** _____     c. not as important as other things or people in a situation

4. **inconsistency** _____     d. a flow of something in large quantities

5. **integrated** _____     e. describes a system that combines elements to create efficiency

6. **latitude** _____     f. always following the behavior and attitudes that people in a society believe to be normal, correct, and right

7. **norm** _____     g. a group of people who have a lot of power and influence because they have a lot of money, knowledge, or special skills

8. **peripheral** _____     h. freedom to choose what you say or do

**2.** *Complete each sentence with the most appropriate key word.*

1. There is a(n) _____ between the prevalence of the mass media and its ability to diffuse innovation.

2. Because social and financial policies were not fully _____, the majority of the population lived in poverty.

3. One invention stimulated the development of other inventions; it was a _____ of inventions.

4. Collaboration among teams of scientists has become the _____ to produce new medicines that can save lives.

5. Now that he is a teacher, he has considerable _____ to teach whatever he thinks is interesting to his students.

6. The _____ approach to marketing suggests that advertising through the mass media is the best way to sell a product.

7. Access to stock market information, once reserved for the financial _____, is now available to everyone.

8. She only played a small role in the development of the cell phone. Her involvement was _____.

# Global Reading

**cattle** *n* a herd of cows and bulls kept on a farm to produce milk or meat

**coal** *n* a hard black mineral that is dug out of the ground and burned to produce energy

**diffuse** *v* to spread ideas or information among a lot of people

**dyke** *n* a wall or bank of earth built to keep back water and prevent flooding (synonym: *break wall*)

**kerosene** *n* a clear oil that is burned to provide heat or light

**tsunami** *n* a very large wave, caused by extreme conditions such as an earthquake, that can cause severe damage when it reaches land

**1.** *Read an excerpt from a sociology textbook and in the chart, list the seven conditions for innovation it discusses.*

| |
|---|
| 1. *internal social inconsistencies that create stress* |
| 2. |
| 3. |
| 4. |
| 5. |
| 6. |
| 7. |

## The Social Conditions That Encourage Innovation

1  What social conditions make high rates of innovation likely and determine whether innovation will diffuse, or be accepted by the majority of a society? Sociologists and others have identified seven structural conditions in societies that create opportunities for innovation and make the diffusion of innovation more likely.

2  Innovation is more likely to be accepted when there are perceived internal inconsistencies that produce social tensions. Note that inconsistencies must be perceived as inconsistencies. Any social condition can objectively exist for a long time without being perceived as stress producing. Poverty, racial discrimination, domestic violence, political corruption, and budget deficits are certainly not new or unique, but until such conditions are widely perceived by people and elites as problems deserving attention, there will be few innovative institutional attempts to deal with these conditions. So when they are perceived as problems, they will generate innovation aimed at reducing social stress and creating more integrated conditions within society. A good example of this is the Great Depression in North America. Due to a market collapse in 1929, combined with a severe drought across all of North America, many people lost their jobs and lived in poverty. The implementation of social welfare in Canada was a direct result of this event.

3 Innovation is likely to be accepted in societies having difficulties with adaptations to the physical environment. When that environmental adaptation is threatened, innovation becomes probable. There is an intriguing hypothesis here, though we know of no research that has studied it systematically; every significant change in the mode of economic production was preceded by an

innovation in the generation of energy, which was in turn stimulated by a near exhaustion of conventional energy sources. Early in American history, for instance, there was an energy crisis of sorts when whales were hunted to near extinction. Without whale oil to provide the major source of oil for lamps, researchers developed kerosene fuel as a substitute. Similarly, the cutting of most trees in Western Europe (especially in England) forced attempts to find new energy sources like coal. Today, the accumulation of greenhouse gases that threaten to alter the climate may stimulate a cascade of innovative energy sources.

4 Innovation is more likely in societies that have broadly as opposed to narrowly defined social norms, rules, and role expectations. Generally, loosely structured societies that allow social norms, rules, and personal roles to change are more likely to innovate. Western societies place a lot of emphasis on individual achievement, working for higher status, and educational success, and people have the ability to move between social classes, so innovation is relatively easy in these societies. In contrast, the Masai, an African society, is an example of a tightly integrated society. Cattle are the main food source, an indicator of economic status, and a means to purchase a bride. So in this kind of society, people are less likely to accept alternative forms of currency; all significant transactions require cattle. Innovation is less likely in this kind of society.

5 Innovation is more likely to be adopted in societies, communities, or organizations that have higher rates of replacement and succession of people. New people who replace older ones are carriers of innovation. When things aren't going well, there are many companies that replace their CEOs, and many sports teams replace their coaches after too many losses.

6 Innovation is more likely to diffuse in cases where different cultures are in close contact with each other. Close contact by itself does not ensure innovation transfer; the innovation should be consistent with the values of the host culture, should be material (rather than ideological), and is most efficient when there are great numbers of people in cross-cultural contact, when the contact is mostly friendly, and when the contact is between social elites and central elements, rather than between peripheral elements of the two societies.

7 Growth in population size and density is likely to stimulate acceptance of innovation. A good example of this on a small scale is small businesses. These small companies must change in structure and organization as they grow bigger. If they fail to innovate, or create change in their organization, they won't be successful at growing their businesses.

8 Innovations are stimulated by catastrophes and disasters. Wars, floods, the recent tsunami in Asia, economic depressions, and infectious diseases are overwhelming events that societies cannot deal with by conventional means. Innovations, both technological and social, are a result. To illustrate, today, because of that tsunami, there are early warning systems, dykes, or break walls to prevent flooding, and media response systems that should prevent the loss of human life in similar conditions. Another example of this is the United Nations. The creation of the United Nations—a global innovation—was the result of World War II.

Source: Harper, C., & Leicht, K. (2007). Sources of innovation. In *Exploring social change: America and the world* (5th ed.). Upper Saddle River, NJ: Pearson Prentice Hall.

**2.** *In pairs, answer the questions. Discuss your answers with the class.*

1. Do you agree that the conditions described in the reading lead to increasing rates of innovation? Why or why not?

2. How does your country demonstrate, or not demonstrate, these conditions?

3. Does your country, or a country you know well, display any of the conditions described in the reading? Would you expect there to be a lot of innovation in your country or a little?

## Focused Reading

### Recognizing the Relationship between Abstract Concepts and Concrete Information

When you read academic texts, it is important to recognize the relationship between abstract concepts and concrete information. Abstract concepts are based on general ideas or principals rather than specific examples or real life events. They are sometimes referred to as theoretical concepts because they are ideas based on theory. Here is an example of an abstract or theoretical concept:

*Conflict theory states that all innovation is a result of competition for scarce resources, concern for status, or struggles for power.*

The opposite of an abstract concept is information that is specific and definite— concrete information. Here is an example of concrete information about the abstract concept above:

*For example, a conflict theorist would say that the ongoing conflict between the United States and the Middle East is based on the desire to control the production of oil, which is a scarce resource in America.*

Concrete information may or may not be introduced by *for example*. If *for example* is used, then the point is most likely concrete information.

Concrete information may relate to abstract concepts in different ways. Concrete information might:

• contradict an abstract concept
• support an abstract concept

In the previous example, the concrete information (about controlling the oil industry) supports the abstract concept (about conflict theory).

*Use information from the text and the skills box to complete the tasks.*

1. Are the seven conditions for innovation that you listed in the chart on page 98 abstract concepts or concrete information?

2. Copy the seven conditions for innovation from the chart on page 98 to the first column of the chart on page 101. Read the text again and fill in the second column.

| Abstract Concept | Concrete Information |
|---|---|
| 1. *internal social inconsistencies that create stress* | *Social welfare in Canada was a result of the Great Depression in North America.* |
| 2. | |
| 3. | |
| 4. | |
| 5. | |
| 6. | |
| 7. | |

3. Which social condition is *not* supported with concrete information?

4. Circle the relationship of the concrete information to the abstract concepts in the reading.

contradict          support

5. What expressions in the reading are used to introduce concrete information? Underline them.

**Checkpoint 1**     PEARSON LONGMAN myacademicconnectionslab

# 3
## Building Academic Listening Skills

In this section, you will practice recognizing relationships among various pieces of information from spoken sources.

For online assignments, go to

## Before You Listen

Over the last two decades, people have slowly become aware that pollution is damaging the global environment. Many people now believe that they need to change their behavior in order to prevent environmental damage that may endanger future generations. This approach to protecting the environment is an example of innovation on a grand scale. How did so many people become aware that the environment requires protection? What forces are encouraging people to change their behavior?

## Key Words

**channel** *n* a system or method that is used to send or receive information

**diffusion** *n* the spread of ideas or information among a lot of people

**inundate** *v* to receive so much of something that you can not easily manage it all

**mass media** *n. pl.* all the people and organizations that provide information and news for the public, including the Internet, newspapers, magazines, radio, and television

**1.** *Work in groups of three. Read the list of forces that are encouraging people to change their behavior in order to protect the environment. These forces are channels of diffusion. What other channels can you think of? Rate the channels of diffusion from most influential (1) to least influential (10).*

_____ mass media (Internet, television, newspapers, magazines)

_____ education systems (elementary and secondary schools)

_____ other people's behavior—social norms

_____ advice from parents

_____ opinions of friends

_____ governmental rules/policies

_____ business policies

_____ protests

_____ intercultural contact

_____ other

**2.** *Now compare your rankings with other groups'. Overall, what do you think is the most influential channel of diffusion?*

# Global Listening

**1.** 🎧 *Listen to the lecture introduction. At the end of the introduction, what does the lecturer say will surprise us? Circle the correct answer. Confirm your answer with the class.*

    a. The mass media is surprisingly influential and has no limits.

    b. The influence of mass media has some limitations and is not as powerful as we might think.

    c. The term *mass media* refers to the Internet, newspapers, radio, television, and the like.

**2.** 🎧 *Listen to the whole lecture. Discuss the questions in small groups.*

1. What does research suggest about the ability of the mass media to produce change?

2. How do mass education and literacy affect the influence of the mass media, specifically the printing press (introduced in the 15th century) and electronic media (introduced more recently)?

3. Why do radio and television have great potential to diffuse innovation? What is the limitation of these forms of mass media?

4. How does lack of interpersonal communication limit the mass media? Why does this suggest that the Internet is (and will be) a powerful channel of diffusion?

5. The professor concludes a point by saying, "What people bring to the media is at least as important as what the media bring to people." What does the professor mean?

*(continued on next page)*

6. Write the points from the list in the appropriate column in the chart.
   - intensifying existing attitudes
   - creating new attitudes
   - reducing the intensity of existing attitudes
   - converting people to new opinions

| The mass media is effective at . . . | The mass media is not successful at . . . |
|---|---|
|  |  |

7. How can the mass media be an effective channel of diffusion with all these limitations?

## Focused Listening

Just as it is important to recognize the relationships among pieces of information when you read, it is also important to recognize the relationships among pieces of information when you listen. For example, you may hear useful information in lectures and in conversations with classmates. You should be able to figure out whether the pieces of information are:

- similar
- contrasting
- concrete examples of an abstract concept
- solutions to a problem
- reasons why something is true
- unrelated

**1.** *Before you can establish the relationship between two sources, you must clearly understand the first source. To demonstrate your understanding, use the summary skills you learned in Unit 4 to summarize the main points of the lecture. Use your answers to the questions in Global Listening on pages 103–104 to help you. Then write your summary in the first row of the chart on page 105.*

**2.** ⌒ *As you leave the lecture hall, you hear three of your classmates talking about the lecture. Listen to the students and take notes in the chart about each expressed opinion. Then decide what relationship each opinion has to the lecture.*

| Lecture's main points: | |
|---|---|
| **Student opinions** | **Relationship to the main lecture:** *similar, contrasting, concrete examples, solutions to a problem, reasons why something is true, unrelated* |
| First student: | |
| Second student: | |
| Third student: | |
| Your own opinion: | |

**3.** Add your own opinion (and the relationship of your own opinion to the lecture) to the last row of the chart.

**4.** Compare your answers with a partner's to confirm your notes about each student's opinion and the relationship of that opinion to the lecture. Discuss your own opinion and its relationship to the lecture. Are you and your partner's opinions similar or different? Why?

**Checkpoint 2**   PEARSON LONGMAN myacademicconnectionslab

## Building Academic Writing Skills

In this section, you will learn how to elaborate on information you present and how to select and present information from various sources. Then you will write a short report about an innovation of your choice and how information about that innovation was diffused. You will synthesize information from the readings and the lectures in this unit. You will also use the vocabulary you have learned.

For online assignments, go to

**myacademicconnectionslab**

# Before You Write

**1.** *Your sociology professor has given you a diagram to help explain the content of the next lecture. Look at the diagram and predict what your professor is going to say about individuals as channels of innovation diffusion.*

Individuals as channels of diffusion → Cosmopolitan leaders ——→ Broad diffusion of new information / Local leaders ——→ Deep diffusion of new information

**2.** 🎧 *Listen to your professor's short lecture about individuals as channels of innovation diffusion. Then complete the tasks.*

1. Was your prediction you made in Exercise 1 about the lecture content correct? Explain.

2. Place the characteristics of cosmopolitan and local leaders into the appropriate columns in the chart. Some characteristics fit into both columns.
   - have large numbers of friends and acquaintances
   - have a wide variety of interests
   - are members of many groups that have different goals
   - are members of many groups with similar goals
   - have a deep reach into a single community
   - have a wide reach into many communities

| Cosmopolitan Leaders | Local Opinion Leaders |
|---|---|
|  |  |

3. Does this short lecture contain abstract concepts or concrete information? Explain.

When you feel you are not strong at communicating in a language, you may not want to say or write very much in that language. To avoid making mistakes, you may use a strategy of not producing a lot of language when you need to communicate. However, this strategy often demonstrates that you are weak in a language, and others may assume, correctly or not, that your language skills are not strong.

Therefore, to show you are strong at using your second (or alternative) language, there are times when you will want to elaborate. Elaborating on ideas or information means giving more details or information about something. Look at these examples:

If you were asked to describe a cosmopolitan leader, you could simply say, *A cosmopolitan leader is a member of many diverse groups.*

This is correct, but if you don't add anything to your description, you may not demonstrate your language skills sufficiently. A more elaborate answer could be this:

> *A cosmopolitan leader belongs to many different groups and has a wide range of interests. Through these groups, the cosmopolitan leader has contact with a wide variety of people. Because these types of leaders are members of a wide variety of groups, they can diffuse information across the groups quickly. This type of leader contrasts with a local opinion leader.*

This more elaborate answer to the question helps to demonstrate that you are a strong user of your alternate language.

**3.** *Elaborate on the sentences.*

1. Local opinion leaders are members of groups that have similar goals.

   **Possible answer:** _____

   _____

   _____

   _____

2. Together, these kinds of leaders have a significant impact on the rest of the population, and they are not limited by the kinds of limitations that the mass media experiences.

   **Possible answer:** _____

   _____

   _____

   _____

**4.** *Compare your answers with another student's. What information did you add to elaborate?*

# Focused Writing

Innovations generally fall into two categories: social and technological.

*1.* *Look at the social and technological innovations in the chart. With the class, brainstorm some extra ideas to add to each category. You will select one of these innovations as the subject of your report.*

| Social Innovations: Ideas That Are Popular or Have Become Laws | Technological Innovations: Things That Have Become Popular |
|---|---|
| • women's right to vote<br>• child labor laws<br>• recycling<br>• bicycle sharing<br>• car sharing<br>• others: | • vaccinations<br>• computers<br>• cell phones<br>• others: |

## Selecting and Presenting Related Information from a Variety of Sources

When you write in an academic context, you need to combine different pieces of information into whatever you are writing—an essay, a report, a response paper, etc. This is called synthesizing information. To synthesize well, you need to identify your pieces of information, discover the relationships among the pieces of information, and express this clearly in writing.

One writer used the chart on page 109 to organize information about the innovation of car sharing. She found this information in her course textbook, on the Internet, and in her sociology lectures. Then she constructed the chart to make sure she synthesized information from this wide variety of sources and so that she could see the relationships among the pieces of information.

*2.* *Examine the chart on page 109 and then read the example student report on page 110. As you read the report, check off (✓) each source of information in the chart. Did the author succeed in synthesizing information from all of the sources?*

**INFORMATION ABOUT CAR SHARING** (from reliable Internet sources)
*Advantages:* environmentally friendly, increases use of public transit, is cheaper than owning a car
*Diffusion:* worldwide—in Asia, Australia, Europe, North America, and the United Kingdom
*Mass media as a channel:* on the Internet; presence not strong in other forms of mass media
*Individuals as channels:* groups of people involved, no key cosmopolitan or local opinion leader; need for individual leader to champion the cause

| Information source | Piece of information | Relationship to car sharing | Included in the Report? (✓ or X) |
|---|---|---|---|
| **Textbook reading:** The Social Conditions That Encourage Innovation | 1. internal social inconsistencies that create stress | not related | X |
| | 2. problems adapting to the physical environment | support | ✓ |
| | 3. broadly defined social norms | not related | |
| | 4. high rates of succession or replacement | not related | |
| | 5. close contact between/among cultures | support | |
| | 6. growth in population size and density | support | |
| | 7. social catastrophe or natural disaster | not related | |
| **Lecture:** Mass Media and Diffusion of Innovation | mass media has limits • dependent on literacy • no human interaction • can't convert people to new opinions | support | |
| **Lecture:** Individuals as Channels of Innovation Diffusion | individuals can have direct effects • cosmopolitan leaders • local opinion leaders | support | |

# The Innovation of Car Sharing

## Introduction

Car sharing is an innovation that allows people to rent cars for short periods of time, sometimes as short as an hour. Car sharing programs provide the convenience of private car ownership without the cost. They reduce the number of cars on the road. In addition, research shows that people who participate in car sharing programs also use public transit more frequently. Car sharing began in Switzerland in 1987, followed by Germany in 1989 and Canada in 1993. Currently, there are car sharing programs in Australia, all across Europe, in North America, in the United Kingdom, and in Israel and Singapore.

## Social Conditions for Car Sharing

The number of car sharing programs is increasing, and this may be attributable to favorable social conditions. For example, concerns about the environment are at the front of many people's minds these days. Scholars have demonstrated that people who use car sharing programs also use public transit, bike, or walk more frequently than those who don't. Therefore, car sharing reduces the number of car trips per person and encourages a healthy lifestyle. As car sharing began in Switzerland and soon became popular across Europe, it is clear that close cultural contact was a factor in encouraging innovation across cultures. Similarly, when car sharing became popular in France, Francophones in Quebec City in Canada began a similar program, demonstrating the transfer of innovation across cultures sharing the same language. Because growth in population size and density is another social condition that encourages innovation, it is no surprise that car sharing programs are also most popular in densely populated cities.

## Diffusion of Car Sharing

You might think that as car sharing is environmentally friendly and financially reasonable, more people would use it. However, while car sharing programs exist on many continents of the world, they are still not mainstream programs. Most information about car sharing programs exists on the Internet. As a result, countries that have little access to the Internet do not have car sharing programs. This is one of the limitations of the mass media in diffusing information about innovations. Of course, cosmopolitan and local opinion leaders could also be influential in encouraging car sharing programs, but as yet, there is no celebrity (politician, sports figure, or actor) who has championed car sharing programs. If a famous figure did begin to promote these programs, their popularity would surely increase.

## Conclusion

Car sharing programs have environmental and financial advantages that should make them even more popular in the future. Currently, diffusion of information about this innovation related to traditional car ownership has been limited to the Internet. This means that access to this information has been restricted to countries that have easy access to the Internet. Furthermore, without a cosmopolitan or local opinion leader to promote car sharing programs, diffusion of information about this innovation will continue to be slow.

## Integrated Writing Task

Here is your report assignment: **Select a significant innovation and write a report about how information about that innovation was diffused.** Reports are divided into sections; unlike academic essays, each report section has its own heading.

*Follow the steps to write your report.*

**Step 1:** Select a social or technological innovation that interests you from the chart on page 94. Use your general knowledge about that innovation, or find reliable information sources about the innovation. Add the information, in point form, to the first row of the chart.

**INFORMATION ABOUT** _____

_____

_____

| Information source | Piece of information | Relationship to _____ | Included in the report? (✓ or X) |
|---|---|---|---|
| **Textbook reading:** Social Conditions that Encourage Innovation | 1. internal social inconsistencies that create stress | | |
| | 2. problems adapting to the physical environment | | |
| | 3. broadly defined social norms | | |
| | 4. high rates of succession or replacement | | |
| | 5. close contact between/among cultures | | |
| | 6. growth in population size and density | | |
| | 7. social catastrophe or natural disaster | | |
| **Lecture:** Mass Media and Diffusion of Innovation | mass media has limits • dependent on literacy • no human interaction • can't convert people to new opinions | | |
| **Lecture:** Individuals as Channels of Innovation Diffusion | individuals can have direct effects • cosmopolitan leaders • local opinion leaders | | |

**Step 2**: Think about the relationship between the information about the innovation you have chosen to write about and the information from the unit readings and lectures. List the relationship in the third column in the chart on page 111.

**Step 3**: Write a first draft of your report. Divide your report into four sections:
- an introductory section that explains the significance of the innovation
- a section on the social conditions that created a context for the innovation
- a section on the channels of diffusion that created awareness of the innovation
- a concluding section that considers the future of the innovation

As you write each piece of information from the table, check it off in the fourth column of the chart on page 111.

**Step 4**: Ask your teacher or a classmate to review your report based on the features listed in the checklist.

| Features of a Report | Yes | No |
|---|---|---|
| Does the title indicate the author's chosen innovation? | | |
| Is the report divided into four sections: introduction, social conditions, channels of diffusion, and conclusion? | | |
| Is there a heading for each section? | | |
| Is the report a synthesis of information from the unit? In other words, does the report contain information from the reading and the lectures in the unit? | | |
| Is the vocabulary specific to the topic of innovation? | | |

**Step 5**: Based on the information in the checklist, revise your report and hand it in.

# UNIT 6

## Physical Science
# Nanotechnology

## Unit Description

**Content:**  This course is designed to familiarize the student with concepts in nanotechnology.

**Academic Skills:**  Fact and Opinion
- Identifying and evaluating information presented to support a position
- Recognizing a speaker's degree of certainty
- Distinguishing between facts and opinions
- Expressing and supporting opinions

## Unit Requirements

**Lecture:**  "The New Small Is Big"

**Readings:**  "Micro Materials That Could Pose Major Health Risks" (from *The Globe and Mail*, M. Mittelstaedt)

"Study Says Carbon Nanotubes as Dangerous as Asbestos" (from *Scientific American*, L. Greenemeier)

**Integrated Speaking Task:**  Preparing and delivering a short oral report about applying precautionary principle to nanotechnology

**Assignments:**  www.MyAcademicConnectionsLab.com

# 1

## Preview

For online assignments, go to

PEARSON LONGMAN
myacademicconnectionslab

## Previewing the Academic Content

Nanotechnology is an emerging field combining the areas of chemistry, science, and engineering. The term *nanotechnology* refers to a wide range of very tiny particles that can be used to enhance many existing products we use every day. "How tiny is tiny?" you might ask. A nanometer is one-billionth of a meter—so small that we can only compare it to the size of a red blood cell or a virus. As small as these particles may be, they have remarkable properties. Some can screen out ultraviolet light, others can fight bacteria, and still others can conduct electricity or transport pharmaceutical drugs to specific parts of the body. However, as with all new technologies, the long-term risks are poorly understood. Could these tiny particles harm human or environmental health? How can we control their production and ensure they are used safely in consumer products? How can we dispose of them once we are finished with them? Should we continue with the development of nanoparticles even if their risks are not clearly understood?

**1.** *Are you using products that contain nanoparticles? You might be. Read the list and check (✓) the products that you use now or have used in the past.*

| PRODUCT | NANOTECHNOLOGY ENHANCEMENT | Do you use this product?<br>✓ = Yes    X = No |
|---|---|---|
| Sunscreens | Screens out ultraviolet (UV) light (most brands) | |
| Tennis rackets, golf clubs, bowling balls | Strengthens without adding weight | |
| Tennis balls | Reduces wear—balls last longer | |
| Car tires | Reduces wear—tires last longer | |
| Sunglasses, car wax, ski wax | Creates a scratch-resistant surface | |
| Breathable waterproof ski jackets | Creates windproof, waterproof, and dirt-repellent jackets that still allow vapor transmission | |
| Wrinkle-resistant and stain-repellent clothing | Prevents clothes from wrinkling, repels liquids and oils | |
| Digital cameras | Creates brighter screen displays, and wider-angle viewing; reduces power consumption | |
| Skin creams | Reduces wrinkles | |
| Odor-free socks | Prevents odor from forming in socks | |
| Cell phones | Improves data transmission speed using less power; improves display screens; reduces unwanted signals | |
| Diesel fuel | Burns fuel more efficiently | |

**conduct** *v* if something conducts electricity, it allows electricity to travel through it

**particle** *n* a very small piece of something

**reinforce** *v* to make something stronger

In this unit, you will learn how to distinguish between fact and opinion, recognize a speaker or writer's degree of certainty, and express and support an opinion.

**2.** *Work in small groups to discuss the questions.*

1. What are some other nanotechnology-enhanced products that you use or have heard of? Why is the enhancement of these products important? Explain.
2. As with most new technologies, there are questions about the long-term risks or possible negative consequences of nanotechnology. What kinds of risks might be associated with nanotechnology?
3. Discuss this statement: *The benefits of a new technology should be developed, even if the risks may be significant.* Does your group agree or disagree with this statement? Be prepared to explain your answer to the rest of the class.

## Previewing the Academic Skills Focus

**1.** *Read the text. Be prepared to express your opinion about the content.*

### Questions and Answers about the Precautionary Principle (from Science and Environmental Health Network)

Governments play a significant role in protecting their citizens from risks. Governments must attempt to prevent external risks, such as wars, and internal risks, such as the marketing of hazardous products or environmental disasters. In order to do this, some governments have adopted the "precautionary principle" to guide their decision making. The precautionary principle is the belief that if an activity (for example, a new technology) may cause harm to human or environmental health, precautions must be taken to prevent harm. The usefulness of the precautionary approach is controversial.

**1. What is the precautionary principle?**

The Wingspread Statement on the Precautionary Principle summarizes the principle this way:

"When an activity raises threats of harm to the environment or human health, precautionary measures should be taken even if some cause and effect relationships are not fully established scientifically."

All statements of the precautionary principle contain a version of this formula:

"When the health of humans and the environment is at stake, it may not be necessary to wait for scientific certainty before taking protective action."

**2. Is there some special meaning for *precaution*?**

*Precautionary principle* is a translation of the German *Vorsorgeprinzip. Vorsorge* means, literally, "forecaring." It carries the sense of foresight and preparation—not merely caution.

The principle applies to human health and the environment. The ethical assumption behind the precautionary principle is that humans are responsible for protecting, preserving, and restoring the global ecosystems on which all life, including our own, depends.

*(continued on next page)*

3. **Why should we take action before science tells us what is harmful or what is causing harm?**

> Sometimes if we wait for certainty, it is too late. Scientific standards for demonstrating cause and effect are very high. For example, smoking was strongly suspected of causing lung cancer long before the link was demonstrated conclusively. By then, many smokers had died of lung cancer. But many other people had already quit smoking because of the growing evidence that smoking was linked to lung cancer. These people were wisely exercising precaution despite some scientific uncertainty.
>
> When evidence gives us good reason to believe that an activity, technology, or substance may be harmful, we should act to prevent harm. If we always wait for scientific certainty, people may suffer and die and the natural world may suffer irreversible damage.

Source: Precautionary Principle—FAQs. Retrieved July 2008, from the Science and Environmental Health Network website: http://www.sehn.org/ppfaqs.html.

## Fact and Opinion

A *fact* is a piece of information that is known to be true. An *opinion* is someone's idea or belief about a particular subject. A fact can be:

- Common general knowledge. For example:
  - The sun rises in the east.
  - Computers have changed the way people work.
- A specific statistic. Usually, the source of the statistic is provided either in the sentence or in a footnote/endnote. For example:
  - The World Health Organization states that infectious diseases killed 14.7 million people in 2002.[1]
- An idea proven through research. Usually, the source of the research is provided either in the sentence or in a footnote/endnote. For example:
  - While foresters have traditionally considered wildfire as an enemy, there is growing evidence that fires may play an important and even a beneficial roll in some ecosystems.[2]

An opinion may be signalled by specific phrases: *I think (that) . . ., From my perspective . . ., In my opinion . . . / In my view . . ., I believe (that) . . ., It seems to me that . . ., As far as I'm concerned . . .*

An opinion may also be provided without these specific phrases. In these cases, opinions can be identified by the use of a modal verb such as *can, could, should, would, may, will,* etc.

- The production process used to create nanoparticles may be dangerous to human health.

---

[1] Wikipedia. Retrived July 8, 2008 from http://en.wikipedia.org/wiki/Infectious_diseases#Morality_from_infectious_diseases.

[2] Kimmins, J. P. (2004). *Forest ecology: A foundation for sustainable forest management and environmental ethics in forestry* (3rd ed., p. 347). Upper Saddle River, NJ: Pearson Prentice Hall

**2.** *Read the statements. Decide if they are facts or opinions. Write **F** (fact) or **O** (opinion). Discuss your answers with the class.*

_____ a. Since the development of the precautionary principle in the 1980s, there has been a growing understanding of how the precautionary principle should be used.

_____ b. In Sweden and Germany, an increasing number of environmental laws are based on the precautionary principle.

_____ c. The use of the precautionary principle as a guide to decision making will prevent the development of new technologies.

_____ d. The application of the precautionary principle will prevent countries from competing effectively in the global market.

_____ e. The 1987 treaty that bans the dumping of toxic substances in the North Sea was premised on the precautionary principle.

_____ f. Technology development that is blocked by the precautionary principle can be replaced by clean technology development that doesn't harm the environment.

**3.** *Paraphrase the answer to the first question from the reading, "What is the precautionary principle?" (page 115). Start your paraphrase with a standard starting sentence identifying the source and the date of the information.*

_____

_____

_____

**4.** *Answer the questions.*

1. There are a number of English proverbs that express the meaning of the precautionary principle. Look at the list of proverbs and circle the ones that sum up the meaning of the precautionary principle. Do you have proverbs that express the meaning of the precautionary principle in your first language? Discuss them with the class.
   a. Better safe than sorry.
   b. A picture is worth a thousand words.
   c. Look before you leap.
   d. A bird in the hand is worth two in the bush.
   e. First do no harm.
   f. A rolling stone gathers no moss.
   g. An ounce of prevention is worth a pound of cure.
   h. You want to have your cake and eat it too.
   i. Err on the side of caution.

2. Which of the two examples demonstrates how to implement the precautionary principle?

   **Example 1:** A sample of water at the local water treatment plant shows high bacteria levels. The person who operates the plant immediately shuts down the plant, takes more water samples, and reviews the water treatment process. The whole city loses its water supply for two days, but nobody becomes sick.

**Example 2:** A sample of water at the local water treatment plant shows high bacteria levels. The person who operates the plant decides to take a number of other samples and wait for the results from those samples before deciding what to do. The extra samples show that bacteria levels remain within the safe range. The city's water supply hasn't been shut off, and nobody becomes sick.

3. What is your opinion about the precautionary principle? Do you believe that we should act to prevent harm before we have scientific proof that harm is being done, or that we should wait for scientific proof to demonstrate that harm is being done before acting? Why? Express your opinion by using some of the expressions from the skills box on page 116.

# 2
## Building Academic Listening Skills

In this section, you will practice identifying and evaluating information presented to support a position. You will also practice recognizing a speaker's degree of certainty when expressing an opinion. For online assignments, go to

PEARSON LONGMAN
myacademicconnectionslab

## Before You Listen

### Identifying and Evaluating Information Presented to Support a Position

In an academic context, you are often asked to identify and evaluate information that is used to support a position or statement. In your search for information on any topic, you will probably find some sources that may not be reliable. Should you believe the information or be skeptical about its accuracy? You may hear the information, read it on the Internet, or see it in a newspaper. What criteria can you apply to the information to make sure that it is reliable?

When you want to evaluate information to decide whether or not it is reliable, ask yourself these questions:

- Does this information fit with what I already know about the topic, or is it different and surprising?
- What is the source of the information—who is the author/speaker? If the information is found on the Internet, is the website reputable?
- Is there a date of publication for the source? Many Internet sources provide no date. This is a sign that the information may be inaccurate or out of date. Books or printed information, particularly on scientific matters, may not be current.
- Has the information been provided and/or reviewed by experts and reputable organizations? What are the credentials of the experts or organizations in the field? For example, an organization called Health on the Net (HON) reviews and certifies Internet websites that have reliable health information. If you find health information on a website that is not certified by HON, then you might wonder if the information is accurate.
- What kind of scientific evidence is there to support the information?
- Is the information speculative? Is it based on things that might or might not happen in the future?

If you don't have acceptable answers to these questions, then you should be skeptical about the accuracy of the information.

1. *Read the sources of information. Do you think these are believable and accurate sources of information, or should you be skeptical about the accuracy of these sources? Write* **Yes** *or* **No**. *Then discuss your opinions with the class.*

_____ 1. an article about nanotechnology published in 1960

_____ 2. a lecture given by your professor

_____ 3. an article on Wikipedia

_____ 4. a chapter from a recently published nanotechnology textbook

_____ 5. a short article from a tabloid

_____ 6. an article from a reputable newspaper

_____ 7. an in-depth television report

_____ 8. a comment about nanotechnology made by a friend who is an economics major

_____ 9. an Internet article with information about nanotechnology that contradicts what you have heard from other sources

_____ 10. an academic journal article

**2.** *Why are nanomaterials so powerful? Work with a partner and scan the diagram. Then read the statements on the next page. Circle* **T** *(true) or* **F** *(false).*

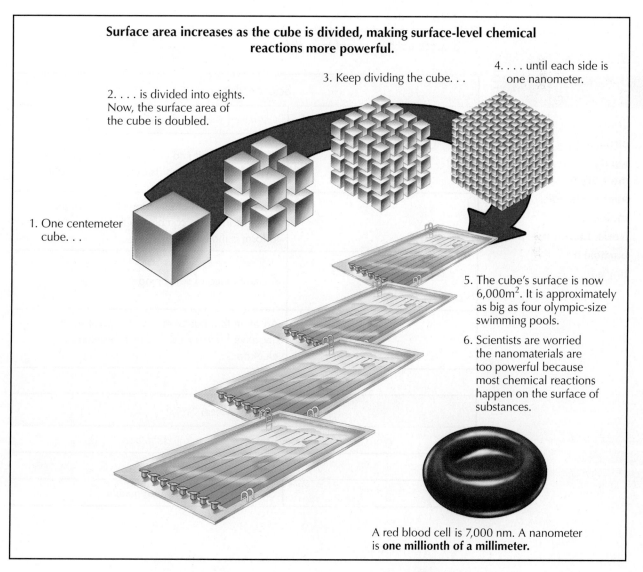

**Surface area increases as the cube is divided, making surface-level chemical reactions more powerful.**

2. . . . is divided into eights. Now, the surface area of the cube is doubled.

3. Keep dividing the cube. . .

4. . . . until each side is one nanometer.

1. One centemeter cube. . .

5. The cube's surface is now 6,000m². It is approximately as big as four olympic-size swimming pools.

6. Scientists are worried the nanomaterials are too powerful because most chemical reactions happen on the surface of substances.

A red blood cell is 7,000 nm. A nanometer **is one millionth of a millimeter.**

1. A one-centimeter cube has a larger surface area than the same cube divided into nanometers.

   T     F

2. A red blood cell is smaller than a nanometer.

   T     F

3. Since most chemical reactions occur on the surfaces of substances, the larger the surface area, the stronger the chemical reaction.

   T     F

4. Scientists are worried about the strength of possible chemical reactions involving nanomaterials.

   T     F

*Now check your answers with the rest of the class and your teacher.*

**3.** *Work with two other students. Group the words with similar meanings into the charts to match each key word to its definition.*

## Key Words

**atom** *n*
**circuit** *n*
**ion** *n*
**mercury** *n*
**minuscule** *adj*
**molecule** *n*
**Nobel Laureate** *exp*
**particle** *n*
**tiny** *adj*

| Scientific Nouns | |
|---|---|
| Word | Definition |
| *molecule* | The smallest unit into which any substance can be divided without losing its own chemical nature |
| | The smallest part of an element that can exist alone or that can combine with other substances to form a molecule |
| | A small piece of something |
| | An atom that has been given a positive or negative force by adding or subtracting an electron |

| Adjectives That Mean Small | |
|---|---|
| Word | Definition |
| | Extremely small |
| | So small it is hard to see; minute |

| Noun That Is a Metal | |
|---|---|
| Word | Definition |
| | A heavy, silver-white poisonous metal that is liquid at ordinary temperatures and is used in thermometers (chemical symbol: Hg) |

| Noun Related to Electrical Systems | |
|---|---|
| Word | Definition |
| | The complete circle that an electric current travels |

| Word Related to Winning a Prize | |
|---|---|
| Word | Definition |
| | Someone who has won a Nobel Prize (a prize given each year to people who have done significant work in various fields such as physics, chemistry, literature, etc.) |

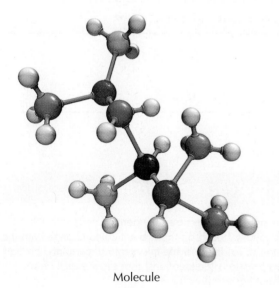

Molecule

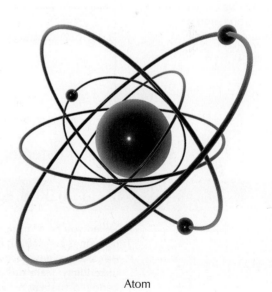

Atom

## Key Words

**fullerene** *n* a nanoparticle composed of 60 carbon atoms. It may be used to deliver antibiotics to resistant bacteria. It is heat resistant and conducts electricity.

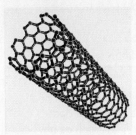

**nanotube** *n* carbon atoms linked together to form a tube. Nanotubes are light and strong, and can conduct electricity.

## Global Listening

**1.** 🎧 *Listen to the beginning of the lecture and answer the questions.*

1. How small is a nanometer?

_____

2. What are nanotechnology and nanoscience about?

_____

3. In 1959, what did Richard Feynman see as the benefits of developing small machines?

_____

4. Why was the development of the atomic force microscope in 1990 so important?

_____

**2.** 🎧 *Listen to the whole lecture. As you hear the beginning of the lecture again, confirm your answers in Exercise 1 (or complete questions that you couldn't answer the first time through). As you listen to the rest of the lecture, fill in the chart. Then share your answers with the class. Develop as inclusive a list as possible.*

| Characteristics of Nanoparticles |
|---|
| • *Strong* |
| **Uses of Nanotechnology** |
|  |

## Focused Listening

### Recognizing a Speaker's Degree of Certainty

When you hear an opinion, you may not always be 100 percent certain that the opinion is correct. An opinion is usually based on facts, but it could change with the discovery of new facts about a topic. To demonstrate this range of certainty through uncertainty, there are common expressions (collocations) that show exactly how certain a speaker or writer is about her or his opinion.

Look at the chart, which shows a range of degrees of certainty and the collocations that can be used to express them.

| Strength of Claim | Statement with Collocation | Approximate Degree of Certainty |
|---|---|---|
| Stronger ↓ Weaker | I believe nanotechnology *will result in* . . . | 100% certain |
| | I believe nanotechnology *should result in* . . . | 90% certain |
| | I believe that nanotechnology *may result in* . . . | 50% certain |
| | I believe that nanotechnology *might/could result in* . . . | 50% certain |
| Stronger ↓ Weaker | I am *certain* that . . . | 100% certain |
| | I am *almost certain* that . . . | 95% certain |
| | I think it is *very probable/highly likely* that . . . | 80% certain |
| | I think that it is *possible* that . . . | 60% certain |
| | I think that it is *likely* that . . . | > 50% certain |
| | I think that it is *fairly likely* that . . . | 50% certain |
| | I think that it is *unlikely* that . . . | 80% certain that something won't happen |
| | I think that it is *improbable/highly unlikely* that . . . | 95% certain that something won't happen |
| Stronger ↓ Weaker | In my view, there is a *definite possibility* that . . . | 90% certain |
| | In my view, there is a *strong possibility* that . . . | 80% certain |
| | In my view, there is a *good possibility* that . . . | > 50% certain |
| | In my view, there is a *slight possibility* that . . . | < 50% certain |
| | In my view, there is a *small possibility* that . . . | 10% certain |

**1.** 🎧 *Listen to five members of a study group discuss the benefits and risks of nanotechnology. Circle the approximate degree of certainty of each student. Notice how the intonation of a statement changes with the degree of certainty.*

1. Student 1's approximate degree of certainty:

   100 percent     90 percent     75 percent     > 50 percent     < 50 percent

2. Student 2's approximate degree of certainty:

   100 percent     90 percent     75 percent     > 50 percent     < 50 percent

Unit 6 ■ Nanotechnology     **123**

3. Student 3's approximate degree of certainty:

    100 percent      90 percent      75 percent      > 50 percent    < 50 percent

4. Student 4's approximate degree of certainty:

    100 percent      90 percent      75 percent      > 50 percent    < 50 percent

5. Student 5's approximate degree of certainty:

    100 percent      90 percent      75 percent      > 50 percent    < 50 percent

**2.** ⌒ *As you leave the classroom, you overhear students talking about the lecture. Listen to what the students are saying and evaluate the information that you hear. Circle the word* reliable *or* unreliable *based on your evaluation. For each statement, explain why. Discuss your answers with the class.*

1. reliable      unreliable

    Why? _____

    _____

2. reliable      unreliable

    Why? _____

    _____

3. reliable      unreliable

    Why? _____

    _____

4. reliable      unreliable

    Why? _____

    _____

**Checkpoint 1**    PEARSON LONGMAN **myacademicconnectionslab**

# 3

**Building Academic Reading Skills**

In this section, you will practice distinguishing between facts and opinions.
For online assignments, go to

PEARSON LONGMAN
**myacademicconnectionslab**

## Before You Read

When the benefits of a new technology are discovered, many enthusiastic individuals, groups, companies, and/or governments are happy to proceed with development, production, and marketing of the technology. Unfortunately, history has shown us that the risks of new technology often are not discovered as early as the benefits.

**1.** *Work in small groups and discuss what you know about the products listed in the chart on the next page. Once these products were thought to be harmless, but they are now known to be highly toxic to humans.*

| Technology/Product | Uses | Benefits | Risks |
|---|---|---|---|
| Asbestos | A soft mineral used to insulate houses, car brakes, and oven wiring | —resists heat<br>—resists fire<br>—does not conduct electricity<br>—strong | —causes inflammation of the lungs and cancer in the linings of the organs |
| Polychlorinated biphenyls (PCBs) | Fluids used to cool electrical transformers and insulate wiring; used in paints, cement, plastic coatings, and pesticides | —resists heat<br>—resists fire<br>—does not conduct electricity<br>—strong | —causes liver cancer, skin disease, and poor brain development in children<br>—persistent environmental pollutant |
| Agent Orange | Chemicals used as herbicides (to kill weeds) and as defoliant (to remove leaves from trees); used by the U.S. military in the Vietnam War | —kills broad-leaf weeds<br>—increases visibility by removing leaves from trees | —causes a variety of cancers and diabetes |

**2.** What other technologies or products used in the past are now known to be toxic? If you can't think of any, try to explain why you can't.

**3.** Express an opinion about whether governments should use the precautionary principle when creating regulations for new technologies. Show your degree of certainty by choosing an expression from the skills box on pages 122–123. Write your opinion in your notebook, and say your sentence out loud to practice your speaking skills. Then share your opinion with a partner.

## Key Words

**backer** n
**err on the side of caution** exp
**fashion** v
**novel substances** exp
**panel** n
**scrutiny** n
**sidestep the rules** exp
**trigger** v
**usurp** v
**wave a yellow flag** exp

**4.** Look at the list of words. One word in each line is **not** a synonym of the other two words. Cross out that word. Then check your answers with the class. If you are not sure which word does not belong, find the boldfaced vocabulary in the reading on pages 127–128, and substitute each of the other two options to see which word makes most sense in the sentence. The one that doesn't make sense is the option that doesn't belong with the other two.

1. panel     council     ~~table~~
2. signal the all clear     wave a yellow flag     proceed with caution
3. novel substances     current information     new material
4. uncover     usurp     take control
5. backer     supporter     thinker
6. deconstruct     fashion     craft
7. err on the side of caution     better safe than sorry     once bitten, twice shy
8. close examination     concerned audience     scrutiny
9. permit     trigger     set off
10. sidestep the rules     prevent damage     avoid regulation

# Global Reading

**1.** *Look at the questions. Read the article from a scientific journal on pages 127–128 and answer the questions based on the information in the reading. Then check your answers with the class. Discuss any differences in your answers.*

1. What warning does the scientific panel's report on nanomaterials give to the public?

   _____

2. Who is on the panel? Do you trust this information? Why?

   _____

3. Why does the report on nanomaterials mention polychlorinated biphenyls (PCBs) and Agent Orange?

   _____

**2.** *Read the statements. Decide if they are true or false. Write **T** (true) or **F** (false).*

_____ 1. Nanomaterials can be found in nature; they are naturally occurring substances.

_____ 2. A nanoparticle can be smaller than a flu virus.

_____ 3. Nanoparticles are created atom by atom.

_____ 4. Nanoparticles have the same properties as the material they are made from.

_____ 5. The panel recommends that nanomaterials be used wherever there may be an advantage to their use.

_____ 6. The panel recommends governments make more rules to control the use of nanomaterials.

_____ 7. In Canada, new chemicals entering the market must be tested to make sure they are safe.

_____ 8. Nanoparticles will always be considered new chemicals and will trigger regulatory tests to make sure they are safe.

**3.** *Work in small groups. Discuss the questions.*

1. Why does the text use the example of the nanoparticle titanium dioxide, used in sunscreens?

2. In the field of medicine, what advantage might nanoparticles provide? Is this advantage worth the risk?

# MICRO MATERIALS THAT COULD POSE MAJOR HEALTH RISKS

By Martin Mittelstaedt  (from *The Globe and Mail*)

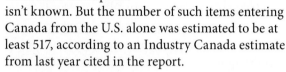

**Panel** issues warning for products with nanomaterials, saying tiny substances in everything from sunscreen to diesel fuel may be toxic

(1) A blue ribbon scientific panel has **waved a yellow flag** in front of a rapidly expanding number of products containing nanomaterials, cautioning that the tiny substances might be able to penetrate cells and interfere with biological processes.

(2) The warning is contained in a report from the Council of Canadian Academies that will be released publicly today. It is one of the most authoritative to date in this country about the risks of engineered nanomaterials, which companies are adding to products ranging from sunscreens to diesel fuels.

(3) The council, which was asked by Health Canada and several other federal agencies to study the state of knowledge about these **novel substances** and the regulatory changes needed to oversee their use, concluded that "there are inadequate data to inform quantitative risk assessments on current and emerging nanomaterials." Their small size, the report says, may allow them to "**usurp** traditional biological protective mechanisms" and, as a result, possibly have "enhanced toxicological effects."

(4) Although **backers** of nanomaterials say they hold enormous promise for developing improved medicines and stronger and more durable products, the report cautioned that many useful items once thought to be harmless, such as polychlorinated biphenyls—the now-banned transformer oils known as PCBs—and the herbicide Agent Orange, were later determined to be extremely dangerous.

(5) Nanomaterials are manmade substances measured in nanometres, or lengths of one-millionth of a millimetre. They can be smaller than a flu virus, which typically is 80 to 120 nanometres across. Over the past decade, they have been increasingly used in such products as cosmetics, wrinkle- and stain-resistant fabrics, sunscreens and sports equipment, including tennis racquets. The full variety of products containing nanomaterials to which Canadians are exposed isn't known. But the number of such items entering Canada from the U.S. alone was estimated to be at least 517, according to an Industry Canada estimate from last year cited in the report.

(6) Some of these offerings should be investigated more closely, says Pekka Sinervo, dean of the University of Toronto's faculty of arts and science, and the chair of the panel. "One can argue fairly strongly that some of those products probably should be looked at on a going-forward basis," Dr. Sinervo said. "It's a new technology. We are concerned."

(7) Health Canada did not respond yesterday to e-mailed questions about the panel's report. The council is an independent academic advisory group funded by the federal government, but operative at armslength from Ottawa. The 16-member panel that wrote the new report included some of Canada's leading scientists and top international experts on nanomaterials.

(8) Scientists have been able to **fashion** these new substances by assembling them almost atom by atom, creating materials that have properties unlike the larger chunks of the matter from which they're made—much like a diamond and pencil graphite are both composed of carbon but have entirely different properties.

(9) One example is titanium dioxide used in sunscreen. Nanoparticles of the material, engineered to have crystal structure, allow visible light to pass though them, but they also absorb ultraviolet light, making them ideal as the active ingredient in sunscreens. Titanium dioxide in a bulk form has a completely different attribute: it is used as the intense white pigment in paint. Dr. Sinervo said sunscreens have been used for years without adverse human

*(continued on next page)*

health impacts, suggesting they are harmless to people while reducing the risks of skin cancer.

(10) But the issue of nanoparticles' overall impact on the environment is still under review. Researchers at Trent University in Peterborough, Ont., for instance, are currently investigating the effects of sunscreens when they get into water, trying to determine if they harm algae,[1] amphibians[2] or fish. They don't expect to complete their research until 2010.

(11) Although there may be risks with nanomaterials, there is research suggesting they could offer major breakthroughs in a variety of fields. One of the most watched is in medicine. Typical of the research was a report earlier this month in the Proceedings of the National Academy of Sciences that found when nano-sized particles were given with chemotherapy, doses of the anticancer drug could be cut by about 95 percent, without any reduction in therapeutic effect. But the new report recommended that, given that the impact of nanomaterials on living things is "poorly understood," regulators **err on the side of caution** whenever there are reasons to doubt the safety of the new substances. This will give scientists time to better understand what risks, if any, they pose.

(12) "In the view of the panel, an assessment of what is known and not known about the health and environmental risks of engineered nanomaterials is urgently needed in both the Canadian and international context, given that hundreds of nanoproducts—consumer products employing nanomaterials—are already being marketed internationally," it said. The report said the federal government doesn't need to **craft** new laws to deal specifically with nanomaterials, but it warned that loopholes[3] exist in regulations that could allow some of these compounds to escape detailed **scrutiny**. Some nanomaterials may not be used in large enough quantities to **trigger** reviews.

(13) Another worry is that these materials may **sidestep the existing rules** covering the evaluation of new chemicals introduced to the Canadian market. New substances must undergo detailed safety evaluations, but the report said companies can argue that many nanomaterials, by merely rearranging atoms into a new shape, aren't really new things at all and therefore not subject to reviews. "Current regulatory triggers are not sufficient to identify all nanomaterials entering the market that may require regulatory oversight," the report said.

---

[1] **algae** *n* very simple plants without stems or leaves that grow in or near water
[2] **amphibians** *n* animals, such as frogs, that can live both in water and on land
[3] **loophole** *n* a small mistake in a law or rule that makes it possible to legally avoid doing what the law says

Source: Mittelstaedt, M. (2008, July 10). Micro materials that could pose major health risks. *Globe and Mail*, A8.

## Focused Reading

### Distinguishing Between Facts and Opinions

Remember that a *fact* is a piece of information that is known to be true. An *opinion* is someone's idea or belief about a particular subject.

A fact can be:
- common general knowledge.
- a specific statistic. Usually, the source of the statistic is provided either in the sentence or in a footnote/endnote.
- an idea proven through research. Usually, the source of the research is provided either in the sentence or in a footnote/endnote.

An opinion is often introduced by specific phrases, such as:

- *I think (that) . . .*
- *I believe (that) . . .*
- *In my opinion . . . / In my view . . .*
- *I am of the opinion that . . .*
- *It seems to me that . . .*
- *As far as I'm concerned . . .*
- *From my perspective . . .*

An opinion may also be provided without these specific phrases or signaled by the use of a modal verb (*can, could, would, should, might, will,* etc.)

For homework, your instructor has asked you to log in to the course website and post an entry on the course discussion forum. You must express your opinion about the safety of nanoparticles based on at least one fact from the class reading.

When you log in to the course website, you find that five of your classmates have already posted their entries. Before you post your own entry, read your classmates' entries to see what their opinions are.

***1.*** *For each of the entries, underline the fact from the reading and circle the opinion. Have all the students included a fact and expressed their opinions?*

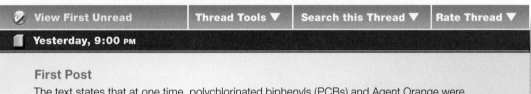

| View First Unread | Thread Tools ▼ | Search this Thread ▼ | Rate Thread ▼ |

**Yesterday, 9:00 PM**

**First Post**

The text states that at one time, polychlorinated biphenyls (PCBs) and Agent Orange were both thought to be safe for human use; however, now everyone knows that they are dangerous to human health and the environment. I think these are both good examples of what can happen when people, governments, and companies proceed too quickly with technological development. From my perspective, nanoparticles are a new technology with potential for dangerous results, and we should err on the side of caution as we develop them for the market.

**Second Post**

The reading begins with the following sentence: "A scientific panel has waved a yellow flag in front of a rapidly expanding number of products containing nanomaterials, cautioning that the tiny substances might be able to penetrate cells and interfere with biological processes." As far as I'm concerned, the word *might* is the key word in this sentence. *Might* indicates that the panel is not sure whether nanomaterials will cause problems or not. Are we going to deny cancer victims the benefits of lower doses of chemotherapy drugs just because some people think there *might* be problems with nanoparticles? I don't agree with that. I believe that we should proceed as quickly as possible to exploit the benefits of nanotechnology.

*(continued on next page)*

### Third Post

How bad could the risks of these tiny particles be? You can't see them, so how much damage could they cause? We've been using titanium dioxide in sunscreens for years, and there haven't been cancer cases resulting from sunscreen use, or even any proof that sunscreen is damaging the environment—for example, the beaches or fish in the water. It seems to me that these particles are completely safe. If we delay further development of nanotechnology, we are depriving people of the advantages that nanoparticles could provide. Why wait any longer?

### Fourth Post

Dr. Sinervo, the dean of the University of Toronto's faculty of arts and science and the head of this scientific panel, is quoted as saying, "One can argue fairly strongly that some of those products probably should be looked at on a going-forward basis. It's a new technology. We are concerned." I am of the opinion that a person in his position knows what he's talking about. If he thinks there may be risks associated with nanoparticles, then there probably are. It just seems reasonable to look before we leap.

### Fifth Post

Nanoparticles are the best thing to ever happen. They will provide us with solutions to problems we already have, and to new problems—ones we haven't even discovered yet. So if nanoparticles are going to cause problems of some kind, we don't need to worry about the problems now. Even *if* nanomaterials cause damage somehow, they also offer the potential to solve those problems later. So we shouldn't worry. Nanoparticles are as safe as we need them to be.

**2.** *Post your own entry. Be sure to include a fact from the text and your opinion based on that fact.*

**Your Post:** _____

_____

_____

_____

_____

_____

_____

**3.** *Show your post to a partner. Discuss whether you can distinguish between the fact and the opinion in each other's entry.*

**Checkpoint 2** PEARSON LONGMAN myacademicconnectionslab

In this section, you will practice expressing opinions and supporting them with details and evidence. Then you will prepare a short oral report about whether or not the precautionary principle should be applied to the development of nanotechnology. You will express your opinion about this statement and justify that opinion with facts from the unit.
For online assignments, go to

myacademicconnectionslab

# Before You Speak

*Read the article about the dangers of nanotubes and answer the questions on page 132. Then confirm your answers with the class.*

## Study Says Carbon Nanotubes as Dangerous as Asbestos

New research shows that long, needle-thin carbon nanotubes could lead to lung cancer.

Inhaling carbon nanotubes could be as harmful as breathing in asbestos, and its use should be regulated in case it leads to the same cancer and breathing problems that prompted a ban on the use of asbestos as insulation in buildings, according to a new study posted online today by Nature Nanotechnology.

During the study, led by the Queen's Medical Research Institute at the University of Edinburgh/MRC Centre for Inflammation Research (CIR) in Scotland, scientists observed that long, thin carbon nanotubes look and behave like asbestos fibers, which have been shown to cause mesothelioma, a deadly cancer of the membrane lining the body's internal organs (in particular the lungs) that can take 30 to 40 years to appear following exposure. Asbestos fibers are especially harmful, because they are small enough to penetrate deep into the lungs yet too long for the body's immune system to destroy.

The researchers reached their conclusions after they exposed lab mice to needle-thin nanotubes. The inside lining of the animals' body cavities became inflamed and formed lesions.[1]

Andrew Maynard, chief science advisor for the Woodrow Wilson International Center for Scholars' Project on Emerging Technologies, based in Washington, D.C., has been researching and warning of the potential health and environmental risks of carbon nanotubes since 2003. He and his colleagues focused their attention specifically on the hypothesis that long, thin carbon nanotubes could have the same impact as similarly shaped asbestos fibers. If you get these things into the lungs, he says, they form scarlike tissue, and the body sees them like a scaffolding,[2] building new cells over them and thickening the walls of the lungs.

The study is not intended to keep nanotechnology from developing further but rather to flag[3] potential dangers of nanotubes in places at manufacturing and disposal sites, the researchers wrote in their paper.

"There is an immediate need to examine how carbon nanotubes are being used and see if there's any chance that people are being exposed to dangerous materials," Maynard says, adding that no one paid attention to the dangers of asbestos until it was too late for a lot of people.

---

[1] **lesion** *n* a wound or a sore
[2] **scaffolding** *n* a set of poles and boards that are built into a structure for workers to stand on when they are building something. In this reading, it means a structure that will act like a frame for cell growth.
[3] **flag** *v* to highlight information that may cause problems

Source: Greenemeier, L. (2008, May 20). Study says carbon nanotubes as dangerous as asbestos. *Scientific American*. Retrieved August 15, 2008, from http://www.sciam.com/article.cfm?id=carbon-nanotube-danger &print=true.

1. What is the source of this information? Do you believe this is accurate information, or are you skeptical? Why?

2. Why are nanotubes compared to asbestos fibers?

3. Do you believe it is dangerous to inhale nanotubes? Use an expression that shows your degree of certainty.

4. Why is it unlikely that the results of this study will prevent the further development of nanotechnology?

5. What is required in the immediate future?

## Focused Speaking

### Expressing and Supporting Opinions

At the university level, you will often have to participate in discussions in which you will need to express your opinions about an issue. When you express your opinions, it is important to support them with details and evidence. Strong support will help people believe your opinion.

Strong support of your opinions should include facts, such as statistics and research results. It should also include explanations and reasons that are clear, logical, and based on facts. In expressing your opinions, you should use words that show a strong level of certainty.

In contrast, you should avoid support that includes facts people can't check easily and opinions of people who are not experts in the area you are discussing.

**1.** *Work in small groups. To help you form an opinion about and discuss the precautionary principle, talk about how it would affect:*

    a. An elementary school that is planning to build a climbing structure in the schoolyard for its students.
    b. A shipping company that wants to ship oil through an aquatic preserve.
    c. A medical research proposal to find a cure for cancer by testing a new drug on human subjects immediately.
    d. A company that wants to import a cheaper product from a foreign country.

*Then discuss with the class whether or not you think the precautionary principle should be applied to the development of nanotechnology.*

**2.** *Once you have defined your position on whether the precautionary principle should be applied to the development of nanotechnology, work with a partner who has a similar opinion to your own. Together, complete the chart. State your opinion and then search for facts in the readings and in your answers to the lecture questions that support your opinion(s).*

| Your Opinion |
|---|
| *As far as I'm concerned, . . .* |

| Facts that Support Your Opinion |
|---|
| |

## Integrated Speaking Task

Here is your oral report assignment: **Should the precautionary principle be applied to the development of nanotechnology?** You will express your opinion about this question, using a degree of certainty that is appropriate to your position, and justify the opinion with facts from the unit. You will also use ideas and key vocabulary from the readings, lecture, and other listening activities in this unit.

Your report will have:
- An introduction in which you state your opinion with the appropriate degree of certainty.
- A body in which you state the facts that support your opinion.
- A conclusion that restates your opinion.

*Follow the steps to prepare your report.*

**Step 1:** Plan the introduction: What is your opinion? What is your degree of certainty?

**Step 2:** Plan the body of the oral report: What facts do you have to support your opinion? Place the most persuasive fact either first or last so the listener is most likely to remember it.

**Step 3:** Plan the conclusion: Restate your opinion and summarize the facts that support your opinion. Do not repeat your introduction, but paraphrase your thesis and summarize your main points. Use parallel structure if appropriate.

**Step 4**: Ask your teacher or a classmate to evaluate your report based on the features listed in the checklist.

| Features of a Report | Yes | No |
|---|---|---|
| In the introduction, does the presenter clearly state his or her opinion about whether the precautionary principle should be applied to the development of nanotechnology? Is the presenter's degree of certainty clear? | | |
| Does the body of the report contain facts that support the presenter's opinion? | | |
| In the conclusion, does the presenter paraphrase his or her thesis and summarize the main points that support the thesis? | | |
| Is the vocabulary specific to the topic of nanotechnology? | | |

**Step 5**: Based on the information in the checklist, make any necessary revisions, practice, and present your oral report to the class.

# UNIT
## 7

## Microbiology
## Fighting Infectious Diseases

## Unit Description

**Content:**   This course is designed to familiarize the student with concepts in microbiology.

**Skills:**   Purpose

- Recognizing a writer's purpose
- Recognizing a speaker's purpose
- Understanding thought groups
- Using intonation
- Understanding sentence stress (rhythm)
- Recognizing how thought groups, intonation, and stress express a speaker's attitude
- Recognizing a writer's secondary purpose
- Taking into account audience needs while preparing a presentation

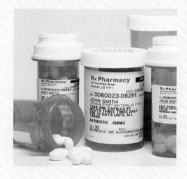

## Unit Requirements

**Lecture:**   "Conditions That Affect the Spread of Infectious Diseases"

**Readings:**   "Resistance to Antimicrobial Drugs" (from *Microbiology: Alternate Edition with Diseases by Body System,* R.W. Bauman, Pearson Benjamin Cummings)

"Preserving Antibiotics' Usefulness" (from "Battle of the Bugs," L. Bren, www.fds.gov)

**Integrated Speaking Task:**   Preparing and delivering an oral presentation about combating the spread of infectious diseases and antibiotic resistance

**Assignments:**   www.MyAcademicConnectionsLab.com

# 1

## Preview

For online assignments, go to

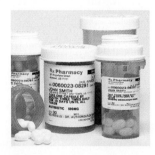

## Key Words

**antibiotic** *n* a drug used to fight infections caused by bacteria

**communicable/ contagious/infectious** *adj* capable of being passed on from one person to another

**contract** *v* to get an illness

**eradicate** *v* to completely destroy something

**resistance** *n* ability to stop something or someone from harming you

**vaccine** *n* a substance that is used to protect people from a disease; **vaccinate** *v*; **vaccination** *n*

## Previewing the Academic Content

Have you ever taken an antibiotic medicine to fight an infectious disease? Did the antibiotic help you feel better? In the past, antibiotics have saved millions of people from suffering and dying from infectious diseases. However, these days, the media are reporting new kinds of contagious diseases: severe acute respiratory syndrome (SARS), West Nile virus, and bird flu to name just a few. These "superbugs" are frightening because they do not respond to drugs. While the fight between humankind and infectious disease has been a long one, we are now in the next phase of the war against contagious diseases—antibiotic resistance. How have social and medical adaptations helped humans fight contagious disease in the past? What adaptations are now required to overcome antibiotic resistance?

**1.** *Match the diseases on the left to their symptoms and other details on the right. Try to do this without using a dictionary. Then check your answers with the class. Which diseases are common in your home country?*

| Disease | Symptoms and Other Details |
|---|---|
| _c_ 1. Chicken pox | a. Caused by a virus that lives in birds. Has infected humans. Does not respond to antibiotic medicine. |
| ___ 2. Small pox | b. Causes inflammation of the small bronchial tubes in the lungs. Symptoms include coughing and fever. |
| ___ 3. Influenza | c. Causes a fever and a red, itchy rash. Usually affects children and lasts two weeks before disappearing. |
| ___ 4. Whooping cough (Pertusis) | d. Causes liquid-filled blisters to form on the face and body. Can result in blindness and death. Eradicated worldwide through the use of a vaccine. |
| ___ 5. Bronchitis | e. Spread by a mosquito. Causes fever, headache, chills, weakness, rash on body, and possibly loss of consciousness. Can be fatal. Is an example of a lower respiratory infection. |
| ___ 6. Severe acute respiratory syndrome (SARS) | f. Causes coughing that can be difficult to stop. Can be fatal. Can be prevented by vaccination. |
| ___ 7. West Nile virus | g. Often referred to as the flu. Causes chills, fever, muscle ache, sore throat, headache. Usually lasts several days. Can cause complications in infants and the elderly. |
| ___ 8. Avian (or bird) flu | h. Infection of the lungs. Causes fever, cough, sore throat, lethargy, and shortness of breath. Can be fatal. |
| ___ 9. Gastroenteric disease | i. Causes immune system failure, which leaves the body open to other infections. Can be fatal. |

_____ 10. AIDS

j. An infection of the lungs. Causes chest pain, coughing up blood, fever, chills, appetite and weight loss, fatigue. Can be fatal.

_____ 11. Tuberculosis (TB)

k. Causes fever, shivering, joint pain, vomiting, convulsions, and brain damage in children. Can be fatal.

_____ 12. Malaria

l. Infection in the stomach and intestines that makes bowel movements frequent and watery. Second leading cause of death in infants

**2.** *The word* disease *collocates with the words listed in the box. Look at the chart. Group the words from the box in the appropriate columns in the chart.*

| | | | |
|---|---|---|---|
| common | deadly | have | life-threatening |
| communicable | develop | heart | rare |
| contagious | eradicate | incurable | serious |
| contract | fatal | is transmitted by | suffer from |

| Adjective + *disease* | Synonyms for *infectious disease* (adjective + *disease*) | Synonyms for *get a disease* (verb + *a disease*) | A synonym for *a disease is spread by* (a *disease* + passive verb + *by* or *through*) |
|---|---|---|---|
| *rare disease* | *contagious disease* | *develop a disease* | |
| | | | **A synonym for *eliminate a disease* (verb + *a disease*)** |
| | | | |

**3.** *Work with a group of three students and discuss the questions in the chart. Write your names at the top of the columns and take brief notes as you listen and speak.*

| Question | Student Name: | Student Name: | Student Name: |
|---|---|---|---|
| 1. What infectious diseases are common in your home country? | | | |
| 2. For which of these diseases do doctors prescribe an antibiotic medicine? | | | |
| 3. For which of these diseases do doctors prescribe non-antibiotic treatments? | | | |
| 4. What kinds of behaviors do you use to avoid infectious diseases? Consider<br>• food<br>• water<br>• sanitation<br>• vaccination | | | |

**4.** *Share your answers with the class. How are people with the same disease treated differently in different countries? On the board, make a list of the kinds of behaviors used to avoid catching infectious diseases.*

In this unit, you will learn how to recognize a writer or speaker's primary and secondary purposes. You will also learn about the use of thought groups, stress, and intonation to express intended meaning.

# Previewing the Academic Skills Focus

## Recognizing a Writer's Purpose

A writer's purpose is the *reason why* he or she writes a text. Generally, a writer has one of three *primary* purposes.

| Writer's primary purpose | Characteristics of a text written for that purpose |
|---|---|
| Inform the reader | Based on facts |
| Persuade the reader | Opinions, strong statements (*it is imperative, it is essential*), modal verbs (*we should, must, could*) |
| Entertain the reader | Informal or colloquial style, high interest, content may be humorous |

In an academic context, the writer's primary purpose is most often to inform the reader, and the readers are most often students. However, you may also read some texts that were written to persuade or even to entertain their readers.

A writer's primary purpose is the writer's most important reason for writing a text; however, the primary purposes can often be integrated. For example, a writer's primary purpose may be to persuade the reader, but the writer may do this by informing the reader about the advantages and disadvantages of different options. Similarly, a writer's primary purpose may be to inform, but the writer may do this by entertaining the reader (by telling a story with a moral, for instance). How writers choose to achieve their primary purposes will vary, often depending on the readers.

**1.** *Work in small groups. Write the types of texts from the box in the appropriate column in the chart. Some texts may belong in more than one column.*

| | | |
|---|---|---|
| advertisements | ~~newspaper editorials~~ | recipes |
| Internet articles | novels | student essays |
| junk mail | operating manuals | ~~textbooks~~ |
| newspaper articles | political fliers | travel magazines |

| Purpose: To Inform | Purpose: To Persuade | Purpose: To Entertain |
|---|---|---|
| *textbooks* | *newspaper editorials* | |

**2.** *Look at the data in Table 1 carefully and then read Paragraph A. Answer the questions about the writer's purpose.*

### TABLE I: Mortality from infectious diseases

| 2002 Rank | Deaths 2002 | Cause of death | Deaths 1993 | 1993 Rank |
|:---:|:---:|:---|:---:|:---:|
| N/A | 14.7 million | All infectious diseases | 16.4 million | N/A |
| I | 3.9 million | Lower respiratory infections | 4.1 million | I |
| 2 | 2.8 million | AIDS | 0.7 million | 7 |
| 3 | 1.8 million | Gastroenteric diseases | 3.0 million | 2 |
| 4 | 1.6 million | Tuberculosis (TB) | 2.7 million | 3 |
| 5 | 1.3 million | Malaria | 2.0 million | 4 |

Source: Adapted from data supplied by the World Health Organization (WHO)

### Paragraph A

Table 1 lists the top five infectious disease killers for the years 1993 and 2002. Since 1993, total deaths have decreased by 1.7 million. Deaths from each of the top five infectious diseases have also decreased, except for deaths from AIDS. Over this time period, deaths from AIDS increased by a factor of four. During this time span, the relative rankings of the diseases has remained almost constant, except for AIDS, which has risen from seventh rank in 1993 to second rank in 2002.

1. What is the writer's primary purpose? How do you know?

2. Does the writer repeat the data from the table in the paragraph? Why?

**3.** *In Paragraph B the writer has a different primary purpose. Read the paragraph and then answer the question.*

### Paragraph B

The data in Table 1 points to several issues of concern. First, because the data shows there are fewer deaths from infectious diseases around the world, governments and health care providers may become complacent[1] about these results. In fact, with the onset of antibiotic resistance, it is possible that the decreasing trend will reverse itself in the future. Second, without greater efforts at intervention, deaths from AIDS will likely surpass those from all other infectious diseases. It is essential that governments and public health organizations, like the World Health Organization (WHO), continue to invest in research on antibiotic resistance and AIDS.

What is the writer's primary purpose in paragraph B? How do you know?

---

[1] **complacent** *adj* pleased with a situation or achievement, so that you stop trying to improve or change things. Used to show disapproval.

# 2

## Building Academic Listening Skills

In this section, you will learn how to recognize a speaker's purpose and attitude about a topic. For online assignments, go to

### Key Words

Humans **fight against** (*v + prep*) disease.

We **battle against** (*v + prep*) disease.

We **wage a war against** (*v + object + prep*) disease.

We **are overcome** (*v—passive*) by disease.

Bacteria **is killed** (*v—passive*) by exposure to antibiotics.

We **combat** (*v*) disease.

The immune system **attacks** (*v*) foreign bacteria.

When we are healthy, we are able to **resist** (*v*) disease successfully.

The immune system is our **first line of defense against** (*exp*) bacteria.

We **keep a disease under control** (*exp*).

A disease can be **out of control** (*exp*).

There is a disease **outbreak** (*n*).

We **are vulnerable to** disease (*adj*).

We **are susceptible to** disease (*adj*).

## Before You Listen

When we talk or write about infectious diseases in English, we often use words that relate to war. We compare the battle against disease to fighting a battle of war. This similarity between fighting disease and fighting a war is a metaphor—a type of comparison in which we describe one thing as being another. If you are aware of this metaphor, you will be able to select appropriate vocabulary when you speak or write about this topic. You will learn more about metaphors in Unit 8.

*Use some of the war-related key words to complete the sentences about infectious diseases. There may be more than one possible answer.*

1. The human immune system is an extraordinary biological system. It is our _____ infectious disease.

2. While humans develop defenses to _____ organisms that cause disease, the organisms are evolving in ways that allow them to _____ our defenses.

3. Most vaccines contain bacteria that have been _____ or inactivated; this is why people do not contract a disease through vaccination.

4. Immune systems will _____ this inactivated bacteria and develop antibodies that will automatically recognize the bacteria in the future.

5. People who are not vaccinated against a disease are the most _____ that disease when there is a disease _____.

6. Professional health care workers and the World Health Organization (WHO) _____ the spread of measles, and they have succeeded in eradicating the disease.

7. In 2003, when there was an _____ of SARS, the WHO worked with doctors around the world to _____.

# Global Listening

In the lecture you will hear an instructor discuss the conditions that affect the spread of infectious diseases. For example, if we are generally in good health, we will be less susceptible to catching infectious diseases.

**1.** *Work in groups of three to brainstorm as many conditions that affect the spread of infectious disease as possible. List them in the first column of the chart. Then combine your answers with other groups' to achieve as inclusive a list as possible. You will work with the other two columns later.*

| Conditions That Affect the Spread of Infectious Diseases | Mentioned in Lecture? ✓/X | Order in Lecture (1, 2, 3, etc.) |
|---|---|---|
| 1. *General health—if healthy, we are less likely to contract a disease* | ✓ | 1 |
| 2. | | |
| 3. | | |
| 4. | | |
| 5. | | |
| 6. | | |
| 7. | | |
| 8. | | |
| 9. | | |
| 10. | | |
| 11. | | |

**2.** 🎧 *Listen to the lecture once. In the middle column, place a check (✓) beside each condition that the instructor discusses. Place an X beside any condition that you have listed that is not mentioned. Then add any conditions that the instructor mentions that you did not have on your list. Confirm your list with the class. You will work with the third column later.*

**3.** 🎧 *Listen to the lecture again. In the third column, write the number that corresponds with the order in which the lecturer mentions the conditions. Then check your order with a classmate's. Did you both get the same order of conditions?*

**4.** *Copy the eight conditions from the lecture into the first column of the chart in the correct order.*

| Conditions That Affect the Spread of Infectious Diseases | Notes from the Lecture |
|---|---|
| 1. *General health* | *If healthy, we resist disease better—opposite is also true* |
| 2. | |
| 3. | |
| 4. | |
| 5. | |
| 6. | |
| 7. | |
| 8. | |

**5.** 🎧 *Listen to the lecture again and take as many point-form notes in the chart on page 143 as you can about each condition. Then work in groups of three and compare your notes. Fill in any gaps you might have. You should now have a complete set of notes on the lecture content.*

> You may hear these words in the lecture and want to write them in your notes. This list should help you with the spelling of these words:
>
> parasites              the Black Death
> schistosomiasis        the bubonic plague

## Focused Listening

### Recognizing a Speaker's Purpose

A speaker's purpose is often called a speaker's intent, and it is the same as a writer's purpose: It is the *reason why* a speaker talks. Generally, a speaker has the same range of *primary* purposes that a writer does.

| Speaker's primary purpose | Characteristics of a text spoken for that purpose |
|---|---|
| Inform the listener | Based on facts |
| Persuade the listener | Opinions, strong statements (*it is imperative, it is essential*), modal verbs (*we should, must, could*) |
| Entertain the listener | Informal or colloquial style, high interest, content may be humorous |

In an academic context, the speaker's primary purpose is most often to inform the listener, and the listeners are most often students. However, you may also listen to some texts that are spoken to persuade or even to entertain their listeners. Just as the primary purposes can often be integrated in writing, they can also be integrated in speaking.

In a longer speech or lecture, a speaker might have several *secondary* purposes, and will divide the talk into sections; each section of the text satisfies each secondary purpose. A speaker's secondary purpose is sometimes called a speaker's *rhetorical* purpose. A speaker may use specific words, phrases, or sentences to achieve his or her secondary purposes. A speaker's secondary purposes may include:

- introducing a new point (*first, next*)
- explaining why something happens (*for this reason, this means that, that is*)
- providing more information (*in addition, also*)
- providing an alternative explanation (*or, on the other hand*)
- providing an example (*for example, for instance, such as*)
- quantifying a general statement (use of numbers)
- emphasizing a point (*it should be noted that, most of all, especially, in particular*)
- contrasting ideas (*but, however, although, while, whereas*)
- creating a picture for the reader/listener (*imagine, picture, is like, looks like*)

**1.** Based on your answers to the questions in the Global Listening (pages 142–144), what was the instructor's primary purpose for giving the lecture? How do you know?

**2.** Listen to the sections from the lecture and answer the questions about the instructor's secondary purpose. Circle the correct answer. Confirm your answers with the class.

🎧 1. The instructor begins the lecture by talking about SARS because _____.
   a. SARS is more important than the swine flu
   b. SARS is a recent example of an infectious disease
   c. SARS supports the point about infectious diseases

2. The instructor says "First of all" because _____.
   a. this is the beginning of the lecture
   b. this is the first point in a list of points
   c. this is the instructor's way of getting the listeners' attention

🎧 3. Why did the instructor say that the disease kills 5 to 8 million people per year and is the leading cause of death for children under the age of five?
   a. to quantify a general statement about the spread of the disease
   b. to explain that children are the most important victims
   c. to contrast with a preceding idea

🎧 4. The instructor talks about the Black Death in China and Europe because _____.
   a. it is an example of an infectious disease that killed a lot of people
   b. it is an example of how susceptible people are to diseases they haven't been exposed to before
   c. it explains why the cultural life in Asia and Europe changed

## Understanding Thought Groups

If you understand why English speakers pause within a sentence (thought groups), raise or lower the pitch of their voices (intonation), and stress specific words, you will understand the speakers' attitudes more easily.

At some point while you are learning English, you may be asked to read aloud so a teacher or tester can assess your pronunciation. One of the elements of pronunciation that the teacher/tester is listening for is whether you pause at the correct points within a sentence. When should you pause when speaking?

Generally, you should pause between thought groups. A **thought group** is often all the words in a clause—a noun, adjective, or adverb clause—or a group of words. They are often separated from a main clause by a comma. You can use a slash (/) to help you mark the separation between thought groups.

Each of these example sentences has two thought groups:

- Good health depends on a clean water supply, / as well as an efficient waste management system.
- Sudden acute respiratory syndrome was a scary disease / because it didn't respond to antibiotics.

When a sentence is written, punctuation marks like commas, periods, and question marks often indicate the end of a thought group. When a sentence is spoken, it is the pauses that show the listener the separation between clauses and phrases. These pauses help the listener understand what you are saying.

**3.** *Mark a slash (/) between the thought groups in the sentences. Then read the sentences aloud to a partner. Practice pausing at the end of each thought group.*

1. Deaths from each of the top five infectious diseases have also decreased, except for deaths from AIDS.

2. Over this time period, deaths from AIDS have increased by a factor of four.

3. During this time span, the relative rankings of the diseases has remained almost constant, except for AIDS, which has risen from seventh rank in 1993 to second rank in 2002.

## Using Intonation

Intonation is the way in which the level of your voice changes to add meaning to a sentence. The end of a thought group can be indicated by a pause, but also by a rising-falling intonation pattern. This rising-falling intonation pattern is often used when the speaker is speaking quickly and does not have time to pause between thought groups. Intonation is usually marked by a line that rises or lowers (like the speaker's voice) just above the words in a thought group.

English speakers tend to raise their intonation on the stressed syllable of the last content word (noun, verb, adjective, adverb, and *wh*-question words) in the thought group and lower their intonation on the syllables that follow.

- First of all, / if we are in good health, / we are more able to resist infectious diseases.

- First, / because the data shows there are fewer deaths from infectious diseases around the world, / governments and health care providers may become complacent about these results.

**4.** *Mark a slash (/) between the thought groups in the sentences. Practice saying your sentences to a classmate. Over each thought group, draw an intonation line to show the rising and falling of your voice at the end of each thought group.*

1. In fact, with the onset of antibiotic resistance, it is possible that the decreasing trend will reverse itself in the future.

2. Second, without greater efforts at intervention, deaths from AIDS will likely surpass those from all other infectious diseases.

3. It is essential that governments and public health organizations, like the World Health Organization, continue to invest in research on antibiotic resistance and AIDS.

English speakers use rising and falling intonation in more places than the end of a thought group. They also raise their intonation on stressed words within a thought group.

In each thought group, the most important words are spoken with more strength than the others. The words that are spoken with more strength are called *stressed words*. When you speak, stressing (or emphasizing) these words creates a rhythm of strong and weak stresses.

In a thought group, content words—or the stressed syllables of content words—are usually stressed. Content words include nouns, verbs, adjectives, adverbs, and *wh*-question words. Function words are usually not stressed. Function words include articles, pronouns, prepositions, and auxiliary verbs.

To show stress when you speak, lengthen the vowel sound in the stressed syllable of the stressed word.

To illustrate stress in writing, stressed words are indicated by capitalizing the letters in the stressed syllable of the stressed word.

These example sentences are marked for thought groups, intonation, and stressed content words.

- SARS and SWINE FLU are exAMples of diSEASes / that SPREAD on a GLObal SCALE.

- And this is the FOcus of today's LECture: / the conDItions that enCOUrage or DIScourage the SPREAD of inFECtious diSEAses.

**5.** *Circle the content words (or the syllables of content words) that should be stressed in each thought group. Then practice saying the sentences with a partner.*

1. Gastroenteritis, / which is a disease of the stomach and intestines, / is caused by improperly prepared foods, / reheated meat and seafood dishes, / and dairy and bakery products.

2. Also, / most of us live in large groups, / very large groups, / and this makes us more vulnerable to infectious disease.

3. Similarly, / large populations of humans tend to attract rats and other rodents / that may also be agents of disease.

Proficient English speakers use thought groups, intonation, and stress when they speak to express their attitudes. A speaker's attitude is the speaker's opinion about an idea, person, or thing. Understanding a speaker's attitude can help you understand what the speaker is saying.

A speaker's attitude or opinion may not be explicit. You may need to listen carefully to both the words the speaker is using and the speaker's thought groups, intonation, and stress to figure out the speaker's opinion.

*(continued on next page)*

Speakers may express:

- Enthusiasm by placing greater stress and raising their intonation on content words more than normal.

  It's WONderful / that the MEAsles disease is now eRAdicated worldWIDE.

- Worry or concern by speaking more slowly, placing greater stress on words that show uncertainty, and using falling intonation.

  I'm NOT SURE / that we can preVENT antibiotic reSIStance.

  In this case, English speakers might also stress the word *can*. Although *can* is an auxiliary (modal) verb and is not usually stressed, in this sentence it has importance because it shows possibility that contrasts with the speaker's uncertainty.

  I'm NOT SURE / that we CAN prevent antibiotic reSIStance.

- Doubt or disbelief by placing greater stress on content words.

  It's unLIKEly / that we can treat AIDS / unLESS DRUG companies reduce the COSTS of their MEdicines.

- Regret or astonishment by placing greater stress on words that quantify a statement.

  By the end of the epiDEMic, / 25 to 40 MILlion people had been killed in Europe, / and WHO KNOWS how many in Asia.

- Possibility by placing stress on and raising intonation on the modal verbs that show possibility (*may, might, could, should*).

  If we imPROVE water quality, / food preparAtion, / and waste management PRACtices, / we SHOULD be able to reduce morTALity rates of diSEAses caused by bacTERia.

- Impossibility by placing stress on words that are negative. English speakers may lower their intonation on negative words to express seriousness.

  At THIS point in time, / there's NO possibility of avoiding the next inFECtious disease epiDEMic.

**6.** *Listen to the sentences from the lecture. Determine the instructor's attitude based on the words, intonation patterns, and stress. Then confirm your answers with the class. (Note: Numbers are in italics because they can't be capitalized to show stress.)*

🎧 1. The WORLD HEALTH OrganiZAtion estimates that *200* MILlion people may be infected with the parasite, / and that *200,000* die EVERY YEAR.

   **Speaker's attitude:** _____

🎧 2. The WHO states that GAStroenteritis kills *5* TO *8* MILlion people per YEAR / and is the LEADing cause of DEATH for children UNDER the age of five! / THIS, when gastroenteritis can be treated SIMply by rehydration.

   **Speaker's attitude:** _____

3. As if this weren't ENOUGH, / LARGE GROUPS of PEople attract / what we call "agents of disease" / —mosQUItoes and RATS.

**Speaker's attitude:** _____

4. MEasles, SMALLpox, influENza, and WHOoping cough / killed MANY of the natives throughout NORTH and SOUTH America, the PaCIfic Islands, and AusTRAlia. / SOME populations were comPLEtely wiped out, / and others had such seVERE disease rates / that their cultures were deSTROYed.

**Speaker's attitude:** _____

**7.** *Now listen to some statements made by students about the Mortality from Infectious Diseases data on page 140. Use the words, stress, and intonation patterns to determine the speaker's attitude.*

1. It's almost imPOSsible to collect data like this from countries all over the world. / I WONder how the World Health Organization colLECted it.

**Speaker's attitude:** _____

2. It's GREAT to have this kind of data. / NOW we can see what we REALly need to do / to imPROve the quality of life for people / all aROUND the world.

**Speaker's attitude:** _____

*What did you notice about how the speakers used stress and intonation to make their purposes clear? Discuss with a partner.*

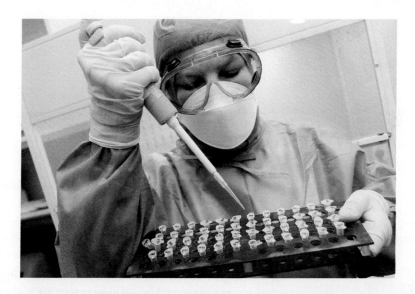

**Checkpoint 1**   PEARSON LONGMAN myacademicconnectionslab

# 3

## Building Academic Reading Skills

In this section, you will learn to recognize a writer's secondary (or rhetorical) purpose. For online assignments, go to

**PEARSON LONGMAN**
**myacademicconnectionslab**

**PEARSON LONGMAN**
**myacademicconnectionslab**

### Key Words

**antibody** *n* a molecule produced by the body to fight an infection

**antimicrobial agent** *exp* any drug that fights pathogens

**chemotherapeutic agent** *exp* any chemical used to fight disease

**germ** *n* the common (non-technical) word for a microorganism that makes you sick

**inhibit** *v* something from continuing or developing

**pathogen** *n* a microorganism that makes you sick, such as bacteria, viruses, fungi, or parasites

**resistant to** *adj* unchanged by the effect of something

**sensitive to** *adj* susceptible or vulnerable

**strain of bacteria** *exp* a particular kind of bacteria with unique characteristics

## Before You Read

**1.** *Study the key microbiology words. Then work with a partner and quiz each other on the meanings of the words.*

**2.** *The figure shows how a strain of bacteria becomes resistant to an antibiotic. With your partner, describe what is happening in pictures a, b, c, and d. Use as many of the key words as possible.*

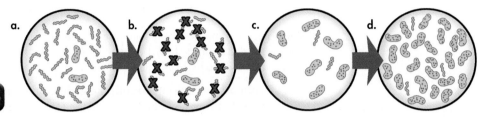

a.      b.      c.      d.

**Description:**

a. *A strain of bacteria contains both antibiotic-sensitive cells and antibiotic-resistant cells. The vast majority of cells is antibiotic-sensitive.*

b. _____

_____

c. _____

_____

d. _____

_____

## Global Reading

**1.** *Read an excerpt from a microbiology textbook. As you read, think about the author's primary purpose.*

### Resistance to Antimicrobial Drugs

**1** Among the major challenges facing microbiologists today are the problems presented by pathogens that are resistant to antimicrobial agents. We focus here on the development of resistance in populations of bacteria, but resistance to antimicrobials is known to occur among viruses as well.

**2** The process by which a resistant strain of bacteria develops is depicted in Figure 7.1. In the absence of an antimicrobial drug, resistant cells are usually less efficient than their normal neighbors because they must expend extra energy to maintain resistance to genes and proteins.

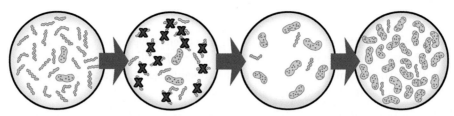

**Figure 7.1**

Under these circumstances, resistant cells remain the minority in a population because they reproduce more slowly. However, when an antimicrobial agent is present, the majority of cells (which are sensitive to the antimicrobial) is inhibited or dies, while the resistant cells continue to grow and multiply, often more rapidly because they then face less competition. The result is that resistant cells soon replace the sensitive cells as the majority in the population. It should be noted that the presence of the chemotherapeutic agent does not *produce* resistance, but instead facilitates the replication of resistant cells that were already present in the population.

## Multiple Resistance and Cross Resistance

**3** A given pathogen can acquire resistance to more than one drug at a time. Such multiresistant strains of bacteria frequently develop in hospitals and nursing homes, where the constant use of many kinds of antimicrobial agents eliminates sensitive cells and encourages the development of resistant strains.

**4** Pathogens that are resistant to most antimicrobial agents are sometimes called superbugs. Superbug strains of *Staphylococcus, Streptococcus, Enterococcus, Pseudomonas,* and *Plasmodium* pose unique problems for health care professionals, who must treat infected patients without effective antimicrobials while taking extra care to protect themselves and other patients from infection.

**5** Resistance to one antimicrobial agent may confer[1] resistance to similar drugs, a phenomenon called cross resistance. Cross resistance typically occurs when drugs are similar in structure. For example, resistance to one aminoglycoside drug, such as streptomycin, may confer resistance to similar aminoglycoside drugs.

## Retarding Resistance

**6** The development of resistant populations of pathogens can be averted[2] in at least four ways. First, sufficiently high concentrations of the drug can be maintained in a patient's body for a long enough time to kill all sensitive cells and inhibit others long enough for the body's defenses to defeat them.

---

[1] **confer** *v* to give (as a property or characteristic) to someone or something
[2] **avert** *v* to prevent something unpleasant from happening

*(continued on next page)*

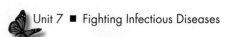

Discontinuing a drug before all of the pathogens have been neutralized promotes the development of resistant strains. For this reason, it is important that patients finish their entire antimicrobial prescription and resist the temptation to "save some for another day."

**7** A second way to avert resistance is to use antimicrobial agents in combination so that pathogens resistant to one drug will be killed by the second, and vice versa. Additionally, one drug sometimes enhances the effect of a second drug in a process called synergism. In one example of a synergistic drug combination, the inhibition of cell wall formation by penicillin (one common antibiotic) makes it easier for streptomycin (another antibiotic) molecules to enter bacteria and interfere with protein synthesis. Synergism can also result from combining an antimicrobial drug and a chemical, as occurs when clavulanic acid enhances the effect of penicillin by deactivating $\beta$-lactamase.

**8** Not all drugs act synergistically; some combinations of drugs can be antagonistic—interfering with each other. For example, drugs that slow bacterial growth are antagonistic to the action of penicillin, which acts only against growing and dividing cells.

**9** A third way to reduce the development of resistance is to limit the use of antimicrobials to necessary cases. Unfortunately, many antimicrobial agents are used indiscriminately, in both developed countries and in less-developed regions where many are available without a physician's prescription. In the United States, an estimated 50 percent of prescriptions for antibacterial agents to treat sore throats, and 30 percent of prescriptions for ear infections, are inappropriate because the diseases are viral in nature. Likewise, because antibacterial drugs have no effect on cold and flu viruses, 100 percent of antibacterial prescriptions for treating these diseases are superfluous.[3] As discussed previously, the use of antimicrobial agents encourages the reproduction of resistant bacteria by limiting the growth of sensitive cells; therefore, inappropriate use of such drugs increases the likelihood that resistant strains of bacteria will multiply.

**10** Finally, scientists can combat resistant strains by developing new variations of existing drugs, in some cases by adding novel side chains to the original molecule. In this way, scientists develop semisynthetic second-generation drugs. If resistance develops to these drugs, third-generation drugs may be developed to replace them. Many health care professionals and research scientists are concerned about how long drug developers can stay ahead of the development of resistance in pathogens.

---

[3] **superfluous** *adj* unnecessary

Source: Adapted from Bauman, R.W. (2006). *Microbiology: Alternate edition with diseases by body system.* San Francisco: Pearson Benjamin Cummings.

**2.** *Complete the tasks with a partner. Then check your answers with the class.*

1. What is the author's primary purpose for writing this text? How do you know?

2. What is the topic (focus) of this particular reading?

3. Read the statements. Decide if they are true or false. Write **T** (true) or **F** (false).

_____ a. Cells that are resistant to an antibiotic exist in any population of bacteria even before they are exposed to the antibiotic.

_____ b. Without exposure to an antibiotic, resistant cells are less efficient and reproduce slowly.

_____ c. When an antimicrobial (antibiotic medicine) is present, sensitive cells are killed, while resistant cells reduce their productivity.

_____ d. When an antimicrobial is present, resistant cells reproduce more quickly because of a lack of competition from sensitive cells.

_____ e. An antimicrobial produces resistance in populations of bacteria.

_____ f. An antimicrobial encourages the reproduction of pre-existing resistant cells.

4. Why does multiple resistance to antimicrobials appear most frequently in hospitals and nursing homes?

5. What is cross resistance, and why does it occur?

6. Fill in the chart with the four methods to prevent antimicrobial resistance.

| Method | How It Works |
|---|---|
| 1. Patients must finish all the antibiotics they are prescribed, even if they begin to feel better before they finish. | *High concentrations of the antibiotic will kill the sensitive cells and allow the body's natural defenses to kill the resistant cells. This eradicates the entire population of bacteria and helps prevent the development of antibiotic resistance.* |
| 2. | |
| 3. Use antimicrobials only when necessary. | |
| 4. | |

7. What is the concern about second- and third-generation drugs?

# Focused Reading

Just as speakers often have a variety of *secondary* purposes, writers also have secondary purposes. Sometimes, secondary purpose is referred to as *rhetorical purpose*. Generally, to express secondary purpose, writers use specific words, phrases, or sentences to:

- introduce a new point (*first, next*)
- explain why something happens (*for this reason, this means that, that is*)
- provide more information (*in addition, also*)
- provide an alternative explanation (*or, on the other hand*)
- provide an example (*for example, for instance, such as*)
- quantify a general statement (use of numbers)
- emphasize a point (*it should be noted that, most of all, especially, in particular*)
- contrast ideas *(but, however, although, while, whereas)*
- create a picture for the reader/listener (*imagine, picture, is like, looks like*)

The writer's secondary purposes are not stated explicitly. You need to consider the words, phrases, or sentences in relation to the rest of the text to figure out why the writer presented this information in the text in this way.

*1. This task requires you to analyze paragraph 6 from the reading on pages 151–152. Each sentence in the paragraph has a secondary (rhetorical) purpose. Study the analysis.*

**Sentence 1:** The development of resistant populations of pathogens can be averted in at least four ways.

**Secondary purpose:** introducing the topic of the next section and indicating there will be four points in this section

**Sentence 2:** First, sufficiently high concentrations of the drug can be maintained in a patient's body for a long enough time to kill all sensitive cells and inhibit others long enough for the body's defenses to defeat them.

**Secondary purpose:** introducing the first point

**Sentence 3:** Discontinuing a drug before all of the pathogens have been neutralized promotes the development of resistant strains.

**Secondary purpose:** explaining why drug resistance develops

**Sentence 4:** For this reason, it is important that patients finish their entire antimicrobial prescription and resist the temptation to "save some for another day."

**Secondary purpose:** emphasizing the point that patients must finish all their antibiotics to prevent antibiotic resistance

**2.** *Determine the writer's secondary purpose for each sentence in paragraph 9 of the reading. Then compare your answers with a partner's. If you do not agree, consult with a third student or your teacher.*

**Sentence 1:** A third way to reduce the development of resistance is to limit the use of antimicrobials to necessary cases.

**Secondary purpose:** _____

_____

**Sentence 2:** Unfortunately, many antimicrobial agents are used indiscriminately, in both developed countries and in less-developed regions where many are available without a physician's prescription.

**Secondary purpose:** _____

_____

**Sentence 3:** In the United States, an estimated 50 percent of prescriptions for antibacterial agents to treat sore throats, and 30 percent of prescriptions for ear infections, are inappropriate because the diseases are viral in nature.

**Secondary purpose:** _____

_____

**Sentence 4:** Likewise, because antibacterial drugs have no effect on cold and flu viruses, 100 percent of antibacterial prescriptions for treating these diseases are superfluous.

**Secondary purpose:** _____

_____

**Sentence 5:** As discussed previously, the use of antimicrobial agents encourages the reproduction of resistant bacteria by limiting the growth of sensitive cells; therefore, inappropriate use of such drugs increases the likelihood that resistant strains of bacteria will multiply.

**Secondary purpose:** _____

_____

**Checkpoint 2** PEARSON LONGMAN myacademicconnectionslab

## Building Academic Speaking Skills

In this section, you will learn how to consider audience needs when preparing oral presentations. Then you will prepare and give an oral presentation about how people can fight the spread of infectious diseases and antibiotic resistance.

For online assignments, go to

**myacademicconnectionslab**

# Before You Speak

## Taking into Account Audience Needs

When you are asked to give a presentation, you may be very nervous. You may be so nervous that you give your presentation and sit down as quickly as possible. While it is normal to be nervous, you must realize that you have a primary purpose for giving your presentation (to inform, to persuade, or to entertain), and your audience has specific needs. The planning of every excellent presentation begins with a careful consideration of your purpose and the audience's needs.

An audience looks for most of the following things from a presenter:

- An entertaining or dramatic beginning
- Understandable content
  - definitions of key vocabulary
  - a presentation outline
  - clear explanations of basic concepts
  - content geared to the audience's level of understanding
  - a clear voice (loud enough and with clear pronunciation)
- Interesting content
- Visual support to help the audience understand the content
- A definite ending
- Recognition from the presenter
  - eye contact

Remember that in almost all cases, your audience wants you to succeed, so they are hoping you will do well.

1. *Work with a partner to discuss how your presentation would change depending on your purpose and audience. Take short notes about these factors in the chart.*

- use of technical terms
- time spent on explaining basic concepts
- need for visuals
- how to achieve your primary purpose

| Presentation Topic: **How Can People Combat the Spread of Infectious Diseases and Antibiotic Resistance?** | | |
|---|---|---|
| Your Primary Purpose | Your Audience | Your Presentation |
| To inform | A group of children | • *don't use technical terms*<br>• *spend more time explaining basic concepts*<br>• *keep it short*<br>• *achieve your primary purpose (to inform) by entertaining—maybe tell a story with a moral* |

| Your Primary Purpose | Your Audience | Your Presentation |
|---|---|---|
| To persuade | A group of classmates and instructors who are well informed about your topic | |
| To persuade | Parents who want antibiotic medicine when their young children develop an illness | |
| To inform | Your classmates who have not read as much as you have about your presentation topic | |

**2.** *Select your presentation partner and your preferred audience (children, well-informed classmates, parents with young children, or less-informed classmates). Think about the topic of your presentation. Then work with your partner to answer the questions. Take notes in your notebook.*

1. What is my primary purpose for this presentation?

2. Who are the people in my audience?

3. How much do they know about my topic?

4. What content-specific terms (new vocabulary) do I need to explain?

5. What visuals could I use to make my presentation more interesting?

6. Is there a joke or a story I can tell to engage my audience at the beginning?

7. How can I logically organize the information in my presentation and show the organization to my audience?

8. What attitude do I want to express at the end of the presentation?

## Focused Speaking

**1.** *Read the news item on page 158. As you read, think about the primary purpose of this text. Be prepared to express your opinion about this question: Is it likely that people will be able to battle antibiotic resistance?*

## Preserving Antibiotics' Usefulness
### by Linda Bren (from "Battle of the Bugs")

1 Two main types of germs—bacteria and viruses—cause most infections. But while antibiotics can kill bacteria, they do not work against viruses—and it is viruses that cause colds, the flu, and most sore throats. In fact, only 15 percent of sore throats are caused by the bacterium *Streptococcus*, which results in strep throat. In addition, viruses cause most sinus infections, coughs, and bronchitis. And fluid in the middle ear, a common occurrence in children, does not usually warrant treatment with antibiotics unless there are other symptoms.

2 Nevertheless, "Every year, tens of millions of prescriptions for antibiotics are written to treat viral illnesses for which these antibiotics offer no benefits," says David Bell, MD, the Center for Disease Control's (CDC) antimicrobial resistance coordinator. According to the CDC, antibiotic prescribing in outpatient settings could be reduced by more than 30 percent without adversely affecting patient health.

3 Reasons cited by doctors for overprescribing antibiotics include diagnostic uncertainty, time pressure on physicians, and patient demand. Physicians are pressured by patients to prescribe antibiotics, says Bell. "People don't want to miss work, or they have a sick child who kept the whole family up all night, and they're willing to try anything that might work." It may be easier for the physician pressed for time to write a prescription for an antibiotic than it is to explain why it might be better not to use one.

4 But by taking an antibiotic, a person may be doubly harmed, according to Bell. First, it offers no benefit for viral infections, and second, it increases the chance of a drug-resistant infection appearing at a later time.

5 "Antibiotic resistance is not just a problem for doctors and scientists," says Bell. "Everybody needs to help deal with this. An important way that people can help directly is to understand that common illnesses like colds and the flu do not benefit from antibiotics and to not request them to treat these illnesses."

6 **What You Can Do to Help Curb Antibiotic Resistance**
- Don't demand an antibiotic when your health care provider determines one isn't appropriate. Ask about ways to relieve your symptoms.
- Never take an antibiotic for a viral infection such as a cold, a cough, or the flu.
- Take medicine exactly as your health care provider prescribes. If he or she prescribes an antibiotic, take it until it is gone, even if you're feeling better.
- Don't take leftover antibiotics or antibiotics prescribed for someone else. These antibiotics may not be appropriate for your current symptoms. Taking the wrong medicine could delay getting correct treatment and allow bacteria to multiply.

Source: Bren, L. (2002). Battle of the bugs: Fighting antibiotic resistance. Retrieved September 12, 2005, from the U.S. Food and Drug Administration database: http://www.fda.gov/fdac/features/2002/402_bugs.html.

**2.** *Write the primary purpose of this text.*

_____

_____

When you express your attitude or opinion in English, you will be better understood if you use the thought groups, intonation, and stress patterns of an English speaker.

**3.** *Now that you have read the news item, do you think it is likely that people will be able to overcome antibiotic resistance? Write a sentence or two expressing your attitude about this question. Mark the thought groups, intonation, and word stress of your sentence. Practice saying your sentence a number of times on your own.*

**Example**

I'm not SURE if people will be able to COMbat antibiOtic reSIStance. / I think people will conTINue to deMAND an antibiOtic / whether it will WORK for them / or NOT.

_____

_____

_____

_____

**4.** *Read your sentence(s) to a classmate. Ask your classmate to guess your attitude. If your classmate could not guess your attitude, work together on improving your thought groups, intonation, and stress. Keep practicing until your classmate can clearly understand your meaning. When you feel you have a good sentence that clearly expresses your attitude, present it to the class and have the class guess your attitude.*

## Integrated Speaking Task

You have listened to a lecture and read texts about fighting the spread of infectious diseases and antibiotic resistance. Use your knowledge of the content, vocabulary, audience needs, and pronunciation features to prepare a short oral presentation in response to this question: **How can people combat the spread of infectious diseases and antibiotic resistance?**

Your presentation will have an introduction, a body, and a concluding statement. In your concluding statement, you will express a positive or a negative attitude about the possibility of eradicating infectious diseases and reducing antibiotic resistance.

*Follow the steps to prepare your presentation.*

**Step 1**: First select an audience for your presentation. Use the chart on pages 156–157 to help you. Next, consider your answers to the questions in the Before You Speak section on page 157. These questions ask you to think about your primary purpose and the needs of the audience that you have selected for this presentation.

**Step 2**: Make a point-form list of the things people (doctors, health care professionals, the World Health Organization, the public) need to do to combat the spread of infectious diseases and antibiotic resistance.

**Step 3**: Write your presentation in your notebook. Write a brief introduction, a body that covers all your points from Step 2, and a conclusion that expresses your opinion about the topic question.

**Step 4**: Focus on the expression of your opinion/attitude in your concluding statement. Mark the stress, thought groups, and intonation contours of the key sentences. Practice saying these sentences a number of times. Check with a classmate to make sure your opinion is clear.

**Step 5**: Transfer all your notes into whatever format you like to use when you give presentations. Many students like to write their presentations in point form on index cards. Other students like to write out their full presentation in order to feel secure. If you write out your full presentation, be sure to practice it enough that you can look at your audience while you speak.

**Step 6**: Prepare visuals appropriate for your audience.

**Step 7**: When you have finished, practice your presentation in front of a classmate or a small group of students. Ask your classmate to give you feedback on your presentation by filling in the checklist.

| Features of an Effective Oral Presentation | Yes | No |
|---|---|---|
| There was a clear introduction to the topic. | | |
| The body of the presentation presented the things people can do to combat infectious diseases and antibiotic resistance. The body included points from the lecture and the two readings in the unit. | | |
| There was a clear concluding statement at the end of the presentation. | | |
| The presenter used thought groups, intonation, and stress to clearly express his or her attitude/opinion. | | |
| The vocabulary was appropriate to the topic and used the metaphor of fighting a war for fighting infectious diseases. | | |
| The presenter clearly considered audience needs by:<br>• providing visuals<br>• being prepared and organized<br>• speaking clearly and loudly enough for the audience to hear<br>• looking directly at the audience<br>• other considerations used by the presenter: _____<br><br>_____<br><br>_____ | | |

**Step 8**: Based on the checklist, make any necessary revisions, practice, and give your presentation to the class.

# Children's Literature
# Characteristics of the Genre

## Unit Description

**Content:**   This course is designed to familiarize the student with concepts in children's literature.

**Skills:**   Inference

- Gathering information to make inferences
- Making inferences about a speaker's intention
- Introducing a specific book in an essay or an oral presentation
- Identifying and using rhetorical devices

## Unit Requirements

**Readings:**   "The Generic Plot Pattern in Children's Literature" (from *The Pleasures of Children's Literature*, 3rd Edition, P. Nodelman & M. Reimer, Pearson Allyn & Bacon)
*The Window* (a children's story)
*Matt and the Killer Whale* (a children's story)

**Lecture:**   "Characteristics of Children's Literature"

**Integrated Writing Task:**   Writing an analytical essay about a children's story

**Assignments:**
www.MyAcademicConnectionsLab.com

# 1

## Preview

For online assignments, go to

### Key Words

**mutter** *v* to speak in a low voice, especially when you are annoyed or confused, so other people can't hear you

**nestled** *adj* pressed against something comforting

**orphan** *n* a child whose parents are dead

**patchwork quilt** *n* a type of blanket made with many colorful squares of cloth that are stitched together

**sill** *n* the part of the cage or frame at the bottom of a door or window

**thrilled** *adj* very excited

**turn tail** *exp* to run away because you are frightened

**zip** *v informal* to move with speed and energy

## Previewing the Academic Content

Most of us can remember a well-loved story or tale from our childhoods. Perhaps you can recall a traditional story retold by a parent or relative, or a storybook with colorful pictures. Whether you remember the tale because of the plot, the characters, or the pictures, you probably have accurate recall after many years. If you discussed these stories with each other, would the tales have similar characteristics? Would the main characters share certain traits, or would the plots parallel each other?

**1.** *Think of a story (or two) that you remember from your childhood and answer the questions.*

1. Who (or what) is the main character? How old is the character? Does the character have parents, or is the character an orphan?

2. During the story, does the main character leave home? Where is the character at the end of the story?

3. Does the main character's attitude change by the end of the story? How?

4. Are there clear opposites in the story, like good versus evil or innocence versus wisdom? What other opposites can you remember?

5. What details do you remember about the story? How would you describe the main action or what the main character looks like?

6. What does the author want children to learn from the story—if anything?

**2.** *Work in groups of four. Discuss your answers to the questions in Exercise 1. Do some of you remember the same stories? Even if you remember different stories, are your answers similar? Why might you have similar answers?*

**3.** *Study the questions and read* The Window *on pages 163–164. Then work with a partner to answer the questions.*

1. Who, or what, are the main characters? How old are the characters? Do the characters have parents, or are they orphans?

2. During the story, does the main character leave home? Where is the character at the end of the story?

3. Does the main character's attitude change by the end of the story? How?

4. Are there clear opposites in the story, like good versus evil or innocence versus wisdom? What other opposites can you see in this story?

5. What are the details about the characters, the action, and/or the setting that you remember after you have read the story? Why do you remember these details?

**4.** *Discuss your answers with the class. Is this story typical of stories for children? Why or why not?*

# The Window by Julia Williams

In a small living room, in a tiny neat apartment, in a tall apartment building, lived two pets. Lucy the parrot lived in a silver cage suspended high on a stand. From her silver cage she could see out the window of the apartment and down over the tops of the buildings and stores below. Cedric the rabbit lived in a red cage in the cozy corner of the living room, far from the window that let sunshine into the room. The two pets were the best of friends.

The children who looked after the pets were often away at school, so Lucy and Cedric talked together to make the days pass pleasantly. To play their favorite game, Lucy gazed out the window, down on the patchwork quilt of rooftops below, and described for Cedric what she saw outside. Oh, how Cedric wanted to see the things Lucy did, but his cage was nestled in the corner of the living room, and he could not see out the window.

"What do you see today?" Cedric would ask with anticipation.

"Cars," said Lucy, "many cars." And she told him about the red, blue, yellow, and white cars that passed on the gray street below. "They move without wings or legs," she said, "and talk by honking to each other. Can you hear them?"

"No," said Cedric sadly.

"I can see the park by the school," said Lucy. "It has green grass and swings. Our children might be playing on the swings."

"What are swings?" asked Cedric.

"They make the children fly without wings," said Lucy.

"Anything else?" asked Cedric, trying to imagine what Lucy was seeing.

"Airplanes," said Lucy. "Silver and white birds that fly without flapping their wings. I don't know how they do it," she muttered. "They fly higher than our apartment building and draw a long feather out behind them."

Cedric loved to listen to Lucy describe what she saw outside, and he longed to see out the window himself one day. He imagined

[1] **yikes** *interjection (informal)* said when something shocks or frightens you

the colorful cars, the flying children, and the feathered airplanes each night before he fell asleep.

Then one day, their children left for school without closing the door to Cedric's cage. "Lucy," called Cedric in excitement, "I can get out of my cage! I'm coming to the window today; I'm coming to the window now!"

Lucy was thrilled for Cedric. They would be able to look out the window together today.

Cedric leaped over the sill of his cage and hopped toward the window. He sat up on his hind legs and placed his tiny front paws on the window frame. "Yikes[1] . . . Lucy," Cedric said, "it's a very long way down."

"Of course it is," answered Lucy. "This window is up high in the sky."

Cedric looked down to the street below and his stomach felt jumpy and his insides felt itchy.

*(continued on next page)*

"Lucy," he whispered, "the cars are honking too much."

"Of course they are," said Lucy. "It's how they talk to each other."

"Lucy," Cedric hesitated, "the children are going to fall off the swings."

"Well, yes," said Lucy. "Sometimes that happens, but they usually get up again."

"Lucy?" Cedric breathed deeply. "The sunlight shining on the airplanes hurts my eyes."

"Really?" questioned Lucy. "I don't see them that way."

Cedric backed away from the window. Suddenly, he didn't want to see out the window. The loud cars, the wingless children, and the flashing airplanes were frightening him. Cedric knew where he wanted to be. He turned tail and zipped back to his cage, where the clean wood shavings smelled like the forest and his rabbit house offered him shelter.

"Lucy," he said. "I'm happy here."

"You're happy in your cage, and I'm happy looking out my window. There's nothing wrong with that," said Lucy.

This unit will help you learn to make inferences based on what a text implies or a speaker's intention. You will also learn to recognize and use a variety of rhetorical devices.

## Previewing the Academic Skills Focus

**1.** Read The Window *again. As you read, think about whether the story was written to teach children something. What does the author want children to learn from the story? Discuss in small groups.*

**2.** *When you answered the question in Exercise 1, what were you doing? Circle the best answer(s). Then discuss your answer(s) with the class.*

    a. forming generalizations

    b. drawing conclusions

    c. thinking critically about the text

    d. guessing at the author's meaning

    e. predicting what comes next

When you read or listen, you may need to make inferences about what you are reading or listening to. When you make an inference, you decide what you think is true based on the information that you have. This truth may not be clearly or explicitly stated by the writer or speaker; it is something that you figure out based on what you have read or heard.

When you answered the question in Exercise 1, you were making inferences about the text. Making inferences is similar to forming generalizations, drawing conclusions, thinking critically, guessing at meaning, and predicting the outcome.

The verbs *make* and *draw* are used with the noun *inference*; the preposition *about* is used afterward. You can *make* or *draw* an inference *about* something from the text or lecture. *Infer* is the verb form of *inference*.

### Examples

1. Based on the children's story *The Window*, you can infer that the author is telling children that home is the best and safest place to be.

2. The literature students drew the inference that in *The Window*, the author contrasts the wisdom of Lucy the parrot with the childlike innocence of Cedric the rabbit.

## 2

**Building Academic Reading Skills**

In this section, you will practice making inferences based on what a text implies. For online assignments, go to

---

**Key Word**

**genre** *n* a particular kind of art, music, or literature that has certain features that all examples of this type share

## Before You Read

**1.** *Here are some genres of music, art, and literature. Add any genres that you can to these lists. Then compare your answers with another student's.*

Music genres: classic, country, pop, rap, _____

Art genres: Renaissance, impressionism, cubism, _____

Literature genres: mystery, romance, biography, _____

**2.** *Find words in the reading on pages 167–168 that have the same meaning as the definitions provided. Use the paragraph numbers and the word forms in parentheses to help you locate the words in the text. Then check your answers with the class.*

1. (1 *n*) a children's story in which magical things happen _____*fairy tale*_____

2. (1 *n*) a long written story that is usually fictional _____

3. (2 *v*) to be appropriate for a particular person in specific circumstances

   _____

4. (7 *adj*) causing problems or additional work _____

5. (7 *n*) something that limits your freedom to do something you want

   _____

6. (8 *adj*) relating to a whole group of things rather than one thing

   _____

7. (8 *adv*) used to emphasize how unimportant something is

   _____

8. (9 *exp*) to be obviously dissimilar _____

9. (9 *v*) to develop in different ways _____

10. (10 *n*) a description of the main parts of something that can be used as a reference (pronounced 'skēmə) _____

### Key Words

**burdensome** *adj*
**constraint** *n*
**diverge** *v*
**fairy tale** *n*
**generic** *adj*
**merely** *adj*
**novel** *n*
**schema** *n*
**suit** *v*
**to bear no apparent relationship** *exp*

**3.** *Use the key words to complete the sentences.*

1. The book and the movie seem completely unrelated. They _____ to one another.

2. The children's preference was for traditional stories or _____ about talking animals.

3. The plot patterns in many children's stories show familiar similarities that readers can use as a _____ to analyze the stories.

4. The rabbit in *The Window* finds that he likes his cage best, despite its _____.

5. "We have books to _____ everybody's interests," said the librarian.

6. That character plays _____ a small role in the _____. She is not a significant character.

7. In the case of the copyright dispute, the judge saw that initially, the plots of the two tales were similar, but by the end, the plots had _____ and bore no apparent relationship to each other.

8. The standard romance plot has a male character who falls in love with a female character, but they cannot be together because of some obstacle; however, by the end of the story, the characters have overcome the obstacle, and they live happily ever after. This is so common that it is a _____ romance plot pattern.

9. Frequently, in children's literature, a character, who has been previously happy, finds new responsibilities to be _____. This change in circumstance forces the character to leave an otherwise comfortable home.

## Global Reading

**1.** *Read an excerpt on the next page from a children's literature textbook once quickly to answer the key question: What is the generic plot pattern in children's literature? Then discuss your answer with the class.*

## The Generic Plot Pattern in Children's Literature

1. Even though children's texts share similar qualities with similar texts written for adults, they also have much in common with one another as texts for children—and that includes everything from short picture books and fairy tales to comparatively long novels. They have enough in common to be identified as children's fiction. Children's literature can, then, usefully be considered a genre of literature in its own right.

2. What defines this genre? As the name *children's literature* suggests, it must be distinguished by qualities that are related to common ideas about children, about what they can understand and what they might enjoy. It seems logical that those assumptions would lead to the creation of a literature designed to suit that audience. In fact, the implied audience of most children's literature is the child defined by these assumptions: The child's major quality is limited knowledge and ability, and the child's major needs are to be protected and educated.

### A No-Name Story: The Basic Pattern

3. The following are descriptions of some texts for children that, based on previous experience of reading children's literature, reflect these assumptions and are typical of the genre of children's literature.

4. In Leo Lionni's *Fish Is Fish*, a fish is left behind in the pond when his childhood friend becomes a frog and goes off to see the world. When the frog returns with stories of glamorous sights, the fish resolves to leave the pond. After the frog saves the fish's life by flipping the fish back into the water, the fish concludes that it's better to stay at home.

5. In Lucy Prince Scheidlinger's *The Little Bus Who Liked Home Best*, a municipal bus becomes envious of the "great silver buses" on the superhighway. After joining them, he becomes confused by the traffic, and when he finally finds his way back, he concludes that home is best.

6. In Marjorie Flack and Kurt Wiese's *The Story about Ping*, a duck avoids punishment for being the last to return home by staying out on the river. Caught by a boy, the duck is threatened with death. After escaping, he happily returns home despite the inevitable punishment.

7. Though the details change, there's clearly a basic pattern underlying these stories: A young creature, an animal or an object with human characteristics, enjoys the security of a comfortable home until something happens to make it unhappy. The small creature leaves home and has exciting adventures. But the adventures turn out to be as dangerous or as discomforting as they are thrilling. Having learned the truth about the big world, the creature finally returns to the security it first found burdensome, concluding that, despite its constraints, home is best.

**Generic Schema**

Figure 8.1 The Home/Away/Home Pattern

8. This story is generic, like the "no-name" canned goods sold in supermarkets. Though not identical to it, many other texts for children relate significantly to it. These stories are not restricted to picture books. They can be found in both classic children's novels and ones written more recently. In Robert Louis

*(continued on next page)*

Stevenson's *Treasure Island*, published over a hundred years ago, the main character, Jim Hawkins, expresses boredom with the quietness of his home. After his exciting but dangerous experiences with pirates, he returns home convinced that nothing could make him wish for adventure again. At the end of *The Amber Spyglass* (2000), the last volume of Philip Pullman's *His Dark Materials* trilogy, the two main characters return not merely to the homes, but also to the home worlds they each left earlier—Lyra in the first book, *The Golden Compass*, and Will in the second book, *The Subtle Knife*. In between, they learn much about why home might be a good place to be.

9   Of course, not all children's literature follows this pattern. Many texts of fiction written for children bear no apparent relationship to it at all. Many poems for children diverge from the pattern simply because they don't tell stories, and have no sequence of narrative events. But the fact that the pattern does recur so often is suggestive. Its characteristics must satisfy many people's ideas about what children's literature is or should be.

10   Furthermore, once the pattern has been observed, it can be used as a schema, so that texts that seem different can be usefully understood as interesting variations on it. For instance, many books reverse the pattern. Instead of having a child leave home to confront danger, they describe a child's bedroom or home invaded by something that clearly belongs elsewhere. For example, in Maurice Sendak's *Where the Wild Things Are*, familiar objects in Max's room grow into a wild forest teeming[1] with monsters. Max's adventure ends when he decides he wants to return to the comfort of his familiar room. In most of these texts, the child is happy to have the calm of home restored in the end.

11   The story of L. M. Montgomery's *Anne of Green Gables* represents a different sort of an inversion on the pattern. A child whose life has been filled with troubling adventures arrives at a safe home at the beginning of the story. And many children's books follow the pattern of fairy tales such as *Cinderella* by describing how children journey away from homes whose security or happiness have been disrupted and finally find a new home representing the old security elsewhere. In yet one more inversion of the generic schema, J. K. Rowling's Harry Potter books start and end in a dangerous home, and Harry has adventures in what seems to be a more secure place in between.

---

[1] **teeming** *adj* full of animals and people who are moving around

Source: Nodelman, P., & Reimer, M. (2003). Children's literature as a genre. In *The pleasures of children's literature* (3rd ed.). Boston: Pearson Allyn & Bacon.

**2.** *Read the textbook excerpt again. Then answer the questions. Compare your answers with two other classmates'. Put your answers to question 6 up on the board to share with your class.*

1. Why is it reasonable to call children's literature a genre?

2. What assumptions about children are reflected in children's literature?

3. Do you know other children's stories that follow the generic plot pattern? What are they?

4. What does the prevalence of this generic story pattern suggest?

5. What is the value of having a schema for children's literature if not all stories follow this pattern?

6. Look at Figure 8.1 on page 167 that represents the generic schema. Then draw the four variations represented by the following children's books.

**Where the Wild Things Are**

**Anne of Green Gables**

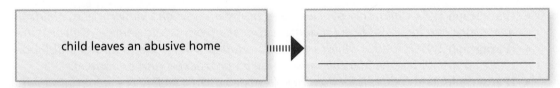

**Cinderella**

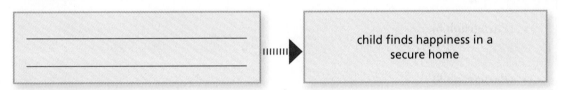

**Harry Potter**

**3.** Think back to the story you recalled from your childhood in the Preview section on page 162. Which plot pattern does your story fit, the generic schema or a variation? Work in your group of three. Briefly retell your story and indicate which plot pattern it represents.

# Focused Reading

As you know, drawing inferences is deciding what is likely to be true based on the information you have. To make your inference, gather as much information as you can from pictures, diagrams, titles, headings, and subheadings, as well as the full text.

**1.** *To help you answer inference questions about the text, first review the information from the reading by making an outline of the text. Then compare your outline with a classmate's. Create a shared outline on the board with the whole class.*

---

- **(Paragraph 1)** *As children's stories have many shared characteristics, children's literature can be considered a genre separate from adult genres of literature.*
- **(Paragraph 2)** *Stories for children reflect adult authors' ideas about childhood: that children are limited/vulnerable and must be protected and educated.*
- **(Paragraphs 3–6)** *Examples of children's stories that follow the generic schema.*
- **(Paragraph 7)**

- **(Paragraph 8)**

- **(Paragraph 9)**

- **(Paragraph 10)**

- **(Paragraph 11)**

---

**2.** *Work with a partner. Discuss the questions.*

1. Why does the author of the text provide so many examples of children's stories?

2. Why does most children's literature present children's characters who are limited and need to be protected and educated?

3. Do you think this generic schema applies only to modern children's stories, or only to children's stories from a single culture? Why?

**3.** *The reading on pages 167–168 does not have a formal academic conclusion. Work with a partner to make inferences about which pieces of information are most likely to be in the conclusion of this reading. For each one, explain why you believe it is appropriate to include it. Then confirm your answers with the class.*

1. Examples of another variation on the generic schema.

2. It is possible that everyone needs to read generic fiction to learn the basic story patterns that underlie all fiction.

3. Readers need to be familiar with the underlying plot patterns in order to appreciate the divergences of the more unusual patterns.

4. Even though many children's stories follow generic patterns, this does not make them uninteresting.

5. Children's stories that do not fit the generic schema should not be considered children's literature.

6. Traditional adult literature follows other generic patterns.

**Checkpoint 1** PEARSON LONGMAN myacademicconnectionslab

# Before You Listen

*To learn which words collocate with the key words, complete the sentences. There may be more than one answer. Then confirm your answers with the class.*

1. You can recap _____.

   (a.) a lecture    (b.) a story    (c.) the main points    d. a computer

2. Characters in children's stories are often limited but have redeeming _____.

   a. qualities    b. finances    c. features    d. vehicles

3. Children may only have a vague _____ about what generic narratives are.

   a. notion    b. idea    c. thought    d. construction

4. Most people have _____ tolerance for long autobiographies.

   a. limited    b. great    c. huge    d. little

5. The _____ protagonists in this story carry the action forward.

   a. main    b. secondary    c. significant

In this section, you will practice drawing inferences based on a speaker's intention. For online assignments, go to

PEARSON LONGMAN myacademicconnectionslab

**Key Words**

**protagonist** *n* main character

**recap** *v* to summarize the main points

**redeeming** *adj* doing or having something that makes you appear less bad

**tolerance** *n* the degree to which someone can suffer pain or difficulty without being harmed

**vague** *adj* unclear because someone doesn't give enough detailed information

# Global Listening

🎧 In this lecture, the professor makes five main points about children's literature. Listen to the lecture and fill in the chart with as much information as possible. Remember to write in point form as you won't have enough time to write full sentences while the lecture is in progress. Then compare your information with another student's. Listen again to fill in any gaps you might have.

| Main Point | Details |
|---|---|
| 1. Descriptive detail | |
| 2. Main characters are limited | |
| 3. Main characters are orphans | |
| 4. | |
| 5. | |

# Focused Listening

## Making Inferences about a Speaker's Intention

Although this may seem obvious, when your instructors lecture, they have a reason for saying everything they say. Every piece of information they tell you is provided for a purpose. However, this purpose—or intention—may not be obvious to you, and the instructors may not make these intentions explicit. Sometimes, you may need to figure out—or infer—the intention of the lecturer so you can understand the lecture better. You may need to answer the question, "Why did he/she say that?"

For example, your instructor may summarize information at the end of the lecture. If you didn't hear or understand the key phrase, "Let's review these points," you may wonder why the instructor is repeating the same information. However, if you realize that

- it is almost the end of the lecture,
- often instructors summarize the main points at the end of a lecture, if they have time,
- repetition of main ideas helps students remember them,

then you will be able to infer that the instructor is summarizing the main points at the end of the lecture for your benefit. (In this case, you should listen carefully and take point-form notes so that you will be able to confirm each of the main ideas in the lecture.)

This is an example of making an inference about the speaker's intention. You inferred that the lecturer is summarizing the main points to help you remember them better.

It is possible to make inferences based on information contained in a sentence or two—micro-level inferences. It is also possible to make inferences based on information contained in a paragraph or a whole story—macro-level inferences.

Examples of micro-level inferences include figuring out if the speaker is:

- Providing examples of a main point
- Showing contrasts to the main point
- Explaining a main point in more detail
- Creating a mental image for the listener
- Providing a simplified image of a complex idea

Examples of macro-level inferences include figuring out if:

- A statement introduces the topic or organization of the lecture
- A statement is true based on information given in a lecture
- There is a logical link between two or more points
- One event was before or after another event
- A story has a moral

🎧 *Listen to the lecture again. Then work with a partner. Circle the best answer to complete each statement. Use your notes from the chart on page 172 to help you. When finished, compare your answers with another pair's. If your answers are not the same, ask to hear the lecture one more time.*

1. The lecturer says, "Now I would like to discuss with you other characteristics of the genre of children's literature" because the lecturer _____.
   a. likes to talk about children's literature
   b. is announcing the topic of the lecture
   c. discussed something else in the previous lecture

2. The lecturer states that children's books have less descriptive detail than adult books and implies that this is because _____.
   a. children prefer action to description
   b. children are bored by visual detail
   c. children like stories about abstract concepts

3. Descriptive details likely to be found in children's literature are details about the (circle three) _____.
   a. landscape
   b. history of a location
   c. noise a machine makes
   d. color of an animal
   e. emotions of a character
   f. looks of a protagonist

4. The purpose of the word *however* when the lecturer says, "The generic story often informs children that they are too limited to cope with the world on their own; however, the characters often have some redeeming quality that saves them" is to _____.
   a. clarify the contrast between adult assumptions and reality
   b. indicate a difference of opinion about a protagonist's qualities
   c. contrast a positive quality with a negative quality
   d. emphasize how limited child protagonists are

5. The lecturer implies that in children's stories, parents are _____.
   a. overprotective
   b. evil
   c. absent
   d. unaware

6. The lecturer says, "This is a good point at which to consider another characteristic of children's literature—it often clearly shows opposition between two themes" because _____.
   a. the previous point was about the opposition of independence and security
   b. the lecturer thought the time was right to mention this point
   c. the speaker says this to introduce a long list of possible oppositions

7. The lecturer uses the word *instead* in the following sentence: "In books such as *Peter Rabbit* or *Where the Wild Things Are*, the complex ideas beneath the surface simplicity aren't explicitly stated. Instead they are implied." The word *instead* shows that the information that follows _____.
   a. develops the preceding idea
   b. contrasts with the preceding idea
   c. provides more explanation of the preceding idea
   d. shows an example of the preceding idea

**Checkpoint 2**  PEARSON LONGMAN myacademicconnectionslab

# 4

## Building Academic Writing Skills

In this section, you will learn about how authors use rhetorical devices to encourage readers to pay attention, to identify with the protagonists, or to visualize details about the story. Then you will use your knowledge of unit content and effective thesis statements to write an analytical essay about a children's story.

For online assignments, go to

**PEARSON LONGMAN**
**myacademicconnectionslab**

# Before You Write

## Introducing a Specific Book in an Essay or an Oral Presentation

When you are studying the field of literature, you must be able to introduce a specific book either in writing or in an oral presentation. There are a few established patterns that you can use to introduce a specific book. In all cases, when you first mention a specific book, you *must* identify both the author and the book title, and sometimes the year the book was published. When you mention the book for the second time, you can simply use the title. Look at the first mention examples of books included in this unit.

**Example 1:** In + author's name + *book title*, + main clause

In Leo Lionni's *Fish Is Fish* (1970), a fish is left behind in the pond when his childhood friend becomes a frog and goes off to see the world.

**Key features of Example 1:**

- Use the author's name in the possessive (*Leo Lionni's*)
- Italicize the book title (*Fish Is Fish*).
- Use a comma after the book title.
- After the comma, start a main clause that makes a statement about the content of the book.
- The date (in parentheses) is optional. It should be included if the date is important to the point you are making.

**Example 2:** In + *book title*, written by + author's name + in date, + main clause

In *Anne of Green Gables*, written by L. M. Montgomery in 1908, the plot is an inversion of the generic pattern.

**Key features of Example 2:**

- Italicize the book title (*Anne of Green Gables*).
- Use two commas: one after the book title and one after the date.
- Do not make the author's name possessive.
- After the second comma, start a main clause that makes a general statement about the content of the book.
- The date—not in parentheses—is optional. It should be included if the date is important to the point you are making.

If you are introducing a fable, a fairy tale, or a traditional story, it is unlikely you will know who the author is or the date when the story was first told or printed. These stories are old and have been retold and rewritten many times by many different authors. This is the only case where it is permissible to leave out the author's name.

**Example 3**

Many children's books follow the pattern of fairy tales such as *Cinderella*. They describe how children journey away from homes whose security or happiness have been disrupted and finally find a new home representing the old security elsewhere.

**Key features of Example 3**

- Italicize the story name (*Cinderella*).
- Follow with a general statement about the content of the book.

*Follow the steps to practice introducing a specific book in writing or an oral presentation.*

**Step 1:** Select three books. You can use any book that you might have with you; you might even use this book. It is best to use a book that you know something about. Your teacher may bring some books that you could use as well.

**Step 2:** In your notebook, write the author, the title, the date of publication, and a sentence about the content of each book. Here are some quick ideas about what to write.

- whether you like or dislike the book and why
- whether you find it interesting or boring and why
- whether you find it informative and why

**Step 3:** Combine this information in a single sentence as if you were introducing the book in an essay. Use the models from the skills box on page 175 to help you.

**Step 4:** When you have finished, practice your sentences orally, as if you were introducing the book in an oral presentation.

# Focused Writing

## Identifying and Using Rhetorical Devices

Rhetorical devices are ways of speaking or writing to create a specific effect. Authors usually want to create these specific effects because they want their readers to:

- Pay attention
- Identify with or recognize qualities in a character
- See a picture of the action, character, or setting

The rhetorical devices listed here are frequently used and discussed, particularly in the field of literature. They are listed according to the specific effect the author is trying to create.

To get readers to *pay attention*, an author might use:

1. **Alliteration**—the use of several words that begin with the same sound. This device is commonly used in poems for children, and even in newspaper and magazine titles.
   **Example**
   Are you **r**eady to **r**ead about **r**hetorical devices?

2. **Repetition**—doing or saying the same thing many times
   **Example**
   A *boogie* is a dance and a *boogie* is a jive and a *boogie's* just another way of saying I'm alive.[1]

3. **Parallelism**—the listing of similar items using similar grammatical forms (see Unit 1 for a more detailed explanation of parallelism)
   **Example**
   In a *small living room*, in a *tiny neat apartment*, in a *tall apartment building*, lived two pets.

---

[1] Lesynski, L. (1999). "Dirty Dog Boogie." Toronto: Annick Press (p. 4).

**1.** *Work with a partner. Identify the rhetorical devices in the examples from* The Window *on pages 163–164 and* Matt and the Killer Whale *(which you will read in the Integrated Task section). Choose from alliteration, repetition, and parallelism.*

| Example | Rhetorical Device |
|---|---|
| 1. Matt swam *deeper and deeper.* | *Repetition* |
| 2. *Down, down, down* he went. | |
| 3. He imagined *the colorful cars, the flying children, and the feathered airplanes.* | |
| 4. Then he set out to find the *deepest, darkest* part of the world's oceans. | |
| 5. He'd *climbed beside mountain goats, rung bells to scare away bears, and looked down on snow geese flying high in the sky.* | |

## Identifying and Using Rhetorical Devices (Cont'd)

To get readers to *identify with or recognize qualities in a character,* an author might use:

1. **Personification**—giving human characteristics to an animal or object OR a character who is the perfect example of a quality because they have a lot of it

    **Example**

    a. "I have been about the world—hopping here and there," said the frog.[1]

    b. In the fable of *Little Red Riding Hood,* the wolf is the personification of evil.

2. **Symbolism**—the use of an object or character to represent an idea or quality

    **Example**

    Symbolism is common in literature and life; white is often a symbol of purity, while roses are a symbol of love.

To get readers to *see a picture of the action, character, or setting,* an author might use:

3. **Imagery**—the use of sensory details to describe ideas or actions in literature

    **Example**

    I thought she was going to burst into flames she was so mad.[2]

4. **Metaphor**—a type of comparison in which the author describes the action, character, or setting by comparing it to something different

*(continued on next page)*

[1] Lionni, L. (1970). *Fish is fish.* New York: Alfred A. Knopf (p. 10).
[2] Gantos, J. (2000). *Joey Pigza loses control.* New York: Farrar, Straus and Giroux (p. 14).

**Example**

The game of baseball comes down to this—a caveman with a stick versus a caveman with a rock. And the pitcher is the caveman with the rock.[3]

5. **Simile**—an expression used to describe the action, character, or setting by comparing it to something else using the word *like* or *as*

**Example**

Then he kicked the dirt *like* he was trying to leave a bruise on the planet.[4]

These rhetorical devices can be useful tools to help you analyze an author's style of writing or to make your own writing more interesting.

---

[3] Gantos, J. (2000). *Joey Pigza loses control*. New York: Farrar, Straus and Giroux (p. 63).
[4] Gantos, J. (2000). *Joey Pigza loses control*. New York: Farrar, Straus and Giroux (p. 67).

**2.** *Work with the same partner. Identify the rhetorical devices illustrated by the examples from children's stories. Choose from personification, symbolism, imagery, metaphor, and simile.*

| Example | Rhetorical Device |
|---|---|
| 1. *Oh, how Cedric wanted to see the things Lucy did.* | *Personification* |
| 2. The angler fish had grinning mouths with *teeth as sharp as needles.* | |
| 3. The killer whale *winked* at Matt. | |
| 4. The airplanes *draw a long feather out behind them.* | |
| 5. Lucy gazed out the window, down on *the patchwork quilt of rooftops below*, and described for Cedric what she saw outside. | |
| 6. One of them jumped high out of the water in front of Matt's kayak, landing with a smack and *a lacy spray of white water.* | |

If you use metaphors and similes when you write or speak, you can create a picture in your readers' minds without having to show them a picture. This makes your writing more interesting and shows excellent mastery of language. Remember, a simile is a comparison using *like* or *as*; a metaphor makes a straight comparison.

**Examples**

1. My brother is so smart. His mind is a computer that processes information at the speed of light. (metaphor)

2. My aunt is like a modern building, with smooth, cool floors of marble and efficient elevators moving people quickly through her life. She never gives me a hug when we meet. (simile in the first sentence)

3. My child's hair is as soft as velvet. (simile)

4. He was so frightened that he was as white as a sheet. (simile)

**3.** Complete the sentences to create metaphors or similes (using either like or as). When you have finished, compare your answers with a classmate's. Have your classmate's metaphors and similes created pictures in your mind? Share the best ones with the class.

1. My mother is _____

   _____

2. My father is _____

   _____

3. My grandmother is _____

   _____

4. My home is _____

   _____

5. My kitchen is _____

   _____

## Integrated Writing Task

Your integrated skills assignment for this unit is to write an analytical essay about a children's story of your choice. Your essay will answer the following question: **Does the children's story that you selected share the characteristics of the children's literature genre?** You will use your knowledge of the content, vocabulary, rhetorical devices, and parallel structure to write your essay.

Before you begin to plan your essay, practice your analytical skills by reading the short story *Matt and the Killer Whale* on pages 180–181. As read, think about whether the story demonstrates the characteristics of the children's literature genre.

**a close call** *exp* a situation where something dangerous almost happens

**angler fish** *n* a type of fish with a huge mouth, sharp teeth, bulging eyes, and often a luminous stem used to attract predators; only found in deep oceans

**bathyscaphe** *n* a kind of submarine, usually rounded, that is used for deep sea exploration

**dorsal fin** *n* the thin part that sticks up from a fish that the fish uses to swim

**high time** *exp informal* used to say strongly that something should happen soon

**kayak** *n* a small, light boat, moved with a paddle, usually for one person

**killer whale** *n* a large black and white dolphin, mostly friendly, sometimes called an orca, sometimes called a killer whale; not a member of the whale family

# MATT
## and the
# KILLER WHALE

by Julia Williams

Matt was a nine-year-old boy who led the life of a mountain goat. All day long, and for days on end, he climbed the steep slopes of Mount Elizabeth, showing mountain climbers the trails that wound their way to the peak. He'd climbed beside mountain goats, rung bells to scare away bears, and looked down on snow geese flying high in the sky. But Matt was tired of all that now; tired of climbing up and looking down. He wanted to travel down, sink deep, and find the bottom of the seas. He wanted to explore the Mariana Trench.

Matt packed his flashlight and some food in a knapsack and said goodbye to his parents. Then he set out to find the deepest, darkest part of the world's oceans. He'd heard it might be hard to get there, but he wasn't worried.

Matt traveled by kayak down the Douglas Channel, paddling with the killer whales along the way. One of them jumped high out of the water in front of Matt's kayak, landing with a smack and a lacy spray of white water. The kayak rocked like a crazy rocking chair in the wake of the killer whale. "Hey," said Matt, "that was a close call. Don't come any closer!"

The killer whale winked at Matt. "That killer whale seems friendly," said Matt.

When Matt reached the Pacific Ocean, he traveled by steam boat. He and the captain fished for their dinner off the back of the boat. Sometimes Matt would see a killer whale's dorsal fin sticking up above the waves, but it was always in the distance.

Very soon, Matt was bobbing on the waves above the Mariana Trench.

"Matt," said the captain, "are you really going to explore the Mariana Trench? You'll need a bathyscaphe, strong lights, long lines! It's dangerous down there."

"I certainly hope so," said Matt. "I'm looking for an adventure. Can I borrow your diving suit?"

Matt pulled on the captain's diving suit, oxygen tank, and old flippers and dove over the side of the boat. Down, down, down he went. At 150 meters below sea level, he snapped on his flashlight so he could see better. The water was dark now, but far below him he could see the stars in the night sky. "Good grief," said Matt, "I thought the sky was above the water!"

As Matt swam deeper, the stars in the night sky below him turned into glow lights, each lighting the way into the mouth of a ferocious angler fish. Their grinning mouths had teeth as sharp as needles. Well, Matt got busy swimming away from those angler fish!

He swam deeper and deeper. The deeper he went, the warmer the water became until he was as warm as toast. "Why am I so warm?" thought Matt. He could see long streams of super-heated water boiling up from the ground. "Ah," said Matt, "these are smoking thermal vents. I'm at the very bottom of the

Mariana Trench; the bottom of the world."

He swam with the crabs and the shrimp for a few minutes, but then decided it was high time to head for the surface. As he swam up through the sea, an angler fish snapped at him. The needle teeth clipped his oxygen line! The remaining oxygen whooshed from his tank. Matt swam as fast as he could, trying to reach the surface before he ran out of air.

Suddenly, a killer whale swam underneath him and pushed him up to the surface! Matt surfaced with a laugh of wonder. "Thanks my friend," said Matt. "That was a close call!"

The killer whale winked at him. That killer whale followed Matt all the way back to the Douglas Channel. When Matt finally climbed back up Mount Elizabeth to his parents' home, his mother said, "Matt, we were a bit worried about you."

"I've seen the bottom of the Mariana Trench, met an angler fish, and was saved by a friendly killer whale," said Matt.

"Sounds like quite an adventure," said his father.

"Yes," said Matt. "I'm going to Niagara Falls next."

**1.** *Work in small groups to analyze Williams's* Matt and the Killer Whale *(2008). Use the chart to help you with the analysis. Then discuss your analysis with the class.*

| Common Characteristic of Children's Literature | Characteristic of *Matt and the Killer Whale* |
|---|---|
| 1. Does the plot follow the typical home/away/home pattern, or is it a variation on the generic schema? | |
| 2. What rhetorical devices does the author use to make the reader pay attention, identify or recognize the qualities in a character, or see a picture of the action, character, or setting? Choose from:<br>• Alliteration/repetition/parallelism<br>• Personification/symbolism<br>• Imagery/metaphor/simile | |
| 3. Does the story share the characteristics typical of children's literature?<br>• minimal but concrete and visual detail<br>• child or childlike protagonists that are limited in some way but have redeeming qualities<br>• orphan protagonists that allow for the exploration of the conflicting desires of independence and security<br>• contrasting themes in clear opposition, like good versus evil | |
| 4. Does the story instruct children? Infer the moral of the story. | |
| 5. Overall, do you think the story is representative of the genre of children's literature? Why? | |

**2.** *Follow the steps to write your essay.*

**Step 1:** Select a children's story to use for this assignment. You may select one you remember from your childhood or one that your teacher brings to class. Collect the information that you need to introduce the book in your essay: author's name, title, and date of publication.

**Step 2:** Recall or read your story carefully. Ask yourself whether the story demonstrates the characteristics common to the genre of children's literature. Use the chart on page 183 to help you think about this.

| Common Characteristic of Children's Literature | Your Story's Characteristics |
|---|---|
| 1. Does the plot follow the typical home/away/home pattern, or is it a variation on the generic schema? | |
| 2. What rhetorical devices did your author use to make the reader pay attention, identify or recognize the qualities in a character, or see a picture of the action, character, or setting? Choose from: <br>• alliteration/repetition <br>• personification/symbolism <br>• imagery/metaphor/simile | |
| 3. Does your story share the characteristics typical of children's literature? <br>• minimal but concrete and visual detail <br>• child or childlike protagonists that are limited in some way but have redeeming qualities <br>• orphan protagonists that allow for the exploration of the conflicting desires of independence and security <br>• contrasting themes in clear opposition, like good versus evil | |
| 4. Does the story instruct children? Infer the moral of the story. | |
| 5. Overall, do you think your story is representative of the genre of children's literature? Why? <br>This will form the thesis of your essay. | |

**Step 3:** Write your essay. This plan may help you:

- Paragraph 1—Introduction to the essay. Be sure to introduce the book using the appropriate information. Is your story representative of the genre of children's literature? Your answer to this question will form your thesis.
- Paragraph 2—Brief summary of your story. This summary will help your readers understand the rest of the commentary on your story.
- Paragraph 3—Discuss the plot pattern. Be sure to include information from the textbook reading in this section.

- Paragraph 4—Highlight the rhetorical devices used in this story. Be sure to include information from Focused Writing on pages 176–179 here.
- Paragraph 5—Discuss whether the story shares the common characteristics of the children's literature genre. Be sure to include information from the lecture here.
- Paragraph 6—Draw an inference about the implied moral of the story.
- Paragraph 7—Write a concluding paragraph.

**Step 4:** Ask your teacher or a classmate to review your essay based on the features listed in the checklist.

| Features of Your Essay | Yes | No |
| --- | --- | --- |
| Is there a clear introduction with a thesis? | | |
| Is the story introduced correctly with the author's name, the title, and the date of publication? | | |
| Is there a brief summary of the story? | | |
| Does the essay explain whether the story is typical of the genre of children's literature? Does the essay refer to information from the reading and the lecture of the unit? | | |
| Does the inferred moral of the story seem believable? | | |
| Are the points supported with specific examples from the story? | | |
| Is the vocabulary specific to the topic of children's literature? | | |

**Step 5:** Based on the information in the checklist, revise your essay and hand it in.

# AUDIOSCRIPT

## UNIT 1

## Urban Planning: Safe Cities

### Global Listening

*Exercise 1, Page 11*

**Professor:** OK, now. Let's think about what large cities were like in the 19th century, that's the late 19th century, 1880, circa 1890, around then. So, you've been reading about the living conditions of residents living in large cities back then. Urban areas at the time, you remember, were dirty, smelly, and noisy; the people who lived there were impoverished, and they suffered from poor health. So what we know of modern cities grew out of disgust and unhappiness with that situation. At the time, city planners believed that it was the city itself that created these horrible conditions: they thought cities were evil, unsafe, and offensive to nature. Therefore in reaction to those conditions, new ideals, new visions emerged of what a healthy city might be. And these ideas have influenced city planning for over a century.

### Lecture: Visions of the Modern City

**Professor:** OK, now. Let's think about what large cities were like in the 19th century, that's the late 19th century, 1880, circa 1890, around then. So, you've been reading about the living conditions of residents living in large cities back then. Urban areas at the time, you remember, were dirty, smelly, and noisy; the people who lived there were impoverished, and they suffered from poor health. So what we know of modern cities grew out of disgust and unhappiness with that situation. At the time, city planners believed that it was the city itself that created these horrible conditions: they thought cities were evil, unsafe, and offensive to nature. Therefore in reaction to those conditions, new ideals, new visions emerged of what a healthy city might be. And these ideas have influenced city planning for over a century.

OK, now. One of these solutions was proposed by Howard, by Ebenezer Howard... Ebenezer Howard. He was English. Uh, Howard looked at the...at all the problems of London, and in 1898, he proposed building new cities in the countryside—he called them "Garden Cities." He thought that the Garden City would be a solution to the problems of big cities, big cities like London. His idea was to take city residents and spread them out over the countryside. The idea was that the poor people of the large city would be able to live close to nature. It's not that they would just lounge around, no; they would still have to work. So, in these cities, the industry would be grouped together in one specific place. I mean, schools, housing,

cultural activities, each would have their own separate places, and a garden—or a public park, something like that—would be in the middle, in the middle of the city. The population of each city would be limited to 32,000 people or so; so essentially, this meant that the Garden City would never become another London. What he, what Howard was doing was separating the different functions of a city into areas, so housing was separate from industry, industry from cultural activities, and so on. You get the idea. In fact, this was the first deliberate planning of a suburban area. For example, Stockholm, Stockholm Sweden, is built this way. And so is Vancouver.

So what about this plan? Sounds pretty good. But let's think about it for a moment. Now, once the town was built, it wasn't easy to make changes. Because it wouldn't account for growth or any kind of changes. So if the industry changed, or the population grew... That's a problem. And because the homes, the residential areas, are separate from the workplaces and from the cultural activities and the like—large suburban areas are empty during the day. And what does that mean? It's the perfect place for property crime.

OK. Now, another approach to the problems of large cities was the "Radiant City." This was developed, this idea was developed by a Swiss architect named Le Corbusier in the 1920s. Got that? His dream city—the Radiant City—was composed of mainly, mainly of skyscrapers, skyscrapers within a park. It was a vertical city—with about 1,200 people per acre—that's 300,000 people per square kilometer. Now that's an extraordinarily high population density. But, here's the key thing... the buildings would occupy only 12% of the ground. And the rest of the land—that's 88%—would be open, remain open for parks and recreation. The idea was to bring the country into the city. City into the country—Howard. Country into the city—Le Corbusier. Le Corbusier's plan also included wide highways for express one-way traffic and underground streets for heavy vehicles. Now, there wouldn't be many small streets because he—Le Corbusier—thought pedestrians should be off the streets... and in the parks. The downtown cores of Toronto, Hong Kong, São Paulo are all examples of this Radiant City idea.

Now, this was a creative solution, but it definitely created some problems. We can see, this makes sense that, it became the basis of our "car culture" of today. Streets were not pedestrian friendly—the spaces were so wide and large that no one could walk anywhere, and most of the roads were highways, so it wasn't safe to walk along them anyway. And Le Corbusier created the same problem that Howard did—he separated out the functions of the city—work from home, etc. creating unsafe city zones.

OK. Another idea, the last one we're going to talk about today, is "The City Beautiful," proposed by Daniel Burnham—Burnham—of Chicago…in 1909. Now his idea was that the inner-city slums, which were the only residential areas in the downtown core, should be cleared away and people should build their cultural center—the civic center—in the middle of the city. Tear down the slums and rebuild. All the important buildings and monuments would be arranged along a single boulevard. The idea was to create the grandest impression possible. Which meant residences were moved into the suburbs, and streets were gently curved, they would be curved, not organized along a grid. Brasilia, Paris, Lisbon, these are all examples of the "City Beautiful." But you know, in many City Beautiful cities—not all—people weren't naturally drawn into the main monument area of the cities, so they did not become busy city centers.

So this is what happens, this is what happens with all three of these models. They all separate housing from business, and industry, and cultural activities. So, this leaves certain areas of the cities empty at certain times of the day—the residential areas in the daytime, the business areas at night. Think about it.

Alright, well now, it's almost time, so for next class, this is what I'd like you to do: I'd like you to think about whether or not living in each of these ideals would be safe and why. Jane Jacobs' book *The Death and Life of Great American Cities* shocked urban planners—the "experts" of the day—with its radical ideas about safety. We're going to talk about that. And also, for next time I want you to read the following pages…

# UNIT 2

## Business: Leadership Behavior

### Lecture: Behavioral Theories of Leadership

**Professor:** OK. To start, let's review what we talked about last class. We talked about trait theories of leadership, and some of the weaknesses of trait research in relation to leadership. Now, you'll recall that the identification of specific traits in successful leaders, like…intelligence, energy, dominance, emotional stability, and the like, while it was useful at describing leaders, did not solve the 'chicken or the egg' problem: that is, it didn't explain which came first. Did the traits create the leaders, or did the leadership position create the traits? And this weakness meant we couldn't apply the research findings to any real-life situations. We couldn't select leaders based on the traits they demonstrated, because we didn't know if the leaders had those traits first, or if they were likely to develop the traits later once they had the leadership position. That was a problem.

Consequently, researchers in the field of leadership began to think that maybe what made a great leader, or an effective and successful one, was *not* the leader's traits. Maybe, what made a leader great was his or her behavior. Now, behavioral theories of leadership try to identify critical behaviors of leaders, in the hopes that we could *train* people to be leaders.

In the 1940s and 50s, researchers at Ohio State University developed a list of more than 1,800 or so specific behaviors that leaders might use. This list included behaviors such as telling employees what to do (being directive), um… another one, being friendly, setting goals for others, and so on. Then the employees were asked to rate their managers on these behaviors—you know—determine whether the manger demonstrated the behaviors, and to what extent. When the researchers put all their data together, they discovered that most leader behaviors were related to one of two main orientations. These two orientations were called consideration and initiation. Consideration and initiation behaviors are complementary. They can both be used at the same time.

Let me give you definitions of consideration and initiation orientations. Consideration behaviors on the part of the leader show that leaders trust, respect, and value good relationships with his or her followers. To complement consideration behaviors, initiation behaviors are what the leader does to get the work done. Assigning individual tasks, looking ahead, setting goals, deciding how the work should be done, and pushing the employees to do their work are all examples of initiation behaviors.

OK, I have a real life example of how consideration and initiation behaviors play out in real life. This is the case of David Pottruck, co-CEO of Charles Schwab and Company—that's a brokerage company—he started out by using initiation behaviors. He was very directive, he used a competitive approach to leading. He didn't show consideration behaviors. As a result, one day, the boss, Charles Schwab, told Pottruck that he had discovered their employees didn't like working with him. The employees felt that Pottruck was forcing his ideas on them, not asking them what they thought, and not asking for their agreement on projects.

As it turned out, Schwab helped Pottruck change his leadership style by hiring an "executive coach" who showed him how to incorporate consideration behaviors into his leadership style. These days, Pottruck shows consideration by explaining problems to his employees and getting their input first. For example, when he realized that the company should probably keep its branch offices open on Saturdays, he explained the need to his branch managers, and also recognized that this might be a big problem for them. Rather than resisting the Saturday openings, his branch managers understood the problem, and agreed to work with him to find the best solutions for their employees. Now Pottruck uses consideration behaviors often to encourage cooperation and teamwork, as well as initiation behaviors to get work done.

But just as behavior research has its strengths, it also has a weakness—just like trait theory did. Behavioral researchers in leadership began to see that the situation the leader was in had a large influence on the kind of behavior that was effective. Therefore, researchers began to look at the situations that caused leaders to behave in certain ways. They discovered a few things.

- When employees experience a lot of stress due to deadlines, or unclear tasks, initiation behaviors will increase employee satisfaction and performance.
- Also, when the job is interesting and rewarding for employees, leaders can use fewer consideration behaviors; the employees are simply motivated by their work, and don't need motivation from their boss.
- When the work is clearly defined, and the employees are experienced, leaders who use consideration behaviors will increase satisfaction. Those who use initiation behaviors will decrease satisfaction.
- When the work is NOT clearly defined—or undefined—or the workers are inexperienced, then they'll appreciate a leader who uses initiation behaviors because the leader gives them guidance in what to do.

So in conclusion, clearly, the situation or the context of the job is very important, too. Leaders should consider the situation as a factor in determining how they should behave. So this information means that we need to look next at situational theories of leadership—that is, how the situation can affect how a leader should behave. Right, so we'll leave it at that for now. Your homework is to read about situational theories of leadership for next class.

## Before You Speak

### Exercise 2, Page 42

**Student:** There are three major styles of leadership that can be used in any leader-subordinate, or employer-employee, situation.

Managers can be autocratic—which means they issue orders and expect the orders to be obeyed without question. Military commanders have to be autocratic leaders, especially on the battlefield. They make the decisions, and everyone else has to follow. This style is good for fast decision making because no one else is consulted. It is also useful in situations where an industry leader has to make a fast decision to beat out a competitor.

The second style of management is the democratic style. These managers generally ask for input from subordinates before making decisions but make the final decisions themselves. In this case, the manager may ask other group members to interview and offer opinions about someone applying for a job, but the manager will make the final hiring decision.

In contrast, the third management style is called the free-reign style (like letting the reins hang loose when you are riding a horse). This kind of manager acts like an adviser to subordinates, and it is the subordinates who are allowed to make decisions. If you were the chairperson of a volunteer committee that was raising funds for a new library or a piece of hospital equipment, you might use the free-reign style.

The relative effectiveness of any leadership style depends largely on the desire of subordinates to share input or be creative.

# UNIT 3

## Environmental Science: Forest Fires

### Lecture: The Benefits of Forest Fires

**Professor:** Well, hello everyone. Some of the statistics on forest fires are quite sobering; they damage or destroy many square kilometers of land each year, and many lives have been lost fighting fires. It's also true that the effects of forest fires can be quite complex—helping some plants and animals survive, while destroying others. However, today we'll talk about the beneficial effects of forest fires.

In the early 1980s, the results of some careful research demonstrated that there were some benefits to forest fires. These results indicated that wildfires were a "natural" event in the lifecycle of a forest, and that wildfires actually helped maintain a healthy forest—so forest fires were, in fact, good for the ecosystem. For example, research proved that wildfires are important to maintaining the diversity of the woodlands and bushlands of eastern and southern Africa, and the eucalyptus forests in Australia.

Let's discuss some of the ecological benefits of forest fires.

First, naturally occurring wildfires—usually started by lightening strikes—are often small—they don't burn much forest, and they don't get too hot. These "small" fires actually protect forests from large scale combined crown, surface and ground fires. This may seem strange, but most small forest fires don't have enough heat to burn the big trees. Trees taller than 6 to 13 feet high have thick enough bark to protect them from burning at low temperatures. This means smaller fires burn away all the accumulated organic matter on the forest floor; you know—years of leaves, twigs and branches—foresters call this stuff "litter"—without damaging the taller trees. In fact, these kinds of low temperature fires can actually strengthen big trees as the fires can burn away all the smaller shrubs and bushes that might compete with the big trees for resources—water and soil nutrients.

So it's a bit ironic. Small forest fires actually reduce the risk of large-scale destructive forest fires. Once the "litter" has been burned away on the forest floor, the forest is safer from high temperature fires—the combined crown, surface and ground fires that can do real damage to the tall trees.

Alright. Second, forest fires improve soil quality. The "litter" on the forest floor would normally decompose very slowly. The fire releases the nutrients in the litter right away—creating an increase in the amount of phosphorus and potassium available to the forest plants, which are key elements to promote tree growth. This makes the soil rich for further seed growth, too. The heat from a fire stimulates soil microorganisms, which again promote growth.

To have a balanced view of the effects of forest fires, yes, we must also consider the damage wildfires have on some plants and animals. The effects of fires on forests are really quite complex, but that's a matter for another lecture. We will be discussing the more complex effects next week.

Let's see, which point are we on now? Oh, oh yes, third, forest fires reduce tree disease and pests. Trees that do burn in low-temperature fires are likely to be trees that have diseases or are infested with pests. These trees are weakened by their conditions, and the fires can eliminate—or at least reduce—the spread of diseases and pests to other trees.

Next, forest fires encourage seed growth. Yes. Low-temperature fires encourage seed growth—or the germination of plants because some trees—usually varieties of pine trees —produce pine cones (with their seeds inside) that need to be exposed to heat before the cone opens and releases the seeds. The heat from the fire opens the pine cones which release their seeds. And the seeds benefit from the improved quality of the soil.

Finally, forest fires have a beneficial effect in that they open up the canopy. In a mature forest, the canopy captures the heat of the sun, and prevents the warmth from reaching the forest floor. A forest burn will open up the canopy and allow the energy from the sun to reach the forest floor. This creates room for some of the bigger animals, like deer and moose, to live in the forest. So it contributes to animal diversity within the forest. The heat of the sun on the forest floor also encourages smaller plants to grow, and this makes the biology of the forest more diverse—you know—it contributes to biodiversity— which makes the forest more resistant to disease and insect pests.

To conclude, these are quite significant benefits. These benefits, combined with the realization that forest fires are a natural part of forest ecosystems, changed forest management practices. As long as fires are far away from homes, communities, and stands of valuable trees, foresters often choose to let the wildfires burn.

Please read the article in your courseware package about the severe forest fires in Canada's British Columbia. This will give you an idea of what happens when fires do approach human habitations.

# UNIT 4

## Art History: Defining Cubism

### Lecture: Cubism as Fashion Art

**Professor:** Hello everyone. Let me remind you—we've been talking about how influential cubism was, as an art movement. Today we want to think about whether we can consider cubism as skillful—especially the later forms of cubism, like synthetic cubism—when Picasso began gluing objects onto the canvas, and cubist construction—when he began building objects.

By the way, I should mention that there will be a new exhibit of cubist art work on display at the art museum downtown this spring. It will feature some of Picasso's more recent sketches

that have never been displayed before. I recommend that you all try to attend when it opens. OK, back to our lecture.

I want you to think about this. All art movements begin with a new idea. An art movement begins as a way of representing new ideas in the clearest possible way. So novelty, or newness, is a key element in art. However, great art must also be skillful. Somehow, the artist must demonstrate some technical skill, right? The work must be skillfully impressive —otherwise it is nothing but invention—like a piece of machinery. Traditionally, art has always been a mixture of novelty and skill. It's a balance—really good art has equal measures of skill and novelty.

Now, let me introduce you to the term "fashion art." Now, fashion art is a whole new ball game. Artists who create fashion art change their art simply because they desire novelty, and they hope that novelty will generate sales. Art becomes fashion art when novelty becomes more important than skill. The balance is lost. Fashion art is new, and will attract buyers because it is different, but there is rarely much skill involved. Oh, another point about fashion art is that it stimulates even more fashion art, since the novelty of the art wears off quickly. That's when the public sees the lack of skill in the art work. Then there is demand for new novelties, and a new stage of art is produced to satisfy the demand.

My hypothesis is that the various forms of cubism—especially when cubism evolved into synthetic cubism and construction —are fashion art. Let's look at some examples, and you can be the judge.

From 1907 to 1911 Picasso was in his analytical cubism stage. We begin by looking at a slide that you should be familiar with, as you read about it in your textbook.

This painting is called *Portrait of Daniel-Henry Kahnweiler*, and it is an excellent example of analytical cubism. You can see here Picasso painting objects and spaces into geometric shapes and cubes that interlock—merging the figure with the background. The perspective is flat. The colors are minimal, but the canvas "shimmers." The true form of the subject is suggested, so the painting is not completely abstract, but "reality" is less important than the concept of the subject. This painting demonstrates both Picasso's novel idea and skill.

Picasso took the cubist idea of breaking up shapes and space into angled planes and applied it to sculpture. Now, here is Picasso's *Woman's Head*, completed in 1909. You can see how he has transferred the idea of cubism from a flat canvas to a three-dimensional object. I would argue that this sculpture still demonstrates some skill, so I wouldn't call this piece fashion art.

But Picasso also wanted to experiment with other forms of representation, and this lead to synthetic cubism. Now we move into what I call the fashion art period of cubism. Picasso was experimenting with his art for the sake of novelty, to generate sales, not to make art more expressive, or to move art forward.

From 1912 to 1914 he worked at synthetic cubism. In his *Still life with Chair Caning*, Picasso took a piece of cloth and painted it to look like the seat of a chair. The word *jou*, which may be a reference to the French word *jouer* (to play) or *jouet* (toy) suggests that Picasso was playing with reality. What do you think? Is it skillful?

His *Guitar* is an open construction. Volume is suggested by a series of flat and projecting planes. Picasso turned the guitar sound hole (in reality an empty space) into a cylinder. Incidentally, you may have seen this image of a guitar around town—even today it is used occasionally. It was used to promote a number of popular music bands in the 1920s, so it certainly caught the popular imagination.

Picasso later moved into collage—a combination of glued paper and drawing.

By gluing paper on canvas, Picasso created *Guitar, Sheet Music and Wine Glass*, and *Man with a Hat*. By the time he reached this stage of cubism, he was no longer creating art that represented the idea of cubism—he was generating pieces of fashion art that were "novel," but lacked skill. This is what I call fashion art.

The textbooks don't make this distinction between art and fashion art. The textbooks will tell you that Picasso's works are all masterpieces. For our next class, be prepared to discuss whether you think Picasso's synthetic cubism and construction cubism are examples of great art, or fashion art.

# UNIT 5

## Sociology: Innovation

### Global Listening
*Exercise 1, Page 103*

**Professor:** Today we're going to discuss how innovation diffuses—in other words—how change spreads. Specifically, we want to look at one of the most significant channels of diffusion—I think you know what that is? Right, the mass media. As you know, the mass media (Internet, newspapers, radio, television, and the like)—the mass media are very influential. That is undeniably true. However, you might be surprised to learn that the influence of the mass media has some limitations.

### Lecture: Mass Media and Diffusion of Innovation

**Professor:** Today we're going to discuss how innovation diffuses—in other words—how change spreads. Specifically, we want to look at one of the most significant channels of diffusion—I think you know what that is? Right, the mass media. As you know, the mass media (Internet, newspapers, radio, television, and the like)—the mass media are very influential. That is undeniably true. However, you might be surprised to learn that the influence of the mass media has some limitations.

OK. So, let's begin. Every day we are inundated by mass media messages trying to get us to do something, to change something, or try some new product. But most research about the mass media suggests that they have limited direct effects for producing change.

Let's look back first. Before the printing press was invented in the fifteenth century, there had to be direct contact between people, and cultures, for information to spread. Once the printing press was invented, there was a new possibility: the diffusion of innovation without physical contact between cultures. However, there was a problem. To receive information, people had to be able to read. Literacy was historically in the hands of just a few people—for example, the rich, the scribes, or monks. So the real impact of print media was dependent on the development of mass education and literacy. And this is the first limitation of mass media—it depends on literacy and education. In the twentieth century, of course, the number of literate people was much larger than it had ever been, but illiteracy is a phenomenon that limits the effectiveness of print media even today in some developing nations. And electronic media still suffers from this limitation. If people can't read, they can't get access to the innovation the media describes.

Radio and television have great potential for the mass diffusion of innovation because they don't require literacy. But like the limitations of print media, the absence of education, and the lack of resources to purchase these items limit the diffusion of information technology. So lack of education, money, and access limit the direct effect of the mass media.

Alright, I can hear you saying it, but in the literate and developed countries, mass media is "king." There can be no other limitations for this channel of diffusion. Right? But let's think about this. Mass media offers one-way communication with limited capacity for feedback from audiences who listen, read, or watch. Recipients of mass communication such as newspapers, magazines, television, and radio can't really ask questions, get clarification, or talk back in any meaningful way. The interesting thing about this is that effective persuasion to adopt change usually requires interactive communication between an individual promoting change and an individual who might adopt the innovation. Direct effects of mass-media communication are limited until they're modified by interpersonal communication among people who tuned to the same media message. You're very likely to discuss media messages with friends, family members, and classmates, and these conversations will critically reshape the impact of the messages. So lack of personal interaction is another limitation of the mass media.

Perhaps this explains the power of the Internet. People can learn about innovations, new technologies and ideas, and discuss them with others all through the same channel. That's a very powerful thing, as you well know.

And there are other factors that limit the ability of the mass media to diffuse innovation. The selective exposure, perception, and retention that people bring to their media exposure limit its ability to persuade people to change. People who initially feel positively about a particular innovation and change are the ones most likely to be receptive to mass communication about it. For example, television messages about voting for a certain political party (whatever the party)… are most likely to have positive impacts on people favorably inclined toward that party in the first place. People are, in other words, most likely to pay attention to and remember information about those things that they feel positive about to begin with. What people bring to the media is at least as important as what media bring to people.

The actual effects of mass media are quite complex. Research suggests that mass media are successful at intensifying or reducing the intensity of existing attitudes and opinions. However, they are not successful, or not very successful, at creating new attitudes and opinions or converting people to new attitudes and opinions. And this limitation is mostly a result of the fact that diffusion of innovation occurs primarily when there is reinforcement through interpersonal communication in an informal group context.

But, for sure, the media can have important long-term effects on social change. They may not be able to get individuals to believe or try new things. They do, however, help socialize people and can shape the culture of knowledge, attitudes, and behavior that people bring to media exposure.

## Focused listening

*Exercise 2, Page 104*

**Student 1:** I don't really believe that the mass media has any limitations. The influence of television and the Internet is so pervasive, they can change anyone's opinion you know, they reach almost everyone on the planet.

**Student 2:** I've never thought about it before, but if I'm not interested in what's on TV one night, I don't bother to watch it. For example, I don't listen to political advertisements; I'm not very interested in politics.

**Student 3:** I'm going out tonight, and I won't be thinking about innovation or channels of innovation diffusion! I'm going to see a movie.

## Before You Write

*Exercise 2, Page 106*

## Lecture: Individuals as Channels of Innovation Diffusion

**Professor:** I talked last class about the mass media—and its limitations—as channels of innovation diffusion, but I also want to touch upon the influence of individuals as channels of innovation diffusion. So this is what you need to know about individuals as channels of innovation diffusion. Individuals, specifically opinion leaders, can have significant direct effects on how the rest of the population perceives innovations.

Scholars have identified two kinds of opinion leaders: cosmopolitan leaders, and local opinion leaders.

Cosmopolitan leaders are people with an extraordinarily large network of friends and acquaintances…think of the people on Facebook who have the most friends—somewhere in the tens of thousands. They almost always belong to a wide variety of established groups, and have a wide range of interests. This allows them to diffuse information about innovations amongst groups. They have so many contacts that they can spread information quickly throughout a broad and diverse spectrum of society.

Local opinion leaders also have large numbers of contacts. However, in contrast with cosmopolitan leaders, the contacts of a local opinion leader are usually within one interest group. Now, local opinion leaders may belong to many groups, and are probably central figures in their groups, but the groups are mostly focused on the same interest or topic. In other words, they have a very deep reach into a single community of people. Cosmopolitan leaders have a wide reach into *many* communities, and local opinion leaders have a deep reach into a *single* community.

Together, these kinds of leaders have a significant impact on the rest of the population, and they are not limited by the kinds of limitations that the mass media experiences.

# UNIT 6

## Physical Science: Nanotechnology

### Global Listening

*Exercise 1, Page 122*

**Professor:** We've all heard of the iPod Nano; your friends tell you they'll be ready in a nanosecond. The prefix *nano-* is becoming commonplace in our vocabulary and our ideas. But what does *nano* actually mean? As science and math students you will know that *nano* means a *billionth*. So when your friend says, "I'll be with you in a nanosecond," he really means he'll be there in one billionth of a second. A nano*meter* is—that's right—a billionth of a meter, or about the length of six atoms. Not very big!

But what do you know about nanotechnology? Nanotechnology is the science of "how molecules do things." It is the science of how molecules, and even atoms, are used to create new materials, new processes, and new machines. These tiny molecules can be put to work to substantially improve our quality of life.

Richard Feynman, the physicist and Nobel Laureate, started the nanotechnology revolution in 1959 when he gave an influential speech entitled "There's Plenty of Room at the Bottom." In his speech he argued that small machines can work more efficiently—using less power—and are cheaper to manufacture. Therefore, he suggested that research should focus on developing technology that is small. He suggested that scientists and medical researchers should look for ways to develop molecules that could perform surgery, devices that could store data on a pinhead, and minuscule generators that could generate power to run computers.

While Feynman's vision was inspirational, researchers just didn't have the tools to work on such a small scale. Until 1990 that is, when a new microscope—the atomic force microscope—was invented. This microscope has a minuscule needle that can move atoms and molecules around. The microscope can be used to manipulate and reorganize atoms. This opened the door to the nanoscale, allowing scientists to develop all kinds of tiny new 'things.'

## Lecture: The New Small Is Big

**Professor:** We've all heard of the iPod Nano; your friends tell you they'll be ready in a nanosecond; the prefix *nano-* is becoming commonplace in our vocabulary and our ideas. But what does *nano* actually mean? As science and math students you will know that *nano* means a *billionth*. So when your friend says, "I'll be with you in a nanosecond," he really means he'll be there in one billionth of a second. A nano*meter* is—that's right—a billionth of a meter, or about the length of six atoms. Not very big!

But what do you know about nanotechnology? Nanotechnology is the science of "how molecules do things." It is the science of how molecules, and even atoms, are used to create new materials, new processes, and new machines. These tiny molecules can be put to work to substantially improve our quality of life.

Richard Feynman, the physicist and Nobel Laureate, started the nanotechnology revolution in 1959 when he gave an influential speech entitled "There's Plenty of Room at the Bottom." In his speech he argued that small machines can work more efficiently—using less power—and are cheaper to manufacture. Therefore, he suggested that research should focus on developing technology that is small. He suggested that scientists and medical researchers should look for ways to develop molecules that could perform surgery, devices that could store data on a pinhead, and minuscule generators that could generate power to run computers.

While Feynman's vision was inspirational, researchers just didn't have the tools to work on such a small scale. Until 1990 that is, when a new microscope—the atomic force microscope—was invented. This microscope has a minuscule needle that can move atoms and molecules around. The microscope can be used to manipulate and reorganize atoms. This opened the door to the nanoscale, allowing scientists to develop all kinds of tiny new 'things.'

The most significant 'things' developed by scientists working on a nanoscale are fullerenes and nanotubes. These are structured nanoparticles created out of carbon atoms. They have incredible properties. They are strong, light, flexible, heat tolerant, and can conduct electricity. These properties are useful in a wide range of fields and that is why nanotechnology is changing our lives in a wide variety of ways.

Let's think about carbon nanotubes. A nanotube looks like a piece of paper—think of it as only one atom thin. The paper looks like chicken wire. Then roll that up into a tube—and we have a nanotube.

Nanotubes are already in products that we buy—for example in car parts, in the dashboard and tires, and in sporting equipment—tennis racquets, skis, bike frames. All of these things benefit from the strength and weightlessness that nanotubes can provide.

Similarly, nanotubes are in the lotions, makeup and hair products that we use. Some cosmetic companies use nanoparticles in makeup to make eye shadow and lipstick last longer. They use nanoparticles in face cream to help our skin absorb the creams more quickly and to penetrate more deeply into the pores of our skin.

It's also likely that when we get dressed, the clothes we wear have nanoparticles in them. We've all seen the shirts that never need ironing, or the pants that simply will not stain. When fruit juice or red wine spills on those pants, the liquid just beads like mercury—and our pants remain clean! That's the result of nanotechnology at work. Oh yes, and we've probably seen the socks that will never get smelly, right? That's nanotechnology. And one company—I think it's Samsung—has developed a washing machine that uses silver ions. Silver ions can eliminate odor-causing bacteria and illness-causing bacteria; it eliminates viruses, algae and fungi—the washing machine disinfects our clothing. All thanks to silver nanoparticles.

Another application of nanotechnology is in the electronics industry. While you won't see the nanotech electronic products just yet—don't bother to look in the Future Shop this week—researchers at all the big electronics companies—such as Hewlett-Packard, Lucent, Intel, and IBM—all want to shrink computer chips to the size of a molecule. Why is that? Because at the moment, we can only make a silicon chip so small before heat from the operation of the chip circuits starts to melt the plastic from which it's made. This heat problem is pushing researchers to look for ways to create tiny chips from materials that won't melt—like those that nanotechnology make possible.

The field of medicine is also studying how nanotechnology can be used to help patients. It is hoped that a fullerene—that's a nanoparticle in the shape of a ball—could be "filled" with medicine, or antibiotic. The fullerene would be attached to a molecule that would connect only with the bacteria, or defective gene, or cancer tumor inside the patient. In this way, medicine could be delivered exactly to the site of the problem. This delivery system would be efficient and might eliminate the nasty side effects of some medicines.

OK. We're out of time for now. You will need to learn more about nanotechnology, its benefits and risks, and develop an opinion about it's usefulness over the next week or so.

## Focused Listening

*Exercise 1, Page 123*

**Student 1:** Nanotechnology is one of the most exciting technologies. I am certain that it will transform the fields of medicine, electronics, and product manufacture in the years to come.

**Student 2:** Whenever a new technology is introduced, there are risks. In my view, there's a good possibility that there are risks associated with nanotechnology.

**Student 3:** I've read some articles about the application of nanotechnology to the field of medicine. I hear that nanotechnology may result in new treatments for cancer patients.

**Student 4:** OK. Well, even if nanotechnology has some drawbacks, there's only a slight possibility that any drawback will prevent the further development of nanotechnology.

**Student 5:** There's a good possibility that nanotechnology will have implications we haven't thought of yet.

*Exercise 2, Page 124*

**Student 1:** We are already using nanotechnology in consumer products like cosmetics, sunscreens, stain-free clothing, and antibactieral washing machines.

**Student 2:** Minuscule machines—made out of molecules—would consume less power and be cheaper to make. It was Richard Feynman who thought of that first. He's famous.

**Student 3:** Nanotechnology? How can something so small have such a large impact on our lives?

**Student 4:** Nanotubes and fullerenes will be used to cure cancer some day. I'm sure the benefits of nanotechnology will save the world.

# UNIT 7

# Microbiology: Fighting Infectious Diseases

## Lecture: Conditions that Affect the Spread of Infectious Diseases

**Professor:** Hello everyone. This is our first lecture on infectious diseases.

Do you remember the outbreak of Severe Acute Respiratory Syndrome (or SARS) in 2003, or the more recent spread of the swine flu? Now, these are cases of infectious diseases that spread on a global scale. How can we keep these infectious diseases under control when they begin to spread? And this is the focus of today's lecture: the conditions that encourage or discourage the spread of infectious diseases.

So, first of all, if we're in good health, we are more able to resist disease, and the opposite is also true—if we're nutritionally deficient, or ill with another disease (like cancer) we're more likely to be susceptible.

A clean water supply and efficient water treatment are essential to preventing all kinds of illnesses. Our water systems can contain parasites that lead to schistosomiasis. Schi-sto-so-mia-sis, which is a disease that damages the bladder, the kidney, the liver, and the intestines. The World Health Organization estimates that 200 million people may be infected with the parasite and that 200,000 die every year.

Now, food preparation also affects our health. Gastroenteritis, ga-stro-en-te-ri-tis, which is a disease of the stomach and the intestines, is caused by improperly prepared foods, reheated meat and seafood dishes, dairy and bakery products. The WHO states that gastroenteritis kills 5 to 8 million people per year, and is the leading cause of death for children under the age of five. This, when gastroenteritis can be treated simply by rehydration.

Also, most of us live in large groups, in very large groups, and this makes us more vulnerable to infectious disease. So, let's look at an example to make this more obvious. When a child is exposed to measles, his or her body requires about two weeks to make antibodies to fight the disease. This means that for the measles virus to survive, it must find a new body every two weeks. And this is easily done in a city where children go to school and meet at play groups.

And here's another impact of living together in groups: we have more contact with waste products. We have to manage our waste so that we have as little contact with it as possible because there are many bacterial diseases and parasitic worms that result from contact with human waste. And of course, we have to minimize our contact with animal waste to prevent the spread of disease.

As if this weren't enough, large groups of people attract what we call "agents of disease"—mosquitoes and rats. The kinds of things we do to support large numbers of humans contribute to the spread of disease. Now, to be specific, when we cut down trees for agricultural purposes or for urban development, we create pools of stagnant water, which are breeding grounds for mosquitoes that carry the protozoa that cause malaria. Similarly, large populations of humans tend to attract rats and other rodents that may also be agents of disease.

Our current levels of travel enhance the ability of a disease to spread as well. Like when SARS and the swine flu began to spread, one of the main problems was that unknowingly infected people traveling from one country to another, spread the disease across borders. These people unknowingly spread the disease to populations that had never been exposed to these diseases before. And if you have never been exposed to a disease before, then you have no antibodies, and you're much more susceptible to contracting the disease.

This is nothing new, of course. One of the most horrific examples of this was the Black Death in Europe (in around 1348 to 1350). The Black Death was bubonic plague, caused by bacteria transmitted by the rat flea, which can spread to humans. An outbreak of bubonic plague was recorded in China in the 1330s, and by the late 1340s it had reached Europe. By the end of the epidemic, a third of Europeans, that's 25 to 40 million, had been killed, and we don't know how many Chinese had died. These deaths changed the economic and cultural life of Asia and Europe forever. Similarly, the native peoples of "The New World" also suffered when the European explorers and colonists arrived after 1492. Measles, smallpox, influenza, and whooping cough killed many of the natives throughout North and South America, the Pacific Islands, and Australia. Some populations were completely wiped out, and others had such severe disease rates that their cultures were destroyed.

So all of these conditions influence the spread of infectious diseases:
- how healthy we are
- whether we have access to clean water
- how we prepare our food
- how closely we live with others
- how much contact we have with waste products
- how closely we live to "agents of disease" like mosquitoes and rats
- how much we travel
- how likely we are to be exposed to a "new" disease

These are all conditions that we can take into account in our constant battle against the spread of contagious diseases. Now, the next challenge humans face in the war against infectious diseases is antibiotic resistance. We need to figure out what to do to combat antibiotic resistance. So, antibiotic resistance will be the focus of your reading for next class.

## Focused Listening

*Exercise 2, Page 145*

### ONE AND TWO

**Professor:** Do you remember the outbreak of Severe Acute Respiratory Syndrome (or SARS) in 2003, or the more recent spread of the swine flu? Now, these are cases of infectious diseases that spread on a global scale. How can we keep these infectious diseases under control when they begin to spread? And this is the focus of today's lecture: the conditions that encourage or discourage the spread of infectious diseases.

So, first of all, if we're in good health, we're more able to resist disease, and the opposite is also true—if we're nutritionally deficient, or ill with another disease (like cancer) we're more likely to be susceptible.

A clean water supply and efficient water treatment are essential to preventing all kinds of illnesses. Our water systems can contain parasites that lead to schistosomiasis. Schi-sto-so-mia-sis, which is a disease that damages the bladder, the kidney, the liver, and the intestines. The World Health Organization

estimates that 200 million people may be infected with the parasite and that 200,000 die every year.

### THREE

**Professor:** Now, food preparation also affects our health. Gastroenteritis, ga-stro-en-te-ri-tis, which is a disease of the stomach and the intestines, is caused by improperly prepared foods, reheated meat and seafood dishes, dairy and bakery products. The WHO states that Gastroenteritis kills 5 to 8 million people per year, and is the leading cause of death for children under the age of five. This, when gastroenteritis can be treated simply by rehydration.

### FOUR

**Professor:** This is nothing new, of course. One of the most horrific examples of this was the Black Death in Europe (in around 1348 to 1350). The Black Death was bubonic plague, caused by bacteria transmitted by the rat flea, which can spread to humans. An outbreak of bubonic plague was recorded in China in the 1330s, and by the late 1340s it had reached Europe. By the end of the epidemic, a third of Europeans, that's 25 to 40 million, had been killed, and we don't know how many Chinese had died. These deaths changed the economic and cultural life of Asia and Europe forever. Now, similarly, the native peoples of "The New World" also suffered when the European explorers and colonists arrived after 1492. Measles, smallpox, influenza, and whooping cough killed many of the natives throughout North and South America, the Pacific Islands, and Australia. Some populations were completely wiped out, and others had such severe disease rates that their cultures were destroyed.

So all of these conditions influence the spread of infectious diseases:
- how healthy we are
- whether we have access to clean water
- how we prepare our food
- how closely we live with others
- how much contact we have with waste products
- how closely we live to "agents of disease" like mosquitoes and rats
- how much we travel
- how likely we are to be exposed to a "new" disease

# UNIT 8

# Children's Literature: Characteristics of the Genre

## Lecture: Characteristics of Children's Literature

**Professor:** Hello everyone. In today's lecture I want to define the characteristics of the genre of children's literature. You have read about the generic plot pattern, and its variations, in your textbook. Now I'd like to discuss with you other characteristics of the genre of children's literature.

Let's think about style first, specifically the amount of descriptive detail that is provided about characters and settings. First, think about children's limited tolerance for descriptive detail. In general, kids aren't very interested in descriptive detail, are they? So the description of character in most children's literature is minimal, at least compared to the description we find in adult literature. But this lack of descriptive detail doesn't make the stories vague. The information that is provided tends to be concrete rather than abstract—to give details about shape, sound, and color that allow readers to imagine physically specific worlds. In *Joey Pigza Loses Control*, for instance, Joey provides not just the abstract information that his mother is "stressed-out" but also some easily visual details: "Her elbows were shaking and her jaw was so tight her front teeth were denting her lower lip." The texts of picture books tend to leave out the visual details of this sort—but do so because the pictures in them offer equivalent concrete and visual information about the way things look.

What about the characters in children's books? Who are the main characters? The main characters are children of course. Child readers are most interested in child, or at least, child-like protagonists. Also, the characters confirm adult assumptions about children—that is to say, the protagonists are limited. The generic story often informs children that they're too limited to cope with the world on their own; however, the characters often have some redeeming quality that saves them. For example, Cinderella is limited by her servant-like status in her step-mother's house, but is redeemed by her goodness and beauty, which attracts the prince. In the traditional folktale *Three Billy Goats Gruff*, the youngest goat avoids being eaten by the monster by telling the monster that his older brother, who would make a bigger and tastier meal, will be coming by later. The youngest goat is limited by his size and strength, but makes up for it with quick thinking.

Another common characteristic of protagonists in children's literature is that they are frequently orphans. Think of Cinderella, Peter Rabbit, Stuart Little, Harry Potter, both Lyra and Will of *The Golden Compass*; also Anne in *Anne of Green Gables*, Dorothy in *The Wizard of Oz*, and Simba in *The Lion King* were all orphans. The prevalence of orphans in children's fiction seems to relate to a central concern that adults have with children's independence and security. Orphans are of necessity independent, free to have adventures without the constraints of protective adults. At the same time, they're automatically faced with the danger and discomfort of lack of parental love. In using orphans as main characters, writers can focus on children's desire for independence, or on their fear of loss of security.

This is a good point at which to consider another characteristic of children's literature—it often clearly shows opposition between two themes. As the use of an orphan as a main character allows, the two opposing themes of independence versus a fear of loss of security is common. You can probably think of other themes that are often placed in opposition in children's stories—the classic example is the contrast of good and evil (think of Harry Potter and Voldemort), but there are many others, for example obedience and disobedience, civilization and nature, restraint and wildness, boredom and adventure, safety and danger, companionship and solitude, old ideas, new ideas, acceptance and defiance, and so on.

Finally, let us think about the meaning of children's stories. Children's stories are action oriented, but they almost always have moral commentary. Remember that most children's stories are written by adults whose primary goal is to instruct children about the adult world. While the stories are action oriented, children's writers almost always want both their characters and their readers to focus on the moral implications of exciting actions. To do this, writers must find ways of expressing the deeper implications in their apparently straightforward stories. Sometimes, the implications are obvious: characters merely state what they have learned from their adventures. But in books such as *Peter Rabbit* or *Where the Wild Things Are*, the complex ideas beneath the surface simplicity aren't explicitly stated. Instead they are implied. By choosing a series of actions that are superficially straightforward but actually complex, Potter and Sendak can both focus on action and imply complex moral situations.

So you can see that children's literature, because of its distinctive characteristics, can certainly be considered a genre in itself. Even if individual stories don't reflect these characteristics, each story can be seen as expressing variations on these common characteristics.

Let me recap the main characteristics we've discussed here. Children's literature generally displays these features:
- minimal but concrete and visual detail;
- child or child-like protagonists, that are limited in some way, but have redeeming qualities;
- orphan protagonists that allow for the exploration of the conflicting desires of independence and security;
- contrasting themes in clear opposition to each other, like good versus evil, and
- stories that are instructive at a deeper level, that allow readers to make inferences about meaning.

Alright. That's all for today. Does anyone have any questions?

# CREDITS

New York; **p. 81** (T) Francis G. Mayer/Corbis, ©2009 Estate of Pablo Picasso/Artists Rights Society (ARS), New York, (B) Kunstmuseum Basel, Switzerland/Peter Willi/ SuperStock, ©2009 Artists Rights Society (ARS), New York/ADAGP, Paris; **p. 84** (L) Art Institute of Chicago, Illinois/A.K.G., Berlin/SuperStock, ©2009 Estate of Pablo Picasso/Artists Rights Society (ARS), New York, (M) McNay Art Museum/Art Resource, NY, ©2009 Estate of Pablo Picasso/Artists Rights Society (ARS), New York, (R) The Museum of Modern Art/Licensed by SCALA/ Art Resource, NY, ©2009 Estate of Pablo Picasso/Artists Rights Society (ARS), New York; **p. 86** (TL) Art Institute of Chicago, Illinois/A.K.G., Berlin/SuperStock, ©2009 Estate of Pablo Picasso/Artists Rights Society (ARS), New York, (TM) Peter Willi/SuperStock, ©2009 Estate of Pablo Picasso/Artists Rights Society (ARS), New York, (TR) Musee Picasso, Paris/Peter Willi/SuperStock, ©2009 Estate of Pablo Picasso/Artists Rights Society (ARS), New York, (BL) The Museum of Modern Art/ Licensed by SCALA/Art Resource, NY, ©2009 Estate of Pablo Picasso/Artists Rights Society (ARS), New York, (BM) McNay Art Museum/Art Resource, NY, ©2009 Estate of Pablo Picasso/Artists Rights Society (ARS), New York, (BR) The Museum of Modern Art/Licensed by SCALA/Art Resource, NY, ©2009 Estate of Pablo Picasso/Artists Rights Society (ARS), New York; **p. 91** (L) Kunstmuseum Berne, Switzerland/A.K.G., Berlin/ SuperStock, ©2009 Artists Rights Society (ARS), New York/ADAGP, Paris, (M) The Museum of Modern Art/ Licensed by SCALA/Art Resource, NY, ©2009 Estate of Pablo Picasso/Artists Rights Society (ARS), New York, (R) Réunion des Musées Nationaux / Art Resource, NY, ©2009 Estate of Pablo Picasso/Artists Rights Society (ARS), New York; **p. 93** (TR) Shutterstock, (T) Shutterstock, (M) Pornchai Kittiwongsakul/AFP/Getty Images, (B) Simon Holdcroft/Alamy; **p. 94** Shutterstock; **p. 96** Shutterstock; **p. 99** Shutterstock; **p. 102** Shutterstock; **p. 103** Shutterstock; **p. 106** Banana Stock/Photolibrary; **p. 113** (TR) Shutterstock, (background) Shutterstock, (T) Shutterstock, (M) Shutterstock, (B) Dreamstime. com; **p. 121** (L) Shutterstock, (R) Shutterstock; **p. 122** (T) Dreamstime.com, (B) Shutterstock; **p. 127** Shutterstock; **p. 131** Shutterstock; **p. 135** (TR) Shutterstock, (M) Corbis/ Jupiterimages, (B) Shutterstock; **p. 136** Shutterstock; **p. 149** Shutterstock; **p. 161** (TR) Shutterstock, (M) Shutterstock; **p. 162** Shutterstock.

**Illustrations**: Gary Torrisi

# AUDIO CD TRACKING GUIDE